Japanese Animation

JAPANESE ANIMATION

East Asian Perspectives

Edited by Masao Yokota
and Tze-yue G. Hu

University Press of Mississippi / Jackson

wwww.upress.state.ms.us

The University Press of Mississippi is a member
of the Association of American University Presses.

Manufactured in the United States of America

First printing 2013

∞

Library of Congress Cataloging-in-Publication Data

Japanese animation : East Asian perspectives /
edited by Masao Yokota and Tze-yue G. Hu.
pages cm
Includes index.
ISBN 978-1-61703-809-9 (hardback) — ISBN 978-1-61703-810-5 (ebook)
(print) 1. Animated films—Japan—History and criticism. 2. Animated
television programs—Japan—History and criticism. I. Yokota, Masao,
1954– editor of compilation. II. Hu, Tze-yue G., editor of compilation.
NC1766.J3J37 2013
791.43'340952—dc23 2012045563

British Library Cataloging-in-Publication Data available

Contents

Section Two

Pioneers of Japanese Animation

Section Three

Popular Culture, East-West Expressions, and Tezuka Osamu

Section Four

Female Characters and Transnational Identities

A Note to the Reader

Except for the author's and the translator's names printed at the beginning of each essay, all Japanese, Korean, and Chinese names in this book are given in the following order: family name precedes given names. For Japanese names, macrons are included in some of the essays as provided by the individual author. However, where names have an established conventional spelling in English, we have retained the spelling (for example, Tokyo, Hankyu, Toei Doga, Showa). All translations from Japanese, Korean, and Chinese are the individual author's unless otherwise noted.

Acknowledgments

We are particularly grateful to our Australian reader Gyöngyi Horvath for generous help throughout, especially with proofreading and grammar corrections as well as the valuable comments given on the whole book in manuscript. She is one contributor working behind the lattice of cross-communication and balance.

We are also indebted to an anonymous reviewer of our work whose constructive criticisms encouraged us to make sections of the book better. Mr. Walter Biggins, the acquiring editor of the University Press of Mississippi, was patient and supportive of our collective project from the beginning.

INTRODUCTION

Frameworks of Teaching and Researching Japanese Animation

—Tze-yue G. Hu

Background of the Project

Over the past quarter century, *anime*, a popular form of Japanese animation (comprising manga and video game characteristics), has engendered tremendous amount of interest both in the academic and nonacademic sectors. This book, however, is not about *anime* per se. It seeks to present a well-rounded study of Japanese animation as a whole consisting of a collection of essays written by scholars and practitioners originating and residing in Japan and the East Asian region.

The beginning of this project and its theme subject, "Teaching and Researching Japanese Animation: Some East Asian Perspectives," dates back to a conference panel session that was part of the twelfth Conference of the European Association for Japanese Studies (EAJS) in 2008. Although a number of the contributors featured in this book collection did not attend the conference, the hatching of this publishing project had already begun with the initial participants who were enthusiastic in presenting their work in a bilingual setting. A longstanding chair and prominent member of the Japan Society for Animation Studies (JSAS), Yokota Masao, was supportive of the panel theme from the beginning. Later as the plan for the book was being developed, various members of the JSAS were requested to submit and contribute past and current work on Japanese animation. Overall, the assembling of this group of contributors took time, and we did not hesitate to include other scholars and animation practitioners whose work would contribute to a more in-depth knowledge and analysis of Japanese animation particularly with Asian perspectives.

Demand for This Publication and Crossing the Language Barrier

The conception of this book volume has its roots in the preparation time of my monograph on Japanese animation, *Frames of Anime: Culture and Image-Building*, which was published by the Hong Kong University Press in 2010. Inevitably, my insights into Japanese animation were partly shaped by my peers' work in Japan, which was usually available only in Japanese. In order to further clarify my exploratory work on Japanese animation and a number of issues as well as areas that I had brought up and raised in my book manuscript, it dawned on me that it would be invaluable to gather the array of works that are available in Japan and get it translated and published in English for the first time for readers worldwide. To be able to refer to the primary research source in English would definitely make research in this subject area less daunting as well as far more accessible, and create fewer chances of misunderstanding and misreading. These are issues that foreign researchers often confront when having to work with research materials available only in Japanese.

The conviction to realize this project also relates to my struggle in accessing sources that are printed only in the Japanese language. I did not come from the traditional discipline of Modern Languages and Literatures Studies where sufficient training in a foreign language is often supported and required. My Film, Media and Cultural Studies background was not adequate enough for me to face a subject so diverse yet so innately connected to Japanese culture and society. Established Western stalwarts of Japanese film art and industry—among others, Donald Richie, Joseph L. Anderson, and David Dresser—had for the greater part "skipped" the chapter on Japanese animation in their artistic and historical studies of the Japanese film industry. Perhaps it was considered as a children's genre, or perhaps they were guided by the dominant domestic film critics and academicians who somehow did not regard the medium with much seriousness. For example, the well-known film critic Satō Tadao, whose writings are often translated into English, hardly mentioned the animation medium in his English-language works. The absence of a discussion of animation was especially glaring in his works charting the growth of the Japanese film industry from a historical perspective.[1]

The JSAS publishes its own annual journal, the *Japanese Journal of Animation Studies;* however, the papers are almost entirely in Japanese except for the brief English abstracts and the occasional publication of a foreign contributor. One cannot fault the society for this as the subject of animation studies is a new academic venture in Japan. Its founding in 1998 was partly due to the rise in popularity of Japanese animation abroad.

The export of Japanese animation, particularly *anime*, has become a staggering international business. It is estimated that "60% of the world's animated television programs" originates from Japan and the peripherals of manga-anime goods like licensed action characters, play cards, and so forth have generated annual sales to the value around US $17 billion (Leheny, 2006: 214). In Japan, the idea of a "Cool Japan" has also captured the imagination of government officials searching for new avenues to reinvigorate a recession-stricken economy. The promotion of Japanese media arts as "soft power" has become an exciting enterprise in realizing Japan's leadership abroad.[2] Surrounding countries also desire to produce and adapt forms of Japanese animation for domestic use, consumption, and even for export motives. One of the aims of this book collection is to give publishing opportunities to regional scholars and animation practitioners to present their works in English. The various papers also show us that because of their countries' proximity to Japan, the influence and import of Japanese animated works and images are at times alarmingly disproportionate, causing paradigmatic rethinking and even strategic measures to be taken. By this, I am referring to the widespread popularity of Japanese animation, particularly the *anime* kind in East and Southeast Asia, especially in the consumption aspects as well as the creative and production methods of making animation in general. For example, in this collection, Koh Dong-Yeon's essay relates how Japanese animation is reconfigured in South Korea in order to adapt to the social-political environment. Kenny K. N. Chow's work, in a different vein, explores the project of recuperating continental East Asian roots of traditional Japanese art and painting so as to educate Hong Kong students in the intra-regional connections of aesthetic thinking in the region.

This book's essays are rooted in the key activities of teaching and researching Japanese animation, with the ultimate objective of sharing one's ideas, thoughts, approaches, and practices in the English printed word so as to reach out to a wider base of international readers. Essentially, teaching is an active pursuit as well as the imparting of knowledge. It also involves the understanding of subjects in a holistic way and shows that the path of learning is multidimensional. As much as the world is fascinated with *anime*, Japanese animation, as a whole, is more than anime—the book brings into focus research aspects that have been neglected before or hitherto, or not seriously investigated upon.

Emergence of Animation Studies and the Epistemological Position of This Volume

The field of film studies has also come a long way in establishing itself as a serious academic discipline within the educational institution. Appearing in the 1950s and growing in popularity in the 1960s, till today, it is still often taught as a subject within a discipline, for example, Language and Literature or English, History, Political Science, and Sociology. On the whole, however, a number of universities and colleges do offer it now as an independent discipline with due recognition of its educational agenda and status. Progressively, animation studies arrived as a dark horse and like the new academic disciplines that sprung into life in the second half of the twentieth century, Gender Studies, Performance Studies, Queer Studies, Cultural Studies, and so on; it has been an educational response of a contemporary world yearning for new forms of knowledge and multidisciplinary thinking. While traditional disciplines continue to promote themselves as nuclei of order, authority, and convention to the advancement and examination of knowledge, the "truths" of human existence are multidimensional as are the layers of nature of which the human kind is only one part.

In the West, the Society for Animation Studies was formed in 1987. The American scholar Harvey Deneroff, the society's founder, often reminds members at annual conferences that it was difficult for him in the past to present his work in cinema and media conferences. His presentations simply just got lost in a panel of speakers where the subject of animation was not the focus, as well as the conference itself where animation seemed too "childish" or a marginal medium to be reckoned with. His determination to establish a society devoted to the study of animation was driven by the desire to lay a meeting ground where scholars and practitioners interested in the subject could find a common home to exchange their ideas and projects theoretically and practically, on a personal or an institutional basis. The society now has more than 220 members worldwide, and it organizes an annual conference at different locations around the world, where members can present their recent research.

It is beyond the capacity of this space to discuss expansively and critically the discipline of animation studies. As mentioned above, it is an emerging field of study. British scholar Paul Ward actually sees it as a field of "multi-sited" knowledge that is not necessarily "a completely coherent field or discipline" (Ward, 2003: np). By that, he is referring at once to the abilities of the animation medium to cross boundaries and the frequent overlapping of subjects and areas pertaining to animation studies research.[3]

How does this collection of papers advance the knowledge of the animation medium? In this edited collection, the backgrounds of the contributors and the contents of their written essays illustrate that although their beginning focal point may be geographically situated in a specific location and academically oriented to the discipline they work in, each contributor is critically aware of the complex materiality of the animation medium and that the intellectualization of the medium cannot be contemplated as a one-sided affair. Indispensably, the adoption of the East-West comparative approach and the acknowledgment of Western influences and cross-current interchanges and adaptations assist us in appreciating the similarities and dissimilarities, which in turn further enrich our research and discovery of the medium. At the same time, the materiality of the animation medium has undergone vast transformation since film, a European invention, became an intrinsic component and mainstay of moving images. Today, digital technology has made hand-drawn animated images seem obsolete and low tech. However, in Japan and in many parts of Asia—for example, in Indonesia, Vietnam, China, and in many Chinese communities around the world—labor-intensive manga adapted animated visuals, puppetry images as reflected on walls, screens, and water ponds, and the rotating candlelit lanterns and its shadows still continue to offer competing charm and delight during festivals and community gatherings.

The cross-fertilization of the animation medium attests to the age-old human attraction to moving images—visually, culturally, technologically, economically, and even hegemonically. In Japan alone, we can see the effects and affectations of the medium. The papers featured in this collection demonstrate the dialogic and engaging aspects of Japanese animation and its multilayered influences. The environment, far and near, natural and man-made, bears much influence and agency on our actions and thoughts both consciously and unconsciously. This volume is concerned particularly with East Asian perspectives of Japanese animation. East Asia is now the fastest-growing region in the world; the potential to share and inform is plentiful. Furthermore, its interregional interactions, intentions, and inclinations (historical, cultural, economic, political, etc.) provide much terrain for continuous exploration and revelation.

Summary of Contents: East Asian Perspectives

As mentioned above, the amount of literature published on the subject of anime is not minute; it has grown steadily through the years. The spectrum ranges from fan publications to "insider's stories"; for example, from *Astro Boy and Anime Come to the Americas* (2009, Jefferson, NC: McFarland and Co.) written by media producer Fred Ladd with Harvey Deneroff, to highly theoretical analyses like Thomas Lamarre's *The Anime Machine: A Media Theory of Animation* (2009, Minneapolis: University of Minnesota Press).

In the local publication scene in Japan, one category of printed literature that has arisen in reaction to the worldwide perception of anime is that which incorporates the information gathering, description, and reflection of this phenomenon. One of the latest publications in this vein is by Sakurai Takamasa, a media producer who has become an "external relations anime ambassador" assisting the Japanese government to promote *anime bunka gaikō*, meaning "anime cultural diplomacy," which is also the title of his book published in 2009 by the Japanese publisher Chikumashobō in Tokyo. The book consists of the author's description and reflection of his meetings with overseas anime fans. On the one hand, Sakurai is pleased and proud to know that anime has brought Japan closer to the world and has created endearing impressions of Japan overseas, especially among youths and young adults. On the other hand, however, he is acutely aware that there are others who dislike anime or have maintained an uninterested attitude toward the medium-genre. In the book, Sakurai self-questions the overriding role of the "bureaucrat or official" (*kan*) in promoting anime abroad versus the common role of "people" (*min*) in undertaking this task. He personally contemplates that while the business of creating anime lies in the domain of the private sector, anime is still, at its essence, very much a cultural product of the Japanese people.[4]

Our present venture is an act of teamwork proposing an independent yet composite amalgamation of teaching and research ideas on Japanese animation as a whole. Thus, this collection essentially seeks to strike a balance of views, analyses, frameworks, and perspectives in presenting a broad variety of studies that are already in progress in Japan and the broader East Asia region. The rigors of teaching and researching are often intertwined due to the dual professional hats that the scholar has to wear and for which he or she has to assume responsibilities. This project casts the spotlight on Japanese animation, the fundamental treatise(s) about humanity and the ideas of "living life" and "giving life" including the educator's cum researcher's roles of experiencing the animation medium, both physical and mental, at the material and abstract levels, as well as advancing speculations of the medium's multifaceted functions and manifestations.

The essays assembled in this publication were not preplanned at an early stage nor were they tailored to meet certain predefined criteria. However, through the course of reviews and submissions, it became obvious that the contributors' works share a common relevance, interest, and involvement. Based on these, contributions are divided into six sections.

The first section contains essays related to the subthemes of "Animation Studies and Animation History in Japan." Animation historian Tsugata Nobuyuki's essay gives us a rundown of Japanese animation history highlighting the "cross-pollination" developments of two opposing forces. Specifically, that of the animated feature films of Studio Ghibli with its aspirational standards of the classic Disney kind and that of the TV manga-anime series that embodies limited animation and its own evolved aesthetic standards. The cross-pollination process has led to secondary trends and the sprouting of new branches of Japanese animation. The appearance of such descriptive terms like "mania," "otaku," and "fanatics" is a product of the resulting segmented nature of Japanese animation and the corresponding fragmentation of the audience along these different segments.

My contribution in this section spotlights the popularity of the Chinese wartime animated film *Princess Iron Fan* (1941), among audiences, the animation production community, and intellectuals in Japan. Reflecting on a rare hand-penned letter by the Wan brothers that was directly addressed to the Japanese reading public, the essay speculates on its historical contents as well as the contexts of this communicative exchange. I relate why the animated film is still highly regarded in Japan despite its virtually forgotten status in mainland China and other overseas Chinese communities. Ideologically, the Chinese Eastern approach had sparked covert inspirational and competitive energies to the Japanese animation community, and the effects can be seen in postwar Japanese animation development, including some of the works of Studio Ghibli and that of the late manga artist Tezuka Osamu.[5]

Koide Masashi's essay comprehensively charts the establishment and the history of the JSAS. As an educator directly involved in the founding and later, the management of the society, he reveals to us astute views of the society's background and its role in promoting animation as a "studies" discipline with inter- and multidisciplinary aspirations. Ikeda Hiroshi's contribution details a veteran animation educator's and an industry insider's historical experiences of advancing the animation medium as a legitimate academic study. The contents of the essay also disclose his initial challenges in attempting to raise the medium's status in the educational sector and other supportive institutional settings in Japan. His paper is in fact a peer reviewer's response to Koide's earlier submission complementing the former's work with more historical and personal information about the uneasy founding period of the society. The contents of his essay and Koide's elaborate to us that the concerned individual's aspirations and the interest group's calls for a specific research solace space occasionally got lost and discouraged in the tides of economic and industrial progress and the inability of authorities to recognize and act upon the value and ramification of arising trends, developments, and issues, as well as foresee a new emerging academic discipline that might serve the public better and elevate the scholarship of education and research.

The second section, "Pioneers of Japanese Animation," considers the historic "legacies" and "roles" of the pioneers of Japanese animation. Sano Akiko's essay provides a succinct discussion of how the indigenous paper-cutout animation of Ōfuji Noburō (1900–1961) was swept aside by the invading trend of American cartoons in the late 1920s Japan. The underlying theme of her research is the contemporary reevaluation of a rich artistic animation heritage that the country once possessed. The next essay is penned by a pioneer animation historian, Watanabe Yasushi, who paints a portrait of Masaoka Kenzō (1898–1988), widely acclaimed as "Japan's first Walt Disney" and the "father of Japanese animation." Watanabe gives biographical details of Masaoka's artistic and creative beginnings.

Providing a critical analysis of Japanese wartime and early postwar animation, my own chapter, "Animating for 'Whom' in the Aftermath of a World War," probes interpretatively into the political and artistic environment in which Masaoka and his younger colleague Kumakawa Masao (1916–2008) worked in. In recent years, more historical materials and old films have surfaced and been restored. I conclude that there are opportunities as well as potential for further constructive interpretations of early Japanese animation.

The three papers in the third section ("Popular Culture, East-West Expressions, and Tezuka Osamu") open the discussion on issues pertaining more to popular culture, East-West expressions, and Japan's "next Walt

Disney," Tezuka Osamu (1928–1989), and his influences in Japan and other parts of East Asia. Yamanashi Makiko's essay discloses to us the rippled effects of the all-female performance troupe Takarazuka on manga-anime artist Tezuka's creative consciousness, especially his infatuations with live-action theatrics including his family's connections to the performer stars. Tezuka's wide repertoire of manga stories and the subjective theatrical spectacles of many of his manga-adapted anime characters and their costume representations could be traced to a fantasized modern Japan as expressed by a young growing-up artist.

Koh Dong-Yeon's research demonstrates the extensive influence of manga-anime stories in South Korea not only as an underground popular culture import but also as a legalized propaganda tool appropriated by the authorities to promote values of industrialization and heroism and the ideals of math and science education. Known as "classical Japanese animation" in South Korea, animated images of *Astro Boy* and *Mazinger Z* exercised ideological impact on young people's minds in the 1970s and 1980s Korea. The backdrop of the "popularity" of Japanese popular culture and the surrounding controversies are also examined in Koh's essay.

Hong Kong's animation film artist and teacher Kenny K. N. Chow's work illustrates the importance of stressing space and location in teaching Japanese animation. The role of the camera is crucial in creating a cultural background. From traditional topographical Chinese painting to iconic *haiku*, Chow's essay is written from the dual perspective of a filmmaker and a teacher as he presents the rich heritage of Japanese animation and additionally designs course lessons for students to experiment the background relations of animating, thereby generating their sensitivity to emotion, viewpoint, and the value of (re)acquaintance with historic East Asian visual arts and even literary arts like *haiku* poetry.

Fantasy is a stable driving force in many animated works. Japanese animation, particularly the *anime* kind, has been considered a terra firma for fantastical storytelling. Female anime characters are recognized for their visual characteristics of long slender legs and big sparkling eyes, while the colorful hairdos and the clothing they adorn indicate the desires of costume-play (*cosplay*) and identity transformation. In the fourth section titled "Female Characters and Transnational Identities," Sugawa-Shimada Akiko's research traces the development of the *goth-loli shōjo* animation genre in Japan and surveys its transformational elements. She discerns the navigated-negotiated spaces and representations and discusses that these seemingly cute female characters assume the act of rewriting gender

identity roles in Japan. Korean animation studies scholar Kim Joon Yang in turn examines the foreign female characters presented in popular works like *Cyborg 009* (1966), *Space Battleship Yamato* (1977), and *The Super Dimension Fortress Macross* (1984). These key manga-anime works have celebrated male-based audiences. Kim's essay takes us back to the crucial boom time of Japanese animation from the late 1960s to the 1980s in Japan. What might we read from the animated "exotic foreign bodies?" His interpretation suggests that what is constructed through the imaginative configurations of the female gender might still be a subtle imperial postcolonial world mentality.

In section five, "Artistic Animation and Expression in Japan," the focus shifts to artistic animation developments and methodologies in twenty-first-century Japan. IKIF's paper explains to us the creative designs of two highly laudable animated projects, *Ghost in the Shell: Innocence* (2004) and the animated film series of *Doraemon* (2004–2009). The husband and wife animation team of IKIF penned the paper in a diary-like journal manner, literally exposing the dialogical and mediating process of creating and planning. Readers have the privileged opportunity to gain insight into the studio's everyday working and decision-making moments, as well as to have a firsthand explanatory glimpse of their animation think tank. The crux of their challenge is IKIF's endeavor to maintain and live up to the "art of animation" rather than merely utilizing 3-D computer graphics to execute the effects and movements. Their joint affiliation with the academic institution and the industry also allows training opportunities for students chosen to work in the projects.

Japan is also well known for its puppet animation. In the past, Japanese puppet animators imparted their animating skills to nearby Asian countries. For example, mainland Communist China benefited from such teaching experiences and collaborative short-film projects were also realized.[6] Yokota Masao's psychological analysis of the late Japan's premier master puppet animator Kawamoto Kihachiro (1924–2010) is no coincidence. Kawamoto's exemplary rendering of traditional East Asian legends and mythological stories in puppet animation is second to none. Hence, Yokota's chapter can be regarded as a tributary biographical account of Kawamoto's Buddhistic philosophical reflections on art and animation and quintessentially, his life's journey and the animated works created.

The last section ("Japan's First Commercial Animation Studio after the Second World War: Toei") contains one important paper that chronicles the commercial animation studio Toei's growth and the social consciousness

of its production staff as they tried to work creatively during the rapid industrialization period of Japan after the war from the 1950s to the early 1970s. Like his contemporaries Miyazaki Hayao and Takahata Isao,[7] Ikeda Hiroshi was among the young Toei animation staff members given the opportunities to direct and express their creative ideas. The editors stress here that his contribution is not presented as a full-fledged essay. It simply contains presentation notes that he originally gave as a lecture in a university in Japan. We have adapted his lecture talk to this collection and have added an appendix containing details of the significant facts and figures raised by Ikeda. His essay is especially relevant to the post-March 2011 earthquake situation of current Japan. Though technology and science may bring conveniences in living as well as producing material wealth, ignorance, and inattention toward their demerits and dangerous aspects may also bring hardship and destruction. The *phantoms* of the present that Japan is facing now are the radiation-leaking nuclear power plant in north-eastern Japan and other issues of environmental pollution. The business corporation[8] and other governmental agencies involved face an extensive task of coping with the massive scale of the problems, which can be said to be man-made. In the light of these recent events, Ikeda's animated feature film, *Flying Phantom Ship* (1969), and the message that it carries is ever more relevant.

Collaborative Book Project

The time is right for *Japanese Animation: East Asian Perspectives*. Professor Yokota and I express our sincere thanks to the extra translation work selflessly contributed by author Kim Joon Yang. Kim took on a much greater role of translating two lengthy essays into English despite the fact that his native language is not Japanese. Author Sugawa-Shimada Akiko also assisted in some of the initial translation work. Friends also helped in the translation process when the need arose and due acknowledgment is given at appropriate places. The essays are all peer reviewed, primarily among the contributors who participated in this collection. But there are other scholars and animators who helped to peer review and offer ideas to this project, too; they are Hee Holmen, Park Giryung, Suzuki Shige (CJ), and Gan Sheou Hui. Their seemingly marginal participation is viewed with no less importance in this project. In fact, their interest and support are encouraging and heighten the diversity and scholarship of the project. It is with much regret that Park Giryung and Gan Sheou Hui were not able to submit their individual chapters as originally proposed partly due to their other work commitments elsewhere and the demands of publishing the research in the English language. It is without doubt that their additional Korean and Malaysian perspectives would have enriched our publication.

The book is as much a research as well as a pedagogic resource where interested parties of Japanese animation can gain an ongoing conversation with the theme-subject. The pragmatic, the theoretical, the traditional, and the experimental approaches are included, herein reflecting the vast range of orientations that the theme-subject offers. This work is a collaborative effort and the published illustrations are original and principal as well, contributing to the further understanding of the chapters presented. The contributors share our view that this book contains vital epistemological and cultural relocation(s) of information, description, and analysis of Japanese animation. It is a project that has just begun to take shape. Just as it is natural for Western scholars to publish their work in English, on the other side of the globe, we endeavor to interconnect as well and emphasize continual dynamic response and penetrating discovery of teaching and researching Japanese animation including its alluring sub-subject *anime*, which has become a fascinating "honeycomb" capturing the imagination of many young and older people around the world.

Not only does the book address and evince the pertinence of viewing Japanese animation as an integral part of Japanese history and culture and Japan's ties to the region, it also serves as a guide to course development and research overhaul for readers looking for fresh paths and directions with East Asian associations. Hence, the East Asian perspectives presented in this collection not only rouse active understanding of the teaching and research parts concerned but hope to inspire and draw new ways of thinking about the overall subject of Japanese animation as well. The smorgasbord of viewpoints offered, whether taken singularly or collectively, speaks of familiar and recurrent contexts reenacted and reinterpreted.[9] However, striding into the unfamiliar, the taking on of challenging standpoints both subtly and vigorously, as well as the introduction of provocative topics that have not been dealt with before elsewhere are also embarked upon in this collection. Our project is far from completed; we expect interest in this theme-subject of teaching and researching Japanese animation to burgeon more proactively defying inward and close boundaries of understanding. After all, the expansive appeal of Japanese animation itself too no longer stops in Japan.

Some Thoughts on the Research Essays and Commentary

—Masao Yokota

Japanese People Are Fond of Drawing and Moving Characters

In general, the activity of drawing is natural to the Japanese people and so is their appreciation of moving or animated characters. Even among older Japanese, they like to read a manga, play a video game, or watch a TV animation during leisure time. In Japan, children can easily draw a manga-style character with big eyes, a small nose, and a small mouth. They also like to express their feeling via simple graphic figures. From birth, almost all Japanese are acquainted with line-drawn characters as displays of such visuals are found everywhere in Japan; for example, in a neighborhood convenience food store, a train station, a mobile phone, and so on. More often than not, these visuals are animated as well. In short, drawings and animated characters are a favorite with Japanese. The former and the latter correspond with the media of manga and animation, respectively. The development and diversity of these two media in Japan are reflected in the essays featured in this volume. These essays not only reveal to us the contributors' efforts in making sense of their dual roles as a teacher and researcher but also their present standpoints for understanding Japanese animation.

Postwar Japanese Animation Development: Two Distinct Roots

Animation in Japan after the Second World War had two distinct roots. One root was the institutional Toei Doga (Toei Animation Studio), and the other was the individual manga artist turned animator Tezuka Osamu. From the very beginning, Toei Doga focused on creating feature animations. Tezuka, in turn, started creating animation television series based on his own manga work.

In the postwar era from the late 1950s onward, Toei Doga led the industrial development of animation in Japan. However, because of working conditions and other labor-dispute issues, its pool of creators began to shrink in the 1960s as one creator after another left Toei Doga to work in other animation production companies.[10] These creators generally obtained work in key artist and animation positions in the production structure of these companies. Because of the movement of trained Toei personnel into the wider animation industry of Japan, it can be said that a certain standard of animation production was thus established outside of Toei.

The first great success of an animation TV series was the well-known *Astro Boy* (1963) based on a manga series of the same title. The author of the manga, the late Tezuka Osamu, had a vision of creating an animation series on his manga work. He had harbored the ambition of becoming an animation creator in the past and was making preparations to realize his ambition at the time when Toei Doga was founding its animation production enterprise. In Toei, there was a structural and systematic production plan of making animation. At that time, every staff member working on a feature animation could know its story background and narrative development and had the opportunity to participate in the creative decision-making process. Tezuka, however, who founded his own animation enterprise, worked on the principle direction that he was the sole creator of the animation. As such, only Tezuka would have known the whole narrative story of the animation series *Astro Boy* when work began on it. He was hence both the original storyteller and manga artist of the story.

Toei Doga thus created an animation production system while Tezuka directed and controlled his staff members by his sheer genius talent. As it stood, manga artist and writer Tezuka was convinced that he could control and create animation via the same methods employed in manga production. However, the production system was more complex than he expected. With time, the animation staff working at Mushi Production, the company founded by Tezuka, realized that they had to use their own initiative without Tezuka's (constant and direct) supervision as the process of animation-making was different from manga-making. Soon after, Tezuka learned to respect his animation staff and creators and consider them independent artists playing vital roles in contributing to the successful adaptations of his manga work. Gradually, they were able to freely create their animation work with originality and developed new expressive styles as well.

It was this hybrid mix of the animation production cum creative system of Toei Doga and that of Mushi Production and its diverse group of creators that subsequently enabled Japanese animation to develop further.

The First Generation of Animation Researchers after the Second World War

One of the researchers of the first generation after World War II is Watanabe Yasushi. A fan of Disney animation and Tezuka's manga, he cowrote the first detailed history of Japanese animation. Indeed, several of the articles featured in this collection make reference to his collaborative work with Yamaguchi Katsunori ("The history of Japanese animation," 1977). As an animation enthusiast, he devotes his time to collecting animation materials. His work has provided scholars with detailed facts of people who created animation as well as places where the works were produced and released. In this volume, his chapter gives us an account of an important animation father figure in Japanese animation history, Masaoka Kenzō and his contributions to the art of Japanese film and animation in general.

The Second and Third Generations of Animation Researchers

Ikeda Hiroshi was previously not only an animation director but also a researcher. At Toei Doga, he had to devise new techniques of expression for his feature animations. However, he was equally interested in the theory of animation as well. He is representative of the second generation of animation studies in Japan. Ikeda has contributed two articles to this volume in relation particularly to his historical experiences and perspectives of animation making and the development of animation studies in Japan.

I was a student of Ikeda's class in Nihon University when he taught animation as a part-time lecturer. He advised me to learn the basic principle of knowledge inquiry in studying animation. It was on his suggestion that I started to take psychology as a major subject in my research to better understand animation, which I have found very relevant in my work. In this volume collection, I wrote an essay on the late animation puppet director Kawamoto Kihachiro using psychological interpretation and theory. I may be considered as a researcher of the third generation, which follows Ikeda. In my youth years, I was fortunate enough to have been able to see not only Toei's animation feature films but also the early works of Tezuka's animation in the 1950s and 1960s.

Koide Masashi and IKIF (referring to Kifune Tokumitsu particularly) belong to the same generation as me. They are both professors of animation techniques and skills. However, Koide is a theorist while IKIF is a director of 3D-CG animation.[11] They together with Ikeda are the cofounders of the Japan Society for Animation Studies. The history of the society's establishment is discussed in detail by Ikeda's and Koide's essays published in this collection.

The Fourth Generation of Animation Researchers and Beyond

Tsugata Nobuyuki is a member of the fourth generation of animation researchers. He has published a few historical books on Japanese animation. He, too, has a strong interest in the animated works of Masaoka Kenzō and Tezuka Osamu. While Watanabe of the first generation was able to watch Masaoka's animation when it was first released in theaters, Tsugata studies Masaoka's animation primarily based on secondary written materials; for example, articles that had been published in film and academic journals. His research on Tezuka's animation has also relied on this method.

Sugawa-Shimada Akiko discusses the *goth-loli* genre in Japanese TV anime and focuses on heroines' dresses as an index of femininity. In turn, Yamanashi Makiko work indicates the starting point of Tezuka's fantasy world; in particular, the theatrical spectacles of the all-female performing community, Takarazuka. She describes how Takarazuka influenced the creative world of Tezuka. All performers in Takarazuka are females. There also are many female Takarazuka fans in Japan. It can be said that these female fans like to imagine that they can play male roles in male outfits. The *goth-loli* dress motif may have played the same role in *goth-loli* anime where its female fans take imaginative pleasure in its visual representations. Though the subjects of discussion in both Sugawa-Shimada and Yamanashi's papers may seem different, there are undercurrent themes that indirectly interact with each other. Their research work also shows the extensive influence of manga-anime in Japanese popular culture. Indeed, they are representatives of a new generation of animation researchers that pays attention to interdisciplinary subjects and methods of analysis.

Sano Akiko's essay on Ōfuji Noburō and his animated works in turn pays tribute not only to his artistic contributions to Japanese heritage and culture but also the animation history of the world. Sano represents another new generation of researchers in Japan who has shown a strong interest in early Japanese pre–Second World War animator-artists. Her work demonstrates a new trend in Japanese animation research as well.

East Asian Perspectives of Japanese Animation

Both Kenny K. N. Chow's and Koh Dong-Yeon's papers mention Tezuka Osamu's manga work. Tezuka utilized the technique of positioning static pictures in TV animated frames of *Astro Boy*. By the 1960s, the industrial-commercial pressure of producing TV anime series in Japan meant that there was not sufficient production time to create full character movements. Notably, this was due to the lack of production time to create full movements of a character. By this, I refer to the industrial-commercial pressure of producing TV anime series in Japan during the 1960s. Noticeably, Tezuka's creative staff members at Mushi Production were fond of using the static picture technique. The static or fixed picture can be compared in its effect on viewers to an image that a *haiku* poem can arouse in its reader. So far, however, no Japanese researcher has tried to compare Tezuka animation work with the world of *haiku* poetry, this is purely my own interpretation. It is interesting to know that Kenny Chow's paper discusses the use of *haiku* poetry in his animation instruction class in Hong Kong.

In Japan, *Astro Boy* and *Mazinger Z* were not broadcast at the same time as the former made its debut in the early 1960s while the latter was produced a decade later. In South Korea, however, there were markedly different viewing experiences as Koh discusses in her research work. As Japanese animation is a foreign import in South Korea, unlike Chow's paper which highlights the artistic aspects of Tezuka animation work, Koh's research critically examines the technological and political messages of Tezuka animation like *Astro Boy* and others and their effects on Korean audiences.

Kim Joon Yang's paper has enabled me to understand certain Japanese animation works from different angles. From his analysis, I learn that the specific TV animation series and their representations (*Space Battleship Yamato* and *Cyborg* 009) were related to identity issues pertaining to geographical–ethnic places like Ezo and Okinawa. I deeply commend and appreciate his efforts in understanding Japan via TV animation. The above-mentioned animation titles are very popular in Japan especially with male anime fans. Kim's analysis gives us valuable insight into the portrayal of transnational and gender identities in Japanese postwar animation.

Toei Doga inherited the techniques of making animation from early Japanese animators who pioneered the art form. One of them was Masaoka Kenzō of whom the late Mori Yasuji, a key animator in Toei Doga, was a former pupil. Before the era of Toei Doga, Mori had worked with Kumakawa Masao, who later helped to train beginners in Toei Doga. Hu Tze-yue G. discusses Masaoka's and Kumakawa's animation that are connected to the wartime and immediate postwar periods of Japan. *Sakura* might have made the Japanese forget the miserable life of a lost world war if it had been released in a theater, and the animated narrative of *Mahō no pen* might have made the Japanese believe in rebuilding a new Japan. Hu's research points out that postwar Japanese animation development can be traced to a few animated works created by pioneer animators who lived through the Second World War. As Japan rebuilt itself in the second half of the twentieth century, the animation medium played an essential role in engaging the public imagination and creating dreams and hopes of the future.

Hu's second paper on the Wan brothers demonstrates to us the "hidden force" behind the establishment of Toei Doga after the Second World War. There was a strong desire to create feature animation like what the Chinese had accomplished during the war. Here, I add that the *dai shokku* (big shock) that the Japanese felt toward the animated *Princess Iron Fan* was due to the small-scale animation production and independent work that existed in Japan at that time. In the early 1940s, the country was able to make feature animation only with the permissive support of Kaigunshō (naval military force) providing the resources and the authority to recruit a large workforce of animators and artists. Hence after the war, Toei played a strong leadership role in integrating these talented people into one establishment with the aim of producing commercial feature animation not only for the Japanese people but also for the worldwide audiences.

My above introduction explanations serve as some of my thoughts and comments of the collected essays while Hu's earlier section coherently explains the main intentions of our publication project. On a practical note, Hu and I trust that the volume will offer scholars, instructors, and animation practitioners a foundational base to grasp and understand the research and pedagogical extent of Japanese animation study in Japan and East Asia, and we are grateful to our contributors for their exemplary work and their participation in this publication.

Notes

1. After Studio Ghibli gained worldwide popularity in the 1990s, the film critic scene also changed; published English articles about the contemporary Japanese film industry occasionally included a paragraph or two about animation films made in Japan.

2. See David Leheny's article, "A Narrow Place to Cross Swords: Soft Power and the Politics of Japanese Pop Culture in East Asia," in *Beyond Japan: The Dynamics of East Asian Regionalism,"* edited by Peter J. Katzenstein and Takashi Shiraishi (Ithaca, NY: Cornell University Press, 2006), 211–33.

3. Paul Ward, "Animation Studies, Disciplinarity, and Discursivity," *Reconstruction* 3, no. 2 (2003). URL: http://reconstruction.eserver.org/032/ward.htm (Accessed February 2, 2011).

4. I thank Asian film scholar Ms. Matsuoka Tamaki for bringing to my attention Sakurai Takamasa's published book.

5. See *Frames of Anime* (2010: 150–54, 96) where I discuss the influence of Chinese animation on some ex-Toei animation staff members including Miyazaki Hayao and Takahata Isao.

6. See Hu (2010: 106). The late puppet animation master Mochinaga Tadahito (1919–1999) is known to have trained a generation of Chinese puppet animators after the Second World War. Kawamoto also collaborated with Shanghai Animation Film Studio to make the puppet film, *To Shoot without Shooting*, in 1988 based on an old Chinese classic tale adapted by a Japanese writer.

7. Miyazaki and Takahata later left Toei and eventually founded Studio Ghibli in the mid-1980s.

8. Tokyo Electric Power Company (Tepco) operates the Fukushima Dai-ichi nuclear power plant, which was damaged by a devastating earthquake and *tsunami* on March 11, 2011.

9. For example, manga continues to exert significant influence in the Japanese animation industry; for example, in the production aspects of creative direction, marketing, and even in terms of audience support. Some of the essays featured in

this collection discuss this influential factor and the genre's deep-seated links to the country's popular culture.

10. Refer to Hu's work (2010) where she discusses the development of the Japanese animation industry after the Second World War. For example, Toei staff members wanted to create animated feature films as they found it more challenging in the creative dimension rather than to work on adapting manga to TV anime series as the latter's storylines and graphic images were preset and designed.

11. 3D-CG animation means three-dimensional computer graphics animation.

Animation Studies and Animation History in Japan

A Bipolar Approach to Understanding the History of Japanese Animation

—Nobuyuki Tsugata

Introduction

Japan's first animated film was produced in 1917. However, while the medium has been in Japan for over nine decades, it was not until the 1960s that Japanese animation actually took off.[1] Most internationally renowned works of Japanese animation, now known by the Japanese word *anime*, have been produced since that era.

Looking back over this ninety-year history, we can distinguish several different epochs that have been marked by two distinct opposing forces. Indeed, Japanese animation appears to have developed through a kind of cross-pollination between these opposing forces. In order to fully grasp the essence of "anime" as such, this chapter considers these opposing forces that contribute to an understanding of the history of Japanese animation.

The 1910s–1920s: Cartoonists versus Entrepreneur

In 1917, animations were produced in Japan for the first time. These were short films lasting about two to five minutes, mainly animated versions of Japanese folk tales or slapstick cartoons of the day. The three creators who produced animations in Japan at that time were Shimokawa Oten (1892–1973, born in Okinawa), Kouchi Jun-ichi (1886–1970, born in Okayama),[2] both former cartoonists, and Kitayama Seitaro (1888–1945, born in Wakayama), who was originally a painter and an entrepreneur who published art magazines.

Each of the above-mentioned pioneers applied different animation techniques, taking inspiration from the French and American animation shorts that were already being screened in Japan at the time. Each produced works independently. For example, Shimokawa produced *Imokawa mukuzo, Genkanban no maki* (Imokawa Mukuzo, The Janitor), while Kouchi directed *Namakura gatana* (The Blunt Sword),[3] and Kitayama directed *Saru kani gassen* (The Crab Gets Its Revenge on the Monkey), all of which were released in 1917.

Of the three, however, Shimokawa and Kouchi were unable to sustain the laborious task of producing animations. After releasing a few films, they reverted to their original work as cartoonists. It is reasonable to think that this was due to their huge financial problems. In contrast, Kitayama produced animation shorts at an extremely productive pace of ten per year. In 1921, he established the Kitayama Film Studio, Japan's first studio specializing in animation. The other two cartoonists were unable to remain in animation production, while Kitayama, originally an entrepreneur, was able to produce many more works over a longer period of time.

Why did this difference arise? One major reason is that Kitayama devised new techniques of producing animated films. He established a mass production system enabling him to produce a large number of works with relative ease. In other words, as an entrepreneur, Kitayama placed priority on producing animations on a commercial basis.

Thus, when the first Japanese animations were produced in the first two decades of the twentieth century, the producers of those animations can be seen as representing the opposing forces of cartoonist and entrepreneur. The victor of this confrontation was the entrepreneur, the one who prioritized commercialization. All these pioneers were commissioned to make animations by different film companies; Shimokawa was commissioned by Tenkatsu, Kouchi by Kobayashi Shokai, and Kitayama by Nikkatsu. They were significantly influenced by the varying attitudes of those companies toward producing animations. As Kitayama was commissioned by Nikkatsu, considering the number of animations produced compared to the other two, it could be that he and the film company Nikkatsu were the most enthusiastic toward animation production.

The 1930s–1940s: Collective versus Individual Production

From the 1930s onward, large Japanese film companies (such as Toho, Shochiku, etc.) increasingly turned toward producing animations, and they started to develop production systems involving large teams of animators. Of the creators who were active in this period, Masaoka Kenzo (1898–1988, born in Osaka) was the most highly acclaimed. Masaoka introduced cel animation and talkies, which were rare in Japan at the time, and created works of high quality. His 1943 film *Kumo to churippu* (The Spider and the Tulip) was, for the sheer beauty of its animation, praised as particularly outstanding among Japanese animations produced during the Second World War. Masaoka also trained a large number of junior animators as part of his system of collective production, and his successors helped Japanese animation back to its feet after the war. In view of these achievements, Masaoka is acclaimed as "the father of Japanese animation."[4]

At the same time, a number of animators attempted to achieve artistic expression through individual rather than collective production. The most notable among them was Ofuji Noburo (1900–1961, born in Tokyo). Like Masaoka, Ofuji also introduced new techniques in the form of cel animation, talkies, and color film from the 1930s onward, a period during which he produced numerous shorts. However, a major difference compared to Masaoka was that, rather than introducing a system of collective production, he continued to produce works mostly on an individual basis. Also, instead of taking commissions from clients, he started to finance his own production. This is a point of major divergence between Ofuji and Masaoka. Moreover, Ofuji started to produce works that contained absurd stories and many elements of eroticism, for which he was criticized or even shunned by the audiences and reviewers of the day.[5]

Though acclaimed in Japan, Masaoka's works remain virtually unknown overseas, even to the present day. Conversely, Ofuji's *Kujira* (The Whale, 1952) and *Yureisen* (The Phantom Ship, 1956), both of them silhouette animations using color cellophane, were screened at the Cannes and Venice film festivals (in 1953 and 1956, respectively) where despite their elements of eroticism, they were highly praised for their uniqueness and the beauty of their animation.

Thus, it can be said that this era already showed two opposing standpoints: one of collective production and one of individual production. It is also evident that the differences between these standpoints could produce differences in the style of the finished works. Notably, due to the large capital needed for any collective production, the content of such works tended to lean toward popular taste. In the case of independent productions, it was (and is) easier to produce work that expresses the animator's artistic sense and individuality.

The 1950s–1970s: Animated Feature Films versus TV Serials

In Japan, American cartoons featuring the characters of Mickey Mouse and Betty Boop, for example, had been released even before the Second World War. This was not the case with animated feature films; for example, *Snow White and the Seven Dwarfs* was not released in Japan until 1950. When they were released, however, *Snow White* and other Disney animated features amazed and moved many of those who saw them, including animation producers. After this, Disney animated features became the benchmark for many creators of Japanese animation.

In 1956, Toei Doga (Toei Animation Studio) was set up for the purpose of producing animated features inspired by the Disney musical and fantasy genres. This was Japan's first large-scale studio devoted entirely to producing animated films. Its first animated feature was *Hakujaden* (White Snake Enchantress, 1958), which was followed by other feature films produced at the rate of one per year. However, colossal sums of money were required to produce animated features, and even so Disney films still remained more popular than those of Toei Animation Studio in Japan at the time. For this reason, Toei Animation Studio had difficulty in returning a profit solely by producing animated features. To prevent running on a loss, it started producing animations for TV commercials, which kept the company afloat.

In January 1963, there was an "incident" that would significantly alter the direction of the Japanese animation industry thereafter. It was the inaugural broadcast of the TV series *Tetsuwan Atomu* (Astro Boy, 1963–1966). The series was produced by Mushi Production, a company established in 1961 by Tezuka Osamu (1928–1989, born in Osaka), Japan's most-respected cartoonist. Though originally a cartoonist, Tezuka was also strongly attracted to animation, and started to think of creating animations himself. However, the animated feature format used by Disney and Toei Animation Studio required massive funding as well as major investment in staff and equipment. Tezuka temporarily abandoned the idea of creating animated films.

Meanwhile, from the late 1950s to the 1960s, numerous American TV animation series were broadcast on Japanese TV. These included *Huckleberry Hound*, *The Ruff and Ready Show*, and *The Flintstones*. As a result, there were two types of animation in Japan at the time: animated features screened in cinemas and series broadcast on TV. Tezuka felt a strong sense of dissatisfaction with the American TV series. This was mainly because the episodes were short, at around five to ten minutes each, and therefore could not express any great variety of narrative or character emotion. He also felt that the technique of limited animation was "abused" and the picture movements were too crude.

Tezuka therefore set out the following principles for animation productions:

1. Rather than producing animated features, Tezuka would produce a TV animation series based on a comic that he himself had created and published. It would be *Astro Boy.*
2. Its content would not be simple, like contemporary American TV series with an episode length of five to ten minutes and consisting of short gags. Instead, each episode would last about thirty minutes, during which complex stories and the emotional expressions of the characters would be fully realized.
3. By rigorously minimizing the number of drawings, he would be able to manage with small production budgets and short lead times.
4. Merchandise would be produced from the principal characters in the series, and the fees received for use of character rights would be diverted to fund further production. (Tezuka was the first to fully introduce this system in Japan.)[6]

By rigorously applying these principles to the production of his works, Tezuka managed to produce a TV animation series in the form of serialized broadcasts of one episode per week, thirty minutes per episode. This had been considered impossible in Japan at the time, but the result was a major success. The on-air season for a single work was between six months and one year, and in some cases longer than that. As a result, the total number of episodes per work-project ran to as many as twenty-six or fifty-two in total. In other words, Tezuka's system made it possible to produce long, complex, and diverse stories in animated form. *Astro Boy* also stood as proof that popular comics (*manga*) serialized in comic magazines could become big hits if converted to TV animation.

Astro Boy and its producer Tezuka had an immeasurable impact on the history of Japanese anime. Tezuka was the first to attempt and achieve major success in serialized broadcasts once a week, thirty minutes per episode, of a popular comic converted to TV animation. This style can still be found in Japanese TV animation today; indeed, the style of Japanese animation now known all over the world as "anime" can be said to have been born then and there. It can also be considered as the greatest achievement of Tezuka, who created this style.

This, however, created problems of its own. One of them was that, spurred by the success of *Astro Boy*, other animation studios all started to produce TV series. This led to a shortage of animators, a sudden increase in the workload on individuals, and, as a result, animators became severely overworked. Another was that while animation production costs were kept low, this meant that the wages paid to animators were therefore very poor. These two points still remain entrenched as a bad practice of the Japanese animation industry to this day, with the exception of some studios and animators. Tezuka Osamu is sometimes blamed for having caused this low-wage system.

Nonetheless, the technique of TV animation created by Tezuka established a twofold approach; namely, that of pursuing story interest and that of emphasizing the emotional expressions of the characters. This provided the impetus for studios other than Mushi Production to create many famous works in the 1970s, including *Mazinger Z* (1972–1974), *Heidi Girl of the Alps* (1974), *Candy Candy* (Candy White, 1976–1979), and *Kido senshi gundam* (Mobile Suit Gundam, 1979–1980).

As described before, the period from the 1950s to the 1970s was, for Japan's animation industry, divided into two opposing forces: animated feature films in the Disney mould, and TV animation series completely unlike Disney productions. Of these, it was the TV series that achieved preponderance.

The 1980s–1990s: Mass Markets versus "Mania"

Some animation producers felt a strong dissatisfaction with the "predominance of TV series" that had become evident by the 1970s. This was rooted in the fact that TV series were cheap to produce and were moreover strongly influenced by the wishes of the sponsors (toy makers, game production companies, etc.) who funded the production. This latter in turn made it harder for animators to create the works they had envisioned.

In 1984, there was another "incident" that would change this status quo once more. It was the release of Miyazaki Hayao's animated feature *Kaze no tani no nausicaa* (Nausicaa of the Valley of Wind). Set in a world one thousand years into the future, when environmental pollution has almost destroyed the planet, it tells a story of a war waged between different kingdoms, and of a girl called Nausicaa, the main protagonist, who tries to save humanity from the war. As such, the film contained a strong message of warning to modern society and appealed to people from a broad range of ages and backgrounds.

In 1985, Miyazaki was instrumental in establishing Studio Ghibli, through which he has produced films such as *Tenku no shiro laputa* (Castle in the Sky, 1986), *Tonari no totoro* (My Neighbor Totoro, 1988), *Kurenai no buta* (Porco Rosso, 1992), *Mononoke hime* (Princess Mononoke, 1997), and *Sen to chihiro no kamikakushi* (Spirited Away, 2001). Today, he has many fans in Japan who would not normally watch anime, but are always keen to see Miyazaki's works. This reveals the extent to which works produced by Miyazaki and Ghibli have become mass-market brands. Ghibli's success also shows that anime, previously assumed to be "for children" or "for fanatics only" in Japan, has come to reach a much broader audience. Miyazaki's achievement lies in that he revived the fortunes of animated feature films, and he did so to the detriment of TV series.

From the second half of the 1980s, the number of TV animation series produced had started to decrease. In fact, with the exception of Studio Ghibli's output, there has been a long-term trend of continuing decline in the industry as a whole. This was because the tastes of anime fans had diversified, bringing with it the consequence that there were now fewer opportunities for a single work to win a large number of fans and become a huge hit.

In 1995, a work that had a major impact on this situation was *Shin-seiki Evangelion* (Neon Genesis Evangelion, 1995–96). Created as a TV series, this work originally targeted obsessive fans of anime, otherwise known as *otaku.* However, the stories with their riddles and secret codes, as well as the style of depicting the complex deep psychology of the characters, started to attract a wider interest and gradually acquired more fans, making this the standout work of the 1990s. *Ghost in the Shell,* directed by Oshii Mamoru, was also released in the same year (1995). In the beginning, it had mainly been conceived as a vehicle for Oshii's fans (and some other anime fanatics). However, when news reached Japan that it had become a hit in America, there was renewed interest in Oshii's work, while the popularity of anime overseas became a hot topic.

As shown in this section, there was again a polarization of opposing forces in Japanese animation in the 1980s and onward. On one side were works aimed at mass markets, as in the case of the Ghibli works; on the other were works produced for a limited fan base only ("mania"). Even in the latter case, it was not unusual for new movements to be spawned and the image of the works or their creators to change, depending on the way word spread about the work. It is this kind of trend that characterizes present-day animation in Japan.

Conclusion

Japanese animation has received a wide range of diverse influences in the course of its development. At the same time, a variety of different opposing forces have also emerged through the decades, and animation developed from a kind of cross-pollination between these opposing trends. In many cases, a secondary trend (or sometimes a completely new trend) appeared suddenly to challenge the mainstream practice, subsequently transforming the Japanese animation industry. The appearance of *Tetsuwan Atomu* in 1963 had the most important influence on the present state of Japanese animation as it paved the way to the mass production of TV anime series and extended the age span of the audience.[7]

In summary, to understand and research the various stages in the development of Japanese animation, we need to be well aware of this characteristic of opposing forces interacting and affecting the developmental trends of Japanese animation.

Notes

1. Editors' note: Television was considered as one of the Three Sacred Treasures in Japan in the late 1950s (the other two were the washing machine and the refrigerator). They were dream appliances that Japanese people wanted to possess, and they were symbolic of a new life after the end of the Second World War as it was portrayed in the comic world of *Astro Boy.* TV was a big hit appliance then that many Japanese households acquired in the early 1960s. Furthermore, the manga of *Astro Boy* had been very popular among children readers since 1952. Thus its animated TV episodes attracted audiences to Japanese animation.

2. Shimokawa Oten published his work as a *mangaka* (manga creator) under the alternate reading of the characters of his name "Shimokawa Hekoten." Likewise, Kouchi Jun-ichi also used the alternate reading of his name "Kouchi Sumikazu."

3. *Namakura gatana* (1917) was also screened under the title of *Hanawa hekonai meito no maki* (Sword of Hanawa Hekonai).

4. Editors' note: Refer to Watanabe's and Hu's chapters in this volume for further details of Masaoka's background and contributions to Japanese animation development in Japan.

5. Editors' note: See Sano's essay in this volume for a comprehensive account of Ofuji's art and animation.

6. Yamamoto Eiichi, *Mushi pro koboki* [History of Mushi Production] (Tokyo: Shinchosha Publishing, 1989).

7. Editors' note: Though Tsugata's writing did not elaborate on the trend of "mania" which he brought up in his work, it is related to the phenomenon of *otaku*. Readers may refer to Azuma Hiroki's *Otaku: Japan's Database Animals*, translated by Jonathan E. Abel and Kono Shion (Minneapolis: University of Minnesota Press, 2009) for a critical analysis of this consumer subculture.

References

Bendazzi, Giannalberto. *Cartoons: One Hundred Years of Cinema Animation*. London: John Libbey & Company, 1994.

Lent, John A., ed. *Animation in Asia and the Pacific*. Bloomington: Indiana University Press, 2001.

McCarthy, Helen. *Hayao Miyazaki, Master of Japanese Animation*. Berkeley, CA: Stone Bridge Press, 1999.

Tsugata, Nobuyuki. "Research on the Achievements of Japan's First Three Animators." *Asian Cinema* 14, no. 1 (2003): 13–27.

———. *Nihon anime-shon no chikara* [Power of Japanese Animation]. Tokyo: NTT Shuppan, 2004.

———. *Anime sakka toshite no tezuka osamu, sono kiseki to honshitsu* [Tezuka Osamu as the animation director, his record and essence]. Tokyo: NTT Shuppan, 2007.

Reflections on the Wan Brothers' Letter to Japan

The Making of *Princess Iron Fan*

—Tze-yue G. Hu

Whether in peace or war, the human condition continually adjusts, adapts, and reacts to new circumstances and contexts. In times of war, the situation tends to present a darker veil on existence, all the more so since the main call of the day is physical survival. In recent years, scholars researching contemporary and historical instances of collaboration between cultures, warring regimes, economic blocs, and the like have highlighted the important role of the individual, his or her interests and experiences in advancing a certain mode of action—a choice, a decision, and the underlying complexity in which a collaborative position took shape, was constructed and maintained. In regard to the Second World War, the intrigues and agendas of various people who survived the war, especially those who held power in one way or another or were made to participate publicly in propagandistic activities, invite and arouse our attention and understanding.

In Louise Young's work *Japan's Total Empire: Manchuria and the Culture of Wartime Imperialism* (1998), the role of the media in stirring war fever and jingoism is discussed. She queries the differing positions of consumers in an imperialistic environment. For example, how do consumers interpret and read the popular media, or do consumers in fact adopt an indifferent attitude in their viewing though they are seen as entertained and informed? Or, to what extent were these propagandistic media products consciously developed and tailored or how much were they simply "the product of the historical moment itself?" (1998: 57). In discussing the history of collaboration in wartime East Asia, Canadian historian Timothy Brook (2005, 2008) spells out the often-negative meanings and images that we attribute to the domain of collaboration. It is as if the subject itself is immoral and so unthinkably unpatriotic as to have ever acted in the collaborative sense at the beginning. Instead, he calls for broad and comprehensive investigation when we study predicaments and motivations that induced rival ethnic groups to work together. In Brook's work, he is concerned in particular with how some Chinese could work with Japanese under the intense Japanese military occupation of China during the Second World War.

Fu Poshek's study of Chinese cinema in occupied Shanghai is also critical of the discourse frame of "moral binarism" whereby the identification of heroes, heroines, and villains has to be geographically and nationally situated. He challenges the "nationalistic representation of the occupation" and asserts a "new notion of ambiguity" and the space of the "grey zone" in our scholarship research over wartime film history (2001: 180). My definition of the "historical moment" is a fluid one; a time and space where a separate landscape or scenario appears, however fleeting it may be, where the realistic hard facts of everyday life become insignificant, less powerful, and even trivial. As Fu has pointed out, documentary evidence of East Asian cinema during the Second World War has only begun to surface in recent years. In regard to the animation medium, the availability of research materials is still very scarce. As mentioned above, politicized and institutionalized readings of war history and media works produced during extraordinary circumstances are not helpful in broadening our understanding of the human condition. How individual Chinese and Japanese forged a survival existence and yet created a meaningful public space for themselves is a topic I shall focus on in this chapter.

Letter from China

This research is about a handwritten letter authored by the Chinese pioneer animators, the Wan brothers, at the height of World War II. Dated September 13, 1942, it was written at the request of the late film critic and executive, Shimizu Akira (1916–1997), soon after he visited them in Shanghai. The contents of the letter together with a short introductory article were published in the 1942 December issue of the film journal *Eiga Hyōron*. Shimizu fully translated the letter into Japanese. This paper explores the spirit of the written letter and its contents including its historical and artistic contexts. A full translation of the letter is published in my monograph, *Frames of Anime: Culture and Image-Building* (2010: 169–73). This paper contains excerpts from the above work (2010: 69–75) and from an article published in Japanese in 2010, "Anime-shon, anime, japanime-shon: kindaika to fantaji-no 'hōko'" [Animation, anime, Japanimation: The baggage of modernization and fantasy] in *Anime wa ekkyo suru* [Anime crossing borders], edited by Kurosawa Kiyoshi et al., vol. 6 of *Nihon eiga wa ikiteiru* [Japanese cinema: New cinema studies series], 31–52, published by Iwanami Shoten, Tokyo. (Copyright 2010 by Iwanami Shoten, Publishers, Tokyo.)

I first came across this letter at the beginning of my research on Japanese animation in the late 1990s. However, I was not able to give due analysis to the letter then, given my limited knowledge of Japanese animation at the time. Moreover, the letter's content is entirely about Chinese animation; on the surface, it has nothing pertaining to the subject of Japanese animation, which I was seeking actively to understand and explore. As time passes and as I delve more deeply into the developmental stages of Japanese animation, I have begun to see the significance of the letter and its underlying messages within the historical background of a world war.[1]

The Animated Film *Princess Iron Fan* and Its Historical Context

By the late nineteenth century, imperialistic Japan increasingly viewed China with disdain, and there was a general and deep sense of dismal hopelessness about the country, given its incapacity to rise and face the challenge of the advancing West and its ongoing internal warlordism and disorder. China, however, produced arguably the first animated feature film in Asia in 1941. Deprived of technological help from abroad, lack of knowledge of other advanced techniques of filmmaking, and a shortage of monetary support, the Wan brothers in China still succeeded in making *Princess Iron Fan* (in Chinese, *Tie shan gong zhu*; in Japanese, *Tetsusen kōshu*). The film played to admiring audiences in China and parts of Southeast Asia. The narrative of the film was based on a traditional Chinese folk legend, *Journey to the West*, and the tale of *Princess Iron Fan* was extracted from parts of this beloved folk narrative.

Critics and film reviewers have tended to emphasize the anti-Japanese war elements embedded in the film. But the film was not so much directed at the Japanese as it was at the Chinese audiences themselves—quintessentially, inspiring the Chinese to aspire to a spirit of unity and unselfishness in the face of adversity, whatever the circumstances might be. By using the animation medium as a platform for artistic expressions, the film displayed an "Eastern answer" to the Disney-influenced type of animation. In an early article published in 1936, the Wan brothers already stressed the importance of utilizing "Chinese traditions and stories, consistent with our sense of sensibility and sense of humour" (Quiquimelle, 1991: 178). In that article, the Wan brothers paid tribute to American cartoons and even admitted that their work had been influenced by Max and Dave Fleischer's animated works. However, they also showed admiration for animated works from other countries notably German and Russian made ones. As Quiquimelle pointed out, they were conscious of aesthetic matters pertaining to "ethnicity," works that authentically bore the stamp of a culture, be it American, German, Chinese, or Russian. In the rare and unusual letter written by the Wan brothers to the Japanese in 1942, again the animators stressed that

> We always had this notion that the Eastern art of film-making should embody Eastern color and taste and it should not imitate and follow wholly the style of Hollywood. Thus, based on this creative aspiration, as seen from the characteristics of *Princess Iron Fan*, in the areas of facial make-up, fashion, action and line-drawing, they all yield originally to traditional Chinese art.

The existence of this letter and the fact that the addressee and the requesting party were the Japanese, speak volumes of the status of the film project in the eyes and minds of the Japanese. Written at the height of the Second Sino-Japanese War (1937–1945) when many parts of China as well as East and Southeast Asia were already under the control of Japanese military forces, the letter strangely did not mention a word about the war or even make indirect reference to the decades' long warfare between the two countries. What the Wan brothers provided in the letter was exactly what the counterpart wanted to know; that is, the production process of *Princess Iron Fan*, the creative and economic problems encountered, and the attempts that were made in overcoming them. In the introductory part, Shimizu reported the tremendous response of the film in China and the astonishing news that even with such a limited market (*shijō ga semaku*), in Shanghai alone, the film could be screened at two cinemas at one time,[2] while in Japan, the film was released in thirty theaters. He also noted that because it was an animated feature film made in such tough economic times, it was necessary to find out the circumstances under which it was made and the hardship the artists had undergone. Image-wise, Shimizu saw it as a "dream" (*yume*) come true and happening at "inland" (*nachi*, meaning China).[3]

The letter was written in *baihua* Chinese and it is in the traditional vertical way of writing. Its length is four and a half pages. The Chinese characters are neatly and clearly written and are meant for Shimizu's easy reading and translation. The breadth and length of the letter are intended to explain comprehensively the production process of *Princess Iron Fan* to Japanese fans. The letter seems to be written by the older twin brother Wan Laiming though it also included the name of Wan Guchan as well.

Ironically, the *other* (meaning China) proved to be ahead in the quest to present a different kind of animation imbued with cultural pride and representation. From basic drawing techniques to background artistic direction, clay model preparation to animators' drawings, coloring, quality control, filming, sound recording, and even aspects of staff illnesses and fatigue, the Wan brothers related them in as much detail as they could showing no intention of hiding any ugly facts or presenting an illusionary "all is well" picture of their production process. The letter ended with a cautionary note that their *Princess Iron Fan* was nothing to be envious about and, in fact, the animators would rather welcome comments and advice from the "Eastern people" (*dongfang renshi*). The names of Wan Laiming and Wan Guchan then appeared at the end of the letter.[4]

It is interesting to note that the Wan brothers did not address the obvious reader as Japanese (*riben renshi*) but instead chose an accommodating broad-based term, "Eastern people," and that this corresponded with the earlier part of the letter, which stressed the indigenous development of "Eastern filmmaking" as opposed to the American approach. In fact, the term *renshi* carries the meaning of "personage" in English. In other words, it denotes a person of rank and distinction with some distinguished power or status. The Chinese characters *dongfang*, in general, refer to the direction and place where the sun rises. Hence, the Wan brothers' usage of these characters politely places the Japanese readers or fans at a special level. Japan is indeed widely known as the "Land of Rising Sun" and is also situated on the far eastern side of mainland China across the sea. There is also a possible reading that indirectly, the Wan brothers were also referring to the prevalent war ideology at that time; that is, the Greater East Asian Co-Prosperity Sphere, which Japan had created and championed during the Second World War. The Greater East Asia Co-Prosperity Sphere concept was an outgrowth of the Asianism ideology. It emphasized

Japan as "the bearer of modernity to the rest of the Asia" (Morris-Suzuki, 1998: 100) and that Japan would lead the Eastern world to freedom from Western domination.

However, it is obvious that what the Wan brothers did not relate in the letter was the great inconvenience and hardship the animators faced in recruiting and managing production staff members due to the invasionary activities of the Japanese military forces in the Jiangsu region. Before the making of *Princess Iron Fan,* the Wan brothers were already engaged in making several short animated film series that contained patriotic messages calling all Chinese to rise up against the invading enemy; animation historian Bendazzi (1994: 182) wrote that the brothers shuttled all around the region making their animated works.[5] Anticipating that the Japanese military forces would pursue them due to the nationalistic message of their work, the Wan brothers operated in studios situated in the cities of Wuhan, Chungking, and Shanghai, and escaped the advancing Japanese military forces whenever they moved near. Later, it was reported that the production of *Princess Iron Fan* was in the French Concession part of Shanghai. But Shimizu's article praised the Wan brothers' perseverance in managing two animation studios during the making of *Princess Iron Fan,* one indeed in Shanghai and another in Suzhou. In other words, it is likely that the film was made in several places, given such difficult wartimes. Moreover, in the letter to the Japanese, the Wan brothers revealed that the film project lasted three years contrary to the common belief that it was made entirely in Shanghai in 1940–1941.

It has been recorded that the Japanese reception of the Chinese-made animated film was a *dai shokku* (big shock). They found it unbelievable that a war-torn and occupied China nearby (*otonari no chūgoku*) could complete such a dedicated film project. Among animation filmmakers and those working in the industry, many recognized it as the "earliest Eastern-made feature animated film," *tōyō de no daichōhen manga* (Yamaguchi and Watanabe, 1977: 40). There were rave reviews and enthusiastic responses praising the luxurious representation of animated images.

Recognizing the Film's Artistic and Hegemonic Positions

In Japan, contemporary printed works about world animation would seldom exclude mentioning the Chinese animated film *Princess Iron Fan.*[6] Contemporary well-known Japanese animation directors like Miyazaki

Hayao, Takahata Isao, and Otsuka Yasuo are known to have held discussions about this film and its impact on Chinese animation.[7] In my interview sessions with a number of veteran Japanese animators and producers who had lived through World War Two, this film often gets mentioned and praised during the course of the conversation. Upon reading a number of printed articles and promotional pamphlets about the film in Japan during the period of 1942, it became apparent that the film critics, producers, and animators were critical of the "path" and "style" Japanese animation was heading in at that time.[8] For example, in appreciating the Chinese animated film and analyzing the state of Japanese animation then, a prominent literary writer, Nakatani Takao, wrote about the importance of referring back to ancient tales and legends as "they are the origins of an ethnic people" (1942: 40). He also mentioned that since the Meiji period (1868–1912) the direction of Japanese literature had a tendency to incline toward the narrow theme of "realism" (1942: 41). In a published article (1942) about a discussion session held on the animated *Princess Iron Fan* film, Seo Mitsuyo, who was the director of the famous animated feature films that were produced soon after, *Momotarō no umiwashi* (1942) and *Momotarō umi no shinpei* (1945), was quoted as classifying the film as an "art film" rather than as a "manga film," for to the director, the latter tended to have more "gags" in its animated content. He was not alone in regarding the film as a *kaiga eiga* (art film). Film critic Takakiba Tsutomu (1942) noted the film's "imaginative and independent animated expressions" and its appeal to both "adults and children audiences." To him, a manga film's narrative is "less complex" and contains more gags and slapstick humor.

Animation studies scholar Sano Akiko (2006) sums up critically the state of Japanese animation development during that period. According to her, Japanese animation then was in dire search of its own artistic animation path besides acknowledging its overenthusiastic orientation toward the "yankee" or Disney kind of animating. One contentious point is: Was it only the "intellectual class" who appreciatively recognized the artistic value of the Chinese animated film *Princess Iron Fan* in the Eastern world? Could it be the case that the Wan brothers' letter had *subverted* the existing political order at that time? The brothers' willingness and sincerity in telling their side of the story must also have been triggered by the spontaneous enthusiasm that Japanese fans had shown via Shimizu's visit to Shanghai. Shimizu also worked as a film executive for Kawakita (see note 3) showing many Chinese and other non-Chinese films in different parts of China. Sano's article also relates that the film was highly popular in Japan due to its fantastical storytelling and energetic animating qualities. Her analysis gives us a glimpse into the popular status of the film and the fervent discussions that were generated as a result.

Shimizu's article and the Wan brothers' letter might have created a kind of interstitial communicative space wherein two supposedly warring parties transcended their real circumstances to communicate about a subject called animation in spite of the knowledge of "who" the enemy was. American music ethnologist and educator Glenn M. Hudak (1999: 447) informs us in his coedited and coauthored book, *Sound Identities*, that music making engages our "consciousness": "an engagement which can 'rattle' the hegemony of everyday life and open up the possibility of a common ground where differences might meet, mingle, and engage one another . . . in the making of a musical 'We.'"

Can we conclude that in a sense the Wan brothers and their animation fans in Japan recognized that art and film could rise above national boundaries? What dominated here was the common identity and experience of human creative endeavors in times of war and nationalism, the realization of the importance of art and scarce resources, experiences of the self and the other, and subtly, the symbolic celebration of an artistic achievement with unique Eastern cultural characteristics. Chinese printed articles about the animated *Princess Iron Fan* tend not to address the film as *the first Eastern animated feature film* but simply refer to it as the "first Chinese-made feature animated film" (Tu, 1997: 105) or "long film animation" (Zhang, 2003: 74) for example.[9] The Japanese honorific description of the film means more, including the incorporation of the Greater East Asian Co-Prosperity Sphere war ideology by openly hailing China as the first Eastern country to produce an animated feature film with Eastern qualities. Outwardly, it is approvingly commending China's ability in upholding the East Asian ideology, both spiritually and creatively. In other words, one may pose the possibility that despite the heinous wartimes, certain transcendental moments and efforts in humanistic understanding can be reached. It underscores animation's power to draw dialogue and even to sustain mutual respect between two opposing parties.

Kempeitai's Intervention

However, a fact remains—namely, that the appreciative gaze from the Japanese side was one of envy and competition. The subsequent *Momotarō* feature film series was Japan's "Eastern" answer to the animating world during the war years. Due to the military government's extensive monetary support, the subject matter of the film series was clearly different from the Chinese one, as the animating narratives focused intensely and realistically about the continual war front. For example, the character design of the various animals and half-human figures featured expressed a pro-Disney-like agenda including representations of the Pacific islanders portrayed that showed obvious racist overtones not unlike early Disney animated works about "savage," "uncivilized," and colored peoples.[10]

It has been raised elsewhere that one must not discount the powerful presence and influence of the Kempeitai, the military police of the Japanese Imperial Army. One can think of the Kempeitai's abilities to solicit "compliant" actions from Shanghai cinema working personnel. In this instance, the Wan brothers might have been threatened or felt the threat of persecution if they did not cooperate in sharing their production process with their Japanese counterparts. This is a valid concern. For example, even Kawakita Nagamasa, who presided over Shanghai's film studios during the occupational era, was under constant surveillance of the military police. His enthusiasm over film art and business, in addition to his close relationship to the cinema scene in Shanghai and his excellent Chinese language background at times, fostered the suspicion of the Kempeitai.

It is beyond the space of this chapter to fully discuss the middle-man role of the film enthusiast and distributor Kawakita Nagamasa (1903–1981) during the Japanese occupation of Shanghai in the 1940s. Readers may refer to Iwamoto Kenji's article (2004), "Ajia shugi no gen'ei: Nihon eiga to daitōa kyōeiken" (Illusion of the Asian doctrine: Japanese film and the Greater East Asia Co-prosperity Sphere) in *Eiga to daitōa kyōeiken* (Film and the Greater East Asia Co-Prosperity Sphere), edited by Iwamoto Kenji, where he gave an introductory account of several Japanese film industry personnel who played significant roles during the wartime era. Till today, in the Japanese film circles, the late Kawakita Nagamasa is remembered as an "international film person" who promoted film as an art form in Japan. Together with his wife, the late Kawakita Kashiko (1908–1993), the couple was known for introducing many foreign films to Japan while at the same time promoting Japanese films abroad.

One may argue that in spite of the looming existence of the Kempeitai, the Wan brothers saw no advantage in resisting the friendship of visiting fan-journalists and film critic writers from Japan. Moreover, the business collaboration between Kawakita and *Princess Iron Fan*'s producer Zhang

Shankun did bring a period of peace and order to Shanghainese cinema despite the occupation. It has been noted that the Japanese authorities had given instructions for the smooth transition and cooperation of the Shanghai motion industry people especially during the early period of the occupation (Fu: 182, Baskett [2004: 161–64]). Hence whether threatened at gunpoint or not, the Wan brothers' act of writing the letter to Japan has to be placed in the context of an ongoing domestic debate within Japan during a time when there was significant disquietude about the country's navigational directions in facing the Western world politically and culturally, in particular the geopolitical ideology and the artistic methods of filmmaking. On the other hand, given the economic hardship of marketing one's film products during a world war, all the more so to the supposed enemy, the Wan brothers must have considered the commercial advantages of writing the letter and the promotional opportunities it would bring in screening the animated *Princess Iron Fan* in Japan.

Conclusion

My reflections on the Wan brothers' letter cross boundaries in terms of space, time, and cross-subject study in its analysis. Since the early 1990s, Japanese animation, specifically the anime kind, has attained a new international name-title, *Japanimation*. However, in view of its ongoing glamour, fame and distinction in the world animation stage, one cannot discount its complexities and its darker phantasmagoric sides in past history. America has invented Mickey and so, too, Japan has invented its own. *Anime*—Japan's answer to the West—has come a long way and the generic realm shows no signs of recess or regress. The power of the visual can be expressed in many ways. Much earlier in the twentieth century, the Japanese already saw and comprehended that Mickey and his friends possessed a host of ideological functions.

The country also saw the innate ideological visions of Chinese animation as created by the Wan brothers. In this collection, Sano's chapter on Ōfuji's *chiyogami* animation demonstrates the local animator-artist's struggle and response to foreign forms of animation, particularly American cartoon animation. Ironically, the wartime animated film *Princess Iron Fan*, even today, has a special status in the Japanese register of world-class animation although the film remains largely unknown and obscure among Chinese communities in mainland China and other parts of the world. In

卡通

著名東方童話—「西遊記」之一．
「鉄扇公主」繪製經過．

萬籟鳴
萬古蟾

隱隱地記得，遠在十七年前，我們已經在開始研究卡通藝術。其中經過不少的艱難和失敗，始達到差強人意的結果。這或者是從事事業者必經過程，而我們的環境裡更是感覺困苦。初步成功以後，共計繪製十四部卡通短片，因為內容含有教育意義，所以得到教育部及教育所的採用，雖然技藝方面的缺陷不容否認，但是那可以說是我們從事卡通事業初期的成功。

最大的問題在於卡通短片不能單獨營業，這未免影響了一切經濟生命線。可是，初步的成功鼓舞起我們的心志。以所服役之電影美工工作的餘暇，繼續埋頭工作。因為缺乏科學知識與鮮有卡通前輩指教，我們就像在黑暗中摸索前進一般的可憐、可笑、好了有自以為完美滿的成績獻演，當時我們得力於所用所服役公司中之機械研究，減少許多困難。的確這也是使得一般畫家，卡通藝術學者不敢嘗試的最大原因，嘗試着枉費心機的並不在少數，說起來我們未免太僥運了吧。

1. Photocopy of the original handwritten letter from the Wan brothers. Author's collection.

short, transnational perspectives and identities can be formed in odd and unimaginable circumstances and contexts.

To conclude, the "spiritual and informative content" of the Wan brothers' letter has proven to be more effectively encouraging and inspirational to the Japanese in the long term; after the end of the Second World War, the dynamic development of Japanese postwar commercial animation alludes to its previously unfulfilled aspirations and unavailable opportunities to excel creatively and globally. For example, the late manga-artist turned animator Tezuka Osamu was known to have watched *Princess Iron Fan* many times besides viewing other old Disney films when he made his first feature animated film, *Saiyūki* (Journey to the West), in 1960 based on his comic work of the same name. In addition, the subtle yet confident form of self-addressing nationalism indirectly expressed in some Studio Ghibli's films, especially those directed by Miyazaki Hayao and Takahata Isao in the mid-1980s to late 1990s, faintly reminds us of their covert appreciation of Chinese animated films and its blazonry of national culture and history (Hu, 2010: 154).[11] That being said, the Eastern color and spirit as expressed in the animated *Princess Iron Fan* and subsequently described in the Wan

2. Copy of publicity material on *Princess Iron Fan* in Japan.

brothers' letter, is not necessarily an original fresh perspective created by the Chinese. As early as in the eighteenth century, the idea of the *wakon yōsai* (Japanese spirit and Western technology) was already implanted in the Japanese drive to modernize and to face the Western world of industrialization (Hu, 2010: 19–20). The letter from the Wan brothers and its contents simply reiterates a familiar modernization concept or goal worth further pursuing from the Japanese end.

Records have shown that the Wan brothers continued to maintain long-lasting friendships with some members of the Japanese film industry after the war. On the Japanese side, for example, the late master-puppet animator Mochinaga Tadahito (1919–1999) had at various times of his postwar animation career revisited China to help train a generation of Chinese puppet animation filmmakers.[12] The collection of the late Shimizu's archival film notes is now owned by the Kadokawa Culture Promotion Foundation. The original handwritten letter from the Wan brothers now rests there. The existence of this letter provides intriguing interpretations; my reflections of its transnational contents and contexts are only a beginning. There is much more to be explored and researched on if the full collection of Shimizu's archival notes could be reviewed and studied concurrently with the Wan brothers' letter. For now, I hope to arouse interest and encourage future explorations on the subject of wartime collaboration and animation filmmaking as well as the humankind's response, motivation, and adaptation to complex situations and circumstances.

Notes

This chapter contains excerpts of my earlier monograph, *Frames of Anime: Culture and Image-Building* (2010), in pages 69–75 of chapter 4, "Development of Japanese Animation up to the End of the Second World War." Reprinted by permission from Hong Kong University Press.

It also contains extracts of my published article in Japanese, "Anime-shon, anime, japanime-shon: Kindaika to fantaji no 'hoko,'" in *Anime wa ekkyō suru*, 31–52, ed. Kurosawa Kiyoshi et al., vol. 6, of *Nihon eiga wa ikiteiru*. Printed in English by permission from Iwanami Shoten (Tokyo), © 2010 by Iwanami Shoten, Publishers.

1. The existence of this letter was first brought to my notice by the Asian film specialist Ms. Matsuoka Tamaki in 1998 and I thank her for sharing this precious information with me.

2. *Princess Iron Fan* was said to be shown in three cinemas in Shanghai during the time of its release. See Quiquemelle (1991: 178).

3. Shimizu Akira was also an employee of the liberal-minded Kawakita Nagamasa (1903–1981), a prominent film distributor in Japan and China during that time. It was probably because of Kawakita's friendship with Zhang Shankun (1905–1957), the financial sponsor of *Princess Iron Fan* and the owner of the film company *Xinhua Yingye Gongsi*, that the Wan brothers agreed to write the letter to the Japanese side. By then, the Shanghai film industry had come under the administrative control of the Japanese military forces, with Kawakita being appointed as a consultant chair presiding behind the scene.

4. The published article also showed pictures of the Wan brothers and the writer.

5. Examples of such films were included in the film series *Anti-Japanese Posters Collection* and *Anti-Japanese War Songs Collection*. See John A. Lent and Xu Ying (2003).

6. See, for example, Okada, Emiko et al., *Anime no sekai* [World of anime] (Tokyo: Shinchōsha, 1988); and Saitani, Ryo, ed. *Sekai to Nihon no anime-shon besuto 150* [Best 150 World and Japanese Animation Films Selected by Professionals] (Tokyo: Fusion Product, 2003).

7. See Takahata Isao, *Eiga wo tsukuri nagara kangaetan koto 1955–91 I* [What I was thinking, while making a film] (Tokyo: Tokuma Publishing, 1991), 144–54).

8. The author expresses her appreciation to animation historian Watanabe Yasushi and animation studies scholar Dr. Sano Akiko for providing further reference materials about the popularity of the animated *Princess Iron Fan* during that period.

9. So far, the author has not conducted research into the Chinese articles about *Princess Iron Fan* written during the war years in order to ascertain the Chinese title description of the film during that period. It is likely that the above-mentioned superlative description of the film was not commonly used by the Chinese. During the Japanese occupation of East and Southeast Asia, many locally produced newspapers and magazines also came to a halt in their publication activities. For example, in Singapore, the author has difficulties locating film reviews of the animated film as Chinese newspapers were no longer in circulation due to the imminent news of arriving Japanese military forces in the second half of 1941.

10. Japanese animation was not alone in harboring racist representations during the war years. What is striking is that there are similarities in racist representations between early Disney and Japanese animated works. It is apparent that Japanese animators picked up this animating influence from Disney. This ideological choice is a subject of study that this essay will not have space to explore. See Nicholas Sammond's "Gentlemen, Please Be Seated: Racial Masquerade and Sadomasochism in 1920s Animation." The paper was presented at the Modern Language Association Annual Convention in Philadelphia, December 27–30, 2009.

11. Here, I am also referring to the Shanghai Animation Film Studio's works made in the late 1950s to late 1970s when the Wan brothers were among the staff members working there. Miyazaki was critically impressed by the production, *Nezha Shakes the Sea* (1979), and he was attracted to Nezha's heroic characteristics, which might have subsequently influenced the characterization of the heroine, Nausicaä, in his directed animation, *Nausicaä of the Valley of the Wind* (1984). See also Takahata (1991: 144–49, see also note 8).

12. See Ono Kosei's article, "Tadahito Mochinaga: The Japanese Animator Who Lived in Two Worlds," *Animation World Magazine* 4, no. 9 (December 1999). http://www.awn.com/mag/issue4.09/4.09pages/onomochinaga.php3 (Accessed on January 5, 2000).

References

Baskett, Michael. "Eiga hitotachi no teikoku: Dai tō-a eiga ken no shosō" [The imperial country of the film people: The aspects of the Greater East Asia film domain]. In *Eiga to Dai-tō-a eiga kyōeiken* [Film and the Greater East Asia Co-Prosperity Sphere], edited by Iwamoto Kenji, 157–79. Tokyo: Shinwasha, 2004.

Bendazzi, Giannalberto. *Cartoons: One Hundred Years of Animation*. London: John Libbey, 1994.

Brook, Timothy. *Collaboration: Japanese Agents and Local Elites in Wartime China*. Cambridge, MA: Harvard University Press, 2005. See also excerpted article at *Japan Focus*, posted on July 5, 2008, http://japanfocus.org/-Timothy-Brook/2798.

Fu, Poshek. "Resistance in Collaboration: Chinese Cinema in Occupied Shanghai, 1941–45." In *Chinese Collaboration with Japan, 1932–45: The Limits of Accommodation*, edited by David P. Barrett and Larry N. Shyu, 180–200. Stanford, CA: Stanford University Press, 2001.

Hudak, Glenn M. "The 'Sound' Identity: Music-Making and Schooling." In *Sound Identities: Popular Music and the Cultural Politics of Education*, edited by Cameron McCarthy et al. New York: Peter Lang, 1999.

Iwamoto, Kenji. "Ajia shugi no gen'ei: Nihon eiga to daitōa kyōeiken" [Illusion of the Asian doctrine: Japanese film and the Greater East Asia Co-Prosperity Sphere]. In *Eiga to daitōa kyōeiken* [Film and the Greater East Asia Co-Prosperity Sphere], edited by Iwamoto Kenji, 7–29. Tokyo: Shinwasha, 2004.

Lent, John A., and Xu Ying. "China's Animation Beginnings: The Roles of the Wan Brothers and Others." *Asian Cinema* 14, no. 1 (2003): 56–69.

"Manga *saiyūki* gahhyō" [Manga *Saiyuki* picture book]. *Eiga Gijutsu* (October 1942): 64–66.

Morris-Suzuki, T. *Re-inventing Japan: Time, Space, Nation.* New York: M. E. Sharpe, 1998.

Nakatani, Takao. "Nisan no kansō" [Two three impressions]. *Eiga Hyōron* (October 1942): 40–42.

Quiquimelle, Marie-Claire. "The Wan Brothers and Sixty Years of Animated Film in China." In *Perspectives on Chinese Cinema*, edited by Chris Berry, 175–86. London: British Film Institute, 1991.

Sano, Akiko. "Manga eiga no jidai—to-ki ikōki kara daisenki ni okeru nihon anime-shon" [Cartoon movie era: Japanese animation from transition period of the talkie to wartime]. In *Eigagakuteki sōzōryoku – shinema sutadiizu no bōken* [Cinematological imagination: An adventure of cinema studies], edited by Katō Mikirō, 96–126. Kyoto: Jimbun Shoin, 2006.

Shimizu, Akira. "Dōwa 'saiyuki' ni shuzai seru: chōhen manga 'tetsusen kōshu' seisaku hōkoku" [Obtaining legendary tale *Saiyuki* material: Feature-length animated film, *Princess Iron Fan* production report]. *Eiga Hyōron* (December 1942): 55–57.

Takakiba, Tsutomu. "Kaiga eiga no tokushusei: chūka no sakuhin *Saiyūki* wo mitte" [Art film special characteristics: Viewing Chinese work, *Saiyuki*]. *Bunka Eiga* (October 1942): 50–52.

Tu, Jia. "Cong zhongguo shuimo donghua shuoqi" [Speaking from China's water and ink painting animation]. In *Donghua dianying yintan shu* [Explorations of animation cinema], edited by Huang Yu-shan and Yu Wei-zheng, 101–13. Taipei: Yuan Liu, 1997.

Yamaguchi, Katsunori, and Watanabe Yasushi. *Nihon anime-shon eiga shi* [The History of Japanese Animation]. Osaka: Yubunsha, 1977.

Young, Louise. *Japan's Total Empire: Manchuria and the Culture of Wartime Imperialism*. Berkeley and Los Angeles: University of California Press, 1998.

Zhang, Huilin. "Some Characteristics of Chinese Animation." *Asian Cinema* 14, no. 1 (2003): 70–79.

On the Establishment and the History of the Japan Society for Animation Studies

—**Masashi Koide**
Translated by Joon Yang Kim

Introduction

This essay is an attempt to present a historical view of the Japan Society for Animation Studies as it was established more than a decade ago. I am the person who has been closely involved with the background management of the society since its founding. In this sense, it can be said that I am in a difficult position to provide objective views of the society. However, I am determined to accept my editors' request, considering that this essay will provide a testimonial discourse or study of the society's establishment. In writing this essay I hope to clear some misunderstandings in regard to its existence within the Japanese academia and any misunderstandings that might be harbored by some nonmembers of the society arising from when it was established.

Here I would like to provide a short introduction of my relationship with the society:

I was involved as an office staff member in the starting up and subsequently the management of the second animation research group of the Japan Society of Image Arts and Sciences (JASIAS) in 1992, the members of which also included the founding members of the Japan Society for Animation Studies. I worked as a secretary-general of the society up until 2011, holding an additional position as vice chairperson of the editorial committee of the JSAS under the first president, Oyama Tadasu (1998–2004 in office), and as vice president of the society since the tenure of the second president, Yokota Masao (2004–2012 in office).

Outline of the Japan Society for Animation Studies

In July 1999, the first issue of the *Japanese Journal of Animation Studies* was published as the official academic journal of the JSAS. The first chairperson of the editorial committee of the society was Nakajima Yoshiaki. The journal's serial volume number reached ten in March 2008, and its publication has been kept regular and sequential, once or twice a year since 1999 (for example, in March 2010, the published issue is vol. 11, no. 1 [Serial no. 12]). In July 1999, at the same time of the first publication of the journal, the first conference—as an annual meeting for reading papers—was held in the Tokyo Metropolitan Museum of Photography, accompanied by the second general meeting; from then on, the general meetings of the JSAS have been held in conjunction with its annual conference. After the second conference in the museum in 2000, the next one was held at Musashino Art University in 2001. This was the first time that one of the schools with which members of the society were affiliated was selected as the conference venue; since then this has been adopted as the venue strategy. The annual conference has been held regularly, the tenth one of which was hosted in Kwansei Gakuin University in June 2008 (the twelfth one was held in Hiroshima Jogakuin University in June 2010). The election of the directors of the society has been held every two years to establish the current seventh directorial board since the very first election in May 2000. The society gained social attention as an academic body for research and was admitted to and became registered with the Science Council of Japan in July 2003 (in its nineteenth term). The tenth anniversary of the JSAS was held in the College of Humanities and Sciences at Nihon University in July 2008.

The society's members are involved in various fields and their backgrounds are cross-disciplinary as well as cross-professional. The first president was Oyama, who is an experimental psychologist (PhD), and the second one is Yokota, who is not only an animation researcher but also a clinical psychologist (MD and PhD). As of March 2012, the number of the members has reached 233.

Prehistory of the Japan Society for Animation Studies

Second Animation Research Group in the JASIAS

The official prehistory of the JSAS began with the formation of the Committee for the Preparation of the Establishment of the JSAS on April 1, 1998.[1] However, it can be said that its unofficial prehistory, including its background and circumstances, go back many years before.

At the center of the momentum for the establishment of the JSAS was a preceding group leading to the subsequent founding of the society. Its members were the late Uchiyama Shotaro, a former professor of Tokyo University of the Arts; Ikeda Hiroshi, a former film director of Toei Doga (the current Toei Animation) who has held the post of professor at Tokyo Polytechnic University and Takarazuka University of Art and Design; and myself. At that time I was a full-time lecturer of Tokyo Zokei University. In 1988, after working three years at that university, in order to encourage academic research on animation in Japan, I asked the board of the JASIAS, of which I was a member, to resume the animation research group which had been in recess, through Hatano Tetsuro, a then professor (presently, a professor emeritus) of Tokyo Zokei University and former teacher, who had long been a director of, and later was to become the president of the JASIAS.

The animation research group was started originally by the late Yabushita Taiji, a film director of Toei Doga, Uchiyama, and Ikeda in August 1975, a year after the establishment of the JASIAS, but the group's activities came to a halt without any specific reason after some meetings. Upon my persistence and after undergoing the process of an interview with the board members in December 1991 led by Uchiyama, who was also an animation specialist, the (*second*) animation research group was commenced officially with the approval of the board in January 1992. The regular meetings of the animation research group over some years were held mainly in the Tokyo facilities of the company Nintendo where Ikeda worked, and what was presented during the meetings later developed into a number of papers presented at academic conferences, some of which were later published as articles. Most of the people who participated in the animation research group later played a central role in the establishment of the JSAS, and also animation as an academic department, major, or course. In Tokyo for example, the two universities that first introduced such academic studies of animation in Japan in 2003 were Tokyo Polytechnic University and Tokyo Zokei University.

Attention should be paid to the matter that the predecessor of the JSAS is not the (*second*) animation research group of the JASIAS. It is not that the former did not start itself in a way of being independent, forming a new group and becoming autonomous from the latter and thus establishing an entirely distinct and separate organization. The (*second*) animation research group of the JASIAS has remained in existence to this day, even after the establishment of the JSAS. As written above, the misunderstanding is caused by the fact that the two groups have common central members. In other words, members of the newly formed JSAS did not break off completely from the JASIAS. Relationships and research networkings have remained in place and continued between the two groups. *(Editors' note: The chairperson of the (second) animation research group of JASIAS is Yokota, who was also the president of the JSAS until 2012.)*

However, there were many cases of those putting off joining the JSAS while being already a member of the animation research group of the JASIAS, or of joining the former and not accepting an invitation to the latter. The founding of the JSAS and the cross-membership or non-cross-membership simply brought to a new recognition the difference between animation studies based on film or image studies, and animation studies as a discipline that is cross-disciplinary or generic and does not specifically presuppose film or image studies. This phenomenon also shed strong light on the "social position" and "a sense of identity" existing at once in a lower branch (as in a research department) of an established society and an independent society.

Despite this, there has been a deeply rooted misunderstanding and the establishment of the JSAS was regarded as a factional activity by some of the directors and members of the JASIAS and it was greeted with great opposition. It remains difficult to say that this misunderstanding has been entirely cleared up, even with the passage of more than ten years.

Committee for the Preparation of the Establishment of the JSAS

Since the founding of JSAS, the society publishes its own newsletter and journal, and it also engages vigorously in social activities such as cooperation in planning exhibitions, lectures, and conferences in museums and in participating in them through providing lecturers or instructors for them. As written above, limits increasingly manifested themselves on animation studies in the category of film or image studies and on animation-related activities in the established society. It can be pointed out that it became increasingly clear that the schema and framework of film or image studies could not sufficiently cope with new concepts of animation brought about by the development of information technology, mechatronics, and robotics. Similarly, the traditional notion of the moving image that presupposes photographic technology and imagery alone as main fields of study was no longer valid, as the new situation of moving images was affected by new forms of digital image technology which underwent rapid development—reflected in the term *digital renaissance*—in the 1990s. The field of animation was after all treated as the "other" or "exceptional" in the established society that was based on traditional film and image studies, and on the existing media of film, photography, television, and video.

Progress in animation studies—in particular, the actualization and accumulation of achievements in the field through organized activities for the first time in Japan, though of small scale—brought the appearance of an inclination to think of an independent society among some of the members who took part in the animation research group. Although it might have been at a level of reverie rather than of an idea, such a movement indicates that the discourse cannot be said to be definitely true that conception of the JSAS was merely due to the breakout of the Pokémon incident,[2] as has been understood in general. Again, from the very beginning, the aims of the establishment of the JSAS had nothing to do with the incident. Yet the Pokémon incident is also alluded to in the phrase "social issues to be evaluated impartially and neutrally in relation to animation," the second clause of "Policy on the Activities of the Japan Society for Animation Studies" adopted in the inaugural meeting of the JSAS. However, in light of previous developments, it can be said that the incident did not have much influence on the conception of establishing the society.

At a scene of a meeting of the (*second*) animation research group during the nineteenth conference of the JASIAS held at Kyushu Sangyo University in June 1993, I stated as a manifestation of my personal vision that by my fortieth birthday I would like to establish a society for animation; by my fiftieth, open an animation department in a university; by my sixtieth, publish its journal; and by my seventieth, establish its research center. I was thirty-five years old at that time. I remember that most of the members except Ikeda did not pay attention to my statement, which seems to have been regarded merely as a hopeful view or optimistic wish. Yet, soon after my statement, as events in the research and education of animation in Japan or in the actions of the government and industries have sped up, the JSAS was established when I was thirty-nine, and animation departments, majors, and courses were opened in three universities including Tokyo Zokei University[3] where I was working when I was forty-five, following the first publication of the *Japanese Journal of Animation Studies*, the JSAS's official academic research journal, when I was forty-one.

It was during this time when the concentration of such an atmosphere surrounding the field was on a steady increase that the so-called *Pokémon* incident broke out in December 1997. It was the appearance of a big social issue related to animation. While not all the members of the animation research group of the JASIAS paid much attention and responded to the accident, Ikeda, one of those who played an important part in starting and managing the group, at that time being responsible for developing Nintendo games, made a strong argument for the necessity of an academic body that would be able to give a suggestion or an answer on impartial, fair, and scientific grounds. It is said that he argued the same in a board meeting of the JASIAS where he was director of the board, but there was no articulate reaction in the JASIAS, nor from the Japan Animation Association (JAA) and other organizations related to film, image, and animation. It was Ikeda who suggested establishing the current JSAS for the first time, almost as if his patience with such a situation had reached its limit. In early 1998, he asked me—as the establishment of the society required opening its office in a university—if it would be possible to hold it in Tokyo Zokei University where I was working. Although I cannot deny that I regarded the establishment as premature on the grounds that there was little accumulation in animation studies and that the strata of researchers in the field was thin, not very differently from the opinions of Hatano Tetsuro, then professor of the Photograph and Cinema Major (which is the present Film Major) from the Department of Design, the Faculty of Art and Design, Tokyo Zokei University, the fact is that I hoped and expected a lot from the idea that a container should not be arranged for contents after they have increased, but that rather it should spur their development.

Discussing the issue with Ikeda, Hatano, and Cho Ikuro, then professor of the Integrated Study of Art and Science Major (which is the present Media Design Major) from the Department of Design, the Faculty of Art and Design, I was determined to ask Umimoto Ken, the then president of my university, to approve setting up the office. Although a negative response was at first given to the request, partly driven by the fact that there was no precedence of such kind, the final approval, after going through some negotiations, was given, made possible by the crucial agreement of Oda Kazuyuki (now an auditor of the JSAS), the director of the educational foundation of Kuwasawa Gakuen, which administers the university.

After that, while preliminary activities provided a step in actually establishing the society, the first difficult issue was to select the key members for the preparation and founding committee, and subsequently make contact and conduct discussions with some ten young researchers and artists to facilitate their participation. They were already members of the animation research group of the JASIAS. Finally, the Committee for the Preparation of the Establishment of the JSAS was formed on April 1, 1998. Four months later, the inaugural meeting of JSAS was held on July 25, 1998.

Early Period of the JSAS

Inaugural Meeting of the Society

Although there might be various opinions and views about the chronological identification of the early period, it is here regarded as the period during which the basis of the society was put in place after the inaugural meeting: that is, setting up subordinate organizations such as committees, enacting bylaws based on the constitution, organizing the conference, publishing the journal, and so on.

In the end, eighty founder members met together after contacting hundreds of people, including participants of the animation research group of the JASIAS, individuals with achievements of research or publication related to animation, as well as others concerned with its education or business. As it was impossible to appoint the president, vice president, and directors by voting, candidates for these posts were chosen ahead by the Committee for the Preparation of the Establishment of the JSAS, and it was arranged to get approval for this at the inaugural meeting.

A candidate for the presidency was Oyama Tadasu, who had been a professor at Hokkaido University and at Tokyo University, the dean of the College of Humanities and Sciences, Nihon University, and a member of the Science Council of Japan; for the vice presidency, Uchiyama Shotaro (then professor at Tokyo University of the Arts), Kazuhiko Goto (then professor at Tokiwa University), and Sumi Shigemasa (then professor at

Keio University); and for the position of directors, ten persons among whom were Ikeda, myself (then assistant professor at Tokyo Zokei University), and Jinnouchi Toshihiro (then assistant professor at Musashino Art University). Ikeda and myself drafted the aims of the establishment of the society, the policy concerning its activities, and its constitution.

The inaugural meeting was held at the Children's Castle of the Child Welfare Foundation (the present Foundation for Child Well-being) where the lecture of contemporary animation had been run, while a conference about the Pokémon accident was arranged and held along with it; the panelists were Ikeda, Koide, Harada Teruo, and Watanabe Sumio. Finally, at the general meeting on July 25, 1998, the JSAS itself came into being with the aims of the establishment, the policy on activities, and the constitution approved and with confidence given to the candidates chosen to be president, vice president, and directors.

Shortly after the Establishment of the JSAS

When founded in July 1998, the JSAS was put in comparatively good order as a new society, including the arrangement in advance to form committees and research departments.

The structure of the organization as a society was settled in September 1998, when the first board meeting was held at Gakushikaikan in Kanda, Tokyo, with the enacting of bylaws as managerial regulations based on the constitution, and with the decision to set up committees for planning and managing, journal editing, research, education business, and international relations, and research departments for theory, history, and psychology, through deliberation on the personnel issues of chairpersons, committee members, chief and second readers for the activities.

The most important in the early period during the preparatory stage was Oyama Tadasu's taking up of the first presidency that resulted in the laying of the foundation of the JSAS. He was a leader in the field of psychology who had a great deal of academic intelligence and experience as a scholar and an educator, and he had experience in managing organizations such as societies and research groups and was also a working member of the Science Council of Japan. Oyama as such directed and led the management of the JSAS with scrupulous care, playing a pivotal role in the new society and discipline. Moreover, he made an active contribution to publicizing the society in conferences or meetings relevant to psychology and the council. Considering its history, scale, and academic achievement, the well-organized basic structure of organization of the JSAS owes much to Ikeda's fundamental conception before its establishment and to Oyama's organizational management after that. Without Oyama's presence and direction in the first presidency over three years amounting to six terms, it would have taken more time to lay such a sound foundation for the society.

The most symbolic case is when the application for the registration of the JSAS was made to the Science Council of Japan in 2003. At the inquiry of briefings at the council, there was for a while a concern that the registration might be rejected by the council as an officer gave a brusque reply as well as a pointless response, asking if there were many cartoon or comic strip artists in the JSAS, on hearing the society's full name. Such a response seems to have been due to authoritarianism, hierarchies, and conservatism that are found in traditional disciplines and their institutions, and the general ignorance and indifference to new areas of study; it surpassed our imagination although it was somehow expected in the inquiry. During the inquiry, when officers asked, "Who is the society's president?" "Oyama" was answered. At that moment, the officers responded with a sudden change of attitude saying, "The psychologist Oyama? Please, apply to us." Later, the registration was admitted without any difficulty despite other known instances where applications from some societies had been rejected many times. The significance of Oyama's presence at the JSAS was recognized, in the sense that his name carried weight with the board of the Science Council; needless to say, the application form and materials were well arranged with due attention paid to them under his direction.

In a situation where even some of the societies related to humanities had no system for peer review, the *Japanese Journal of Animation Studies*, the first issue of which was published in 1999, a year after the establishment of the JSAS, had clear regulations of contribution and a system of peer review from the beginning, edited with methods and forms in accordance with journals of traditional disciplines and under the proper direction of the first chairperson of the journal editorial committee, Nakajima Yoshiaki, a psychologist and then professor at the Graduate School of Osaka University and currently a professor at Waseda University, and Oyama. Regarding the reputation of the journal, members accustomed to contributing to existing journals said that if an article passed the peer review process of the JSAS it would be able to pass that of other societies as well.

In tandem with the social tendency of the time of introducing information and electronic technology from the beginning, the JSAS made an effort for high efficiency by managing the office work of the society via frequent use of personal computers and the Internet. The JSAS Newsletter took up the e-mail system as its primary way of communication from the moment of its first publication in October 1998, soon after the establishment of the society, and was distributed by fax as an interim measure for the members who had no e-mail address. The official home page of the society was set up on the Web site of Tokyo Zokei University two days before the inaugural meeting, later followed by an independent Web site (http://www/jsas.net) hosted on a hired server. The application form for membership as well was made in electronic format from the very beginning.

Animation Research and Three Academic Generations Thereof in Japan

In Japan for a long time, animation research in a wide sense, not confined to an academic sense, has been mainly dilettantish. Even now it is much based on dilettantes' views and stances or centered on their preference without dealing with animation artists and their works as objective entities.[4] Most publications on sale are of such kind. They cannot be regarded as academic achievements or data though they can play the roles of being primary or secondary materials for some academic subjects.

In 1941, *Discussion on Cartoon Animation: Manga Eigaron* was published in Japanese, making it the first book specializing in animation in Japan and a pioneer work in animation research in the country, although the book itself does not take a form of a treatise. Its author was Imamura Taihei, known as an original and devoted film theorist and reviewer. After World War II, reviewers and writers of animation began to appear in the first instance around *Fun and Fancy Free*, the pioneer dilettante magazine formed from the background of the import of foreign animation like Disney, which was banned during the war. Some specialist publications also appeared with contents similar to reviews: *Introduction to Animation* (1966) by Mori Takuya, *The History of Japanese Animation* (1977) by Yamaguchi Katsunori and Watanabe Yasushi, and *History of World Animation* (1986) by Tomono Takashi and Mochizuki Nobuo.

Even in a situation where there was no differentiation between research and review, or between academic and commercial publications, and there was above all no sufficient, social recognition of animation as an subject of academic research, this so-called first generation of animation research had an incomparable knowledge and insight, whose academic deficiency cannot nonetheless be defended with respect to organization or form in writing and publications. Hayashi Joji[5] undertook remarkable activities from within the JASIAS, and yet made too early an appearance at a time when there was no social basis for the academic research of animation. Such quality of animation research was barely performed in the corners of film and image studies, and Hayashi, despite certain achievement in obtaining a post as a full-time researcher of the subject with conspicuous difficulty, was not able to keep his research activities going for long.

In the light of this situation, the second animation research group of the JASIAS seems to have been conscious of the question of how the group members should make mind, method, and format for academic research to take root in the field of animation. An emphasis was constantly placed on the development of reports of the group in favor of writing papers or reading at conferences. This is where the appearance of the second generation of animation research was witnessed, in the sense that its members were deeply aware of and specifically aimed for an academic approach. What became obvious after the establishment of the JSAS is the appearance of young researchers who obtained degrees, taking animation as their main subject in graduate schools. Of the generation that was in a graduate course when the society was established, some have already obtained their full-time posts in university, or others have begun to publish their own books. There is an anticipation that the academic research of animation in Japan should be brought to an obvious change by the appearance of the "third-generation researchers," each member of which has been sufficiently trained as a researcher in a graduate school without any academic and social opposition to researching the subject.

Background and Meaning of the Establishment of the JSAS

Social Background

The social background of the establishment of the JSAS is the nexus of the huge growth of the animation industry resulting from the expansion of general markets, the qualitative improvement of Japanese commercial animation as demonstrated by the outstanding works of Miyazaki Hayao, and the growing social recognition and elevation of the evaluation of animation since the 1990s. Although there was no specialized department or research course at that time, there was a steady increase in animation research by undergraduate and graduate students. In addition, film studies or film history classes ceased to be rarities in universities. This is also due to the progress of reformation in national universities after the revision of the University Establishment Standards, followed by the successive opening of classes like Animation Studies, Cultural Studies of Animation, Cartoon/Comics Studies, and Cultural Studies of Cartoon/Comics mainly in private universities. It is also worth referring to the increased social recognition as well as attention paid to animation both in industry and culture, as shown by a number of exhibitions held for cartoon/comics or animation in places such as public museums. What also cannot be ignored here is that there is a spread in the reach and appeal of animation from a primarily teenage audience to adult audience groups. Both groups seldom show prejudice against animation, having being brought up in an intimate relationship with the subject via cinema and television.

It is not hard to imagine that if it should have been attempted before, during the early 1990s, there would have been difficulties in bringing together enough members to maintain the organization of the JSAS as a society. Its establishment would have seemed much more surprising and strange to people than now. Moreover, only a small number of people would have been "deserving" of its membership. As it stands, it can be pointed out the researchers were intrinsic to the establishment of the society.

Intrinsic Background: Studies or Gaku

For the English name of the Japan Society for Animation Studies, Ikeda's original suggestion was actually "Japan Animation Society." On the surface, this might not have much significance. In the international scene, the title name of the society seems to be in tune with those of overseas societies of the same subject such as the Society for Animation Studies and the Korean Society of Cartoon and Animation Studies (KOSCAS). In Japanese, the society's name title reads as "Nihon Anime-shon Gakkai."

However, the name represents the body of the organization. The choice of "Society for Animation Studies" means that the society declared and established itself as a society for animation studies. Indeed, when the society was founded, there were many members who recognized a standpoint of a society with such a title name and such members not only belonged to traditional disciplines but also had rich experience participating in other societies. Although some members did not accord the recognition, there are ways to achieve the aims of the society, and its policy on research activities can be made distinctive by encompassing the meanings of animation-*gaku*[6] and animation studies. After all, due attention is given to the academic research of animation, a discipline taking animation as the subject of academic research. At present, the difference is not actualized, merely because the society itself is still in its early stages of development, and because most of the members do not have a firm enough grasp of the differences between the two for that.

Animation studies is not a unified discipline relying on a unified methodology and research approach; rather it encompasses interdisciplinary research, and relies on various methodologies and research approaches based on a variety of disciplines. Animation-*gaku*, in my opinion, relies on a systematized, organized knowledge and methodology based on a certain principle and theory. The two differ much from each other in basis and aims, though sharing in common animation as the subject of academic research.

The choice of animation studies for the name of the society, as I pointed out above, involves constructing the frame of a society in a situation in which academic research of animation is not established systematically. There should be an establishment of animation-*gaku* as a systematized, organized discipline, through accumulation of research by means of multi-methodologies and approaches of various disciplines. The judgment is that it was too early to advocate animation-*gaku*. Thus, the establishment of the JSAS and the construction of animation-*gaku* can be said to be the reintegration or reconstruction, from a new perspective and standpoint, of the academic research of animation that is open to division.

A press release was later provided to the mass media and journalist meetings for the establishment of the JSAS. This led to coverage by a lot of the mass media from general newspapers like the *Asahi Shinbun* and the *Mainichi Shinbun* to *Animage* (a commercial animation magazine). Their reports were not entirely in accordance with the statements and intentions of the society, but one of them pointed out that the establishment of the JSAS is steeped in the diversification and enhancement of disciplines and their subsequent specialization would be a consequence.

Composition and Characteristics of the JSAS Members

Any person and student of graduate level and above is eligible for the regular membership of the JSAS, as "an individual who pays attention to animation and is involved in it for research or business in a direct or indirect way" as specified in the constitution, without requirements like a degree or a post in education or research. For this reason, the membership profile of the society encompasses a wide spectrum; it is cross-professional, consisting not only of scholars, researchers, and graduate students, but also artists and creators, educators, producers, and businesspersons at a more hands-on level. The research interests are cross-interdisciplinary and specialists from various fields such as film and image studies, aesthetics and fine arts studies, literature, psychology, social sciences, engineering, and more are eligible for membership. In other words, the society does not focus on just animation research in a narrow sense. From the beginning, the JSAS might well have had something in common with the predecessor (JASIAS). For example, most of the preparing committee members for the establishment of the former were affiliated to the latter, and Ikeda was involved in drawing up the constitution of both societies.

There was unfavorable comparison–"cohabitation between doctor and patient"—with the JASIAS that was originally established by scholars and researchers in cooperation with artists and practitioners in 1974, resulting in the creation of a unique society embracing practice as well as research, and in which various professions were integrated with the comprehensive concept of image, instead of individual medium like film, photograph, or video. There is no denying that the JSAS is a subconscious extension of the JASIAS. The number of researchers at first was not large enough to constitute a sizable membership, and the new animation society would have had difficulty in satisfying requirements as an organization if it had not accepted practitioners as well as theoreticians and researchers.

The field of animation has more areas undifferentiated between academic and nonacademic research than that of film and image, and has an issue of gray zones such as dilettantish scholars and scholarly dilettantes. Now that the JSAS has set the academic direction as its own organizing principle, and has registered itself with the Science Council of Japan (as if) it had confirmed the principle after its own establishment, the members are required to separate animation from the concept of hobby or dilettantism. At the same time, if we trace back where the researchers, not confined to the field of animation, originated from, and how they developed so far, it is often possible to find that the starting point was a simple interest or taste in the area. The problem is how each researcher should objectify it, developing it to academic research standard with methodology and professionalism. There is no denying that the JSAS is loose in such a respect, as the field of animation studies itself is a developing one.

Establishment of the JSAS and Higher Education in Animation in Japan

Rise of the Higher Education in Animation

Tokyo Designer Gakuin College is the first *senmon gakko,* a vocational school in Japan that began the practical training of animation as a professional craft in the mid-1960s.[7] At the higher education level, Nihon University was the first one to open a lecture class on animation in the College of Art in the 1970s. It is not that animation was not at all studied in the universities before that; it was already offered in classes relevant to graphic design in Tama Art University and Joshibi University of Art and Design in the 1950s to 1960s. While animation-related classes began to be introduced as an optional item in art/design-specific universities, as those for the skills of animation opened in Tokyo Zokei University in 1981, they were basically identified as what is called a "special liberal" rather than as a main special major.

In the 1990s, a movement surfaced for the introduction of animation as a major subject in many universities, especially with an easing of the University Establishment Standards. Initially the introduction did not always make smooth progress, owing in part to the opposition of faculties despite boards being in favor of it. It can be said that this is due to the authoritarianism, class consciousness, and conservatism typical in universities, academic circles, and the bureaucratic world in Japan. It also pertains to issues related to the discrimination against popular cultures and arts; for example, the issue of classifying high art and low art that had been considered to have become meaningless a long time ago in a twentieth-century mature mass society. There was also a movement in "winter universities" to increase enrollment due to a dwindling birth rate as if it actually had an understanding of the social significance of animation. Tokyo Polytechnic University is a first case example where practical reasons (before arriving at the recognition of the artistic and academic significance of animation) were behind a positive decision for the establishment of a department of the subject; it was in response to the decreasing number of student applicants and the resultant internal reorganization and conversion of Women's Junior College, an affiliate of the school.

Academic organizations such as the JSAS as well as the Society for Animation Studies and the Korean Society of Cartoon and Animation Studies abroad also had an affirmative effect on the introduction of new departments or majors of animation in each university. Tokyo Polytechnic University even requested a letter of reference from the president of the JSAS in applying for the introduction of the subject from the Ministry of Education, Culture, Sports, Science and Technology.

In April 2003, there were further establishments: the Department of Animation in the Faculty of Arts of Tokyo Polytechnic University; the Animation Major in the Department of Design of Tokyo Zokei University; and the Animation Course (by Correspondence) in the Art and Design Faculty of Kyoto University of Art and Design. These were the first cases of independent introduction of the subject of animation in Japanese universities. Later, the year 2006 saw the establishment of the Department of Animation in the Faculty of Manga of Kyoto Seika University, and the year 2008 that of the Department of Animation of the Graduate School of Film and New Media of Tokyo University of the Arts. As of now, more than ten undergraduate or graduate schools have faculty departments conducting majors or research courses specific to the subject.

Present Situation and Homework for the Higher Education of Animation in Japan

In Japan, there are circumstances that cannot be considered satisfactory for the subject of animation to flourish in the context of university education as compared to South Korea. So far, the department or major of the subject has been introduced to more than ten schools in Japan. In South Korea, however, more than a hundred schools have done so, and the student enrollment situation is relatively good.[8]

For now a characteristic of Japanese university education of animation is that the fundamental principle is to teach practical things, to train artists and creators in practice- or skill-oriented schools such as colleges of the fine arts. Faculty staff, either full time or adjunct, mostly consists of practitioners or artists. In that sense, they do not seem to differ much from vocational schools, *senmon gakko*. In other words, there is a tendency for courses to be centered on practical learning, skills, and application in Japanese university education on the subject of animation.

Considering the adoption and adaptation of the animation subject in university education and its instructional differentiation from vocational schools, many universities have, of course, opened proper lecture classes for theory, history, and the like in their animation curriculums, and some which have introduced animation as a department or major have also employed lecturers in a full-time capacity; however, there is no original academic research coming from the staff or the students. Primarily, the education of animation in Japanese universities aims at training students in the skill and knowledge for the basic production of animation, so that all of them might be experts (artists or creators) in the field after graduation; as for theory and history of animation in such education, they are mostly treated as knowledge that is regarded as "specialist liberal arts" or is useful for production and creation. Most of the animation students do not think that this kind of education is strange, nor raise a question about it, because their aim is to be experts in the production of animation. Some lectures are comparatively advanced, so to speak, possibly intended for young budding animation scholars, but there is no systematic introduction of lectures, as a group, regarding the theory and history of the subject. After all, there are classes for techniques, methodologies, and basic technologies as requirements for being producers and creators, but none for the methodologies needed for the production of knowledge for nurturing scholars. For this reason, there is no denying that it seems to be merely an "added-on" that most of the practice- or skill-oriented universities simply incorporate the education of scholars and researchers, as well as critics and reviewers, along with that of artists and creators in their teaching. Yet so far no system has been organized for the development of a new cohort of animation researchers and scholars despite an expected possibility that some of the students who completed their practical courses might wish to delve further into research, as seen in the fields of film and image studies that are thirty years ahead with respect to education.

However, it can be said there is an emerging environment for the academic development of animation studies in that there is a steady increase in the number of undergraduate and graduate students who take animation as their research subject in the departments or majors already established in faculties related to human sciences such as aesthetics, fine arts studies, and art history; and in that the same phenomenon appears in those related to social sciences such as economics and sociology. At the same time, increasing attention is being paid to the industrial and economic aspects as well as the social issues of animation, along with cartoon/comics, games, and other contents. It should be emphasized that at present, there isn't any department or major of animation studies that takes animation itself as a subject of academic research in a substantial sense.

Thus, requirements for promoting the academic research of animation cannot be satisfied by the JSAS alone; substantial activities have to be enriched in the research and education institutions of animation. In all, greater efforts need to be made in order to actualize the meaning of educating and researching animation in universities or graduate schools, and not in vocational and various other schools.

In reflecting on the present situation and a near-future outlook, it is difficult to expect the realization of the department of animation as a source of a discipline for theory alone in a field where the practical learning and the skills of animation have precedence, both in mind and practice. An immediate expectation is that there should be further expansion of animation as a research subject in many disciplines that support animation studies, such as aesthetics and art history, economics and sociology, psychology, and engineering, and the establishment of the major or course for theory and critique, as an academic annex in the practice- or skill-oriented departments of animation.

Present Situation and Homework of the JSAS

At present, the members who joined ten years ago at the time of its establishment constitute some three quarters of the membership of the JSAS, while the percentage of founding members on the board has decreased to about half. Compared with ten or more years ago, it has become commonplace to teach and research animation in universities even though the emphasis is on practical learning and skills. The number of publications that advocate animation research has increased, as has the number of people who identify themselves as animation researchers, marking a notable achievement in the field. With these developments, the JSAS membership has expanded further.

To reiterate, at the inaugural meeting of the JSAS on July 25, 1998, the four policies adopted for the activities of the society were the following:

1. To organize animation researchers and build a field for enriching and expanding animation research in Japan.

2. To evaluate impartially and neutrally social issues related to animation; that is, to establish an entity organization with social impartiality, contributing right and valid judgments, and to take measures in regard of the above-mentioned qualities without any bias toward specific interests.
3. To have ties with international animation research activities, particularly serving as a representative organization of Japan in relation to international academic bodies of animation; for example, to act as a domestic body ready to hold a conference for the Society for Animation Studies in Japan.
4. To offer a central agency-field for animation educators and researchers involving the evaluation of achievements of those who educate and research animation as their primary or additional occupation.

Considering the society's activities since its establishment, there has been a fulfillment through the continued existence of the society, its annual conferences being held every year, and the continued regular publication of the journal. However, there has been no realization of an international conference with the Society for Animation Studies (SAS) in Japan as originally intended at the establishment of the JSAS. In the past, three members of the animation research group of the JASIAS[9] had attended and presented papers at SAS annual conferences at the University of Utrecht, Netherlands, in 1997; Chapman University in the United States in 1998; and in Concordia University, Montreal, Canada, in 2001. In retrospect, our founding views were to establish the JSAS as a domestic organization, aiming at launching and supporting animation research for a number of issues and with the cooperation with the SAS, make social contributions as an international academic organization for a wide range of animation research.[10]

From now on, international activities in research and relations will become more and more vigorous while the desire to hold an SAS conference in Japan is still under discussion. In recent years, the JSAS has enhanced its relationship with the Korean Society of Cartoon and Animation Studies especially in the area of developing links and partnerships with international animation research activities. As for the policy (2) to evaluate impartially and neutrally social issues related to animation, there actually remains a question whether it would be possible to take sufficient, organized measures under the present conditions in cases of social significance such as that brought up by the Pokémon incident. In a sense, the JSAS can be said to be midway to achieving its aims.

In hindsight, when the JSAS was established in the late 1990s, a number of animated works have already occupied high rankings as successful films (called the top ten box-office hits) in the film industry of Japan.[11] Also, there has been an unprecedented situation whereby more than eighty television animated programs were produced per year. In the field of technology, the introduction of computer graphics has become generalized in animation production, while the production of digital animation is on the point of paving a way of further expansion in face of the digitalization of television broadcasts. At present, digital animation by means of the computer continues to make a whole new way of interactive communication possible. As an industry, too, as shown in flight simulation and computer games, it has already begun to reform human societies, accelerated by needless to say a rapid expansion in the number of the education scenes of CG animation in universities and vocational schools.

There has been a number of research subjects related to animation: the issue of the protection of copyright holders caused further by the confusion due to the convergence between broadcast and telecommunication, as well as the digitalization of information; the need for the establishment of a code of "visual morality" brought about in past and present discussions by the frequent occurrence of the juvenile crimes of violence with murderous weapons; and others.

Regarding the issue of expressions in comics, animation, and others being regulated by the amendment of "the Tokyo Metropolitan Government's ordinance on wholesome development of young people under 18," which has drawn attention to itself at a social level in 2010, the JSAS has not presented to the Japanese public "an impartial and neutral evaluation of social issues related to animation," and in the meantime, the amendment was approved in the plenary session of the Tokyo Metropolitan Assembly. It is reasonable to keep a cautious attitude as an academic organization; however, the Japan Society for Studies in Cartoon and Comics and others contributed to a certain degree in pointing out the state of the issue for society, avoiding a hasty deliberation and approval in such a way that the president manifested objection through the swift resolution of the board, though they could not eventually stop its approval. There were a lot of implications from the difference that came to the surface between the Japan Society for Animation Studies and the Japan Society for Studies in Cartoon and Comics in both membership and mind, and from a difference, too, between the world of cartoon/comics and publication and that of animation and its industry in their relationship to administrative agencies, in considering how different comics and animation are from each other in Japan. Regardless of the society's founding principle of evaluating impartially and neutrally social issues related to animation, it cannot be said that there were socially strong demands on the Japan Society for Animation Studies, and the observation is that there is a much better realization of what the society's presence and raison d'être are in the field of animation.

In my view, the academic basis of the society or the aim of its academic development, discussed only by some members at its establishment, has not been sufficiently investigated so far with a question as to whether it should take the route of animation studies or animation-*gaku*. Likewise, the JSAS journal has to face the issue of combining scholarship and journalism in academic research of animation, which was also discussed only by some members at the first publication. Since animation is strongly bound up with practical and phenomenal aspects and with factors such as fluidity and timeliness, it is unreasonable to confine the subjects of the academic research of animation to what are classical, historical, and fundamental. At the same time, it is necessary for the society to aim to promote and keep a holistic academic mind in its own attitude and stance, identifying itself as an institution of academic organization that is recognized by the public as such and not as a group of reviewers or journalists, or that of dilettantes or amateurs.

Among the members of the JSAS, it is not that sufficient investigations or discussions have not been conducted about the social issues that arise; rather, the fact is that many of the members seem not to be interested in or aware of them. This can be construed as highlighting that the academic research of animation is on the path of development, and that the level of consciousness of scholarship is far from as mature as required, though the quantity of research papers and publications through the years has increased exceptionally.

Notes

1. Editors' note: Refer to Ikeda Hiroshi's article for further background history of animation research and study in Japan.

2. This incident is also known as the Pokémon shock or panic. On December 16, 1997, 750 people had photosensitive epilepsy (PSE) or similar symptoms when they

were watching the 38th episode, Computer Soldier Polygon, of Pocket Monster (known as Pokémon, an abbreviation of the original title), the animated television program broadcasted by TV Tokyo and its network: these people were admitted to hospitals, and some 140 of them had to remain there for further observation.

At an early stage after the outbreak of the incident, it was not known that the cause was PSE, which can occur as a result of watching film and moving images as well as animated television programs, and there was criticizing of Pokémon itself, the bashing of which was then at its height. There was also a tendency to deal with animation alone as the issue and not with moving images generally; however, this was put to rest when the actual cause was made clear.

After the incident, the animated series was compelled to stop its screening on TV and in the meantime, the television station TV Tokyo, together with other television broadcasters and the National Association of Commercial Broadcasters in Japan, conducted an investigation as well as research, setting up guidelines for preventing the recurrence of such an incident. As for the government, the Ministry of Welfare (the present Ministry of Health, Labor and Welfare) set up the Group for a Clinical Research of Photosensitive Epilepsy, while the Ministry of Posts and Telecommunications (the present Ministry of Internal Affairs and Communications) proceeded to prepare guidelines, introducing the Conference for Broadcasts and Audiovisual Functions.

Guidelines were set up, including that the flashing of image or light, the reversal of pictures in high contrast, and a sudden switch of pictures should not be made more than three times in one second. These guidelines greatly affected the production of animated television programs both in expression and technique. The notice also cautioned that interior lighting should be made bright while watching television, and that the audience should keep themselves at a distance from the television monitor on display. (Readers may refer to the reference sources for further reading of the incident.)

3. These are Animation Major, Department of Design, Faculty of Art and Design, Tokyo Zokei University, Department of Animation, Faculty of Arts, Tokyo Polytechnic University and Animation Course, Department of Information Design, Art and Design Faculty (by correspondence), Kyoto University of Art and Design.

4. Here, the word dilettante is understood as referring to people like fans, buffs, amateurs, hobbyists, who enjoy, love, and prefer things as entertainment, in particular for pleasure and not as a profession or specialization. They tend to place more emphasis on the quantity of information as opposed to a specific way of looking at or understanding subjects like artists and their works.

5. He completed a doctoral course at a graduate school of Waseda University. His main interests were Disney and prewar Japanese films. With presentations of his research at annual conferences of the JASIAS, he had two articles, "Limited Animation" and "Animated Cartoon as an Instrument of Education and Enlightenment," published in *Iconics: Japanese Journal of Image Arts and Sciences* (respectively, no. 8, 1978, and no. 12, 1979). Owing to personal circumstances, he went back to his native town, ceasing further research on the topic.

6. The Japanese word *gaku*, which means knowledge or study, is much like -ology or -ics in English. For example, biology and linguistics in Japanese are *seibutsu-gaku* and *gengo-gaku*, respectively, where *seibutsu* amounts to bio- and *gengo* to lingu-. There are more academic fields named with *-gaku*, as the usage of the Japanese suffix is different from that of the two English suffixes; for example, *chiri-gaku* in Japanese is not geology but geography, where *chiri* already means the latter English word. In this sense, the author in the essay also keeps in mind the possibility of an English name with the suffix -ology to replace the term animation studies, but is not yet sure that he has found it. This is why *-gaku* is not translated in English here. (The footnote is the translator's explanation.)

7. The vocational school's curriculum usually consists of two years of learning. (The footnote is the translator's.)

8. The prosperity of animation education in South Korean universities is thought to be strongly backed up by the government's cultural and industrial promotion of comics and animation since the late 1990s besides a large percentage of the pupils entering universities, which reaches no less than 89.8 percent (50.7 percent in Japan) in 2004. It can be argued that one of the most important reasons for this is that the South Korean university system consists of four-year schools (called *daehakkyo* in Korean), and two- or three-year schools (called *daehak* or *jeonmun daehak* in Korean), and in a flexible way most of them have departments or majors for subjects that are offered in Japanese vocational schools (called *senmon gakko* in Japanese), which are distinguished from the university in Japan.

9. Editors' note: They were Yokota Masao, Koide Masashi, and Nomura Koji.

10. Editors' note: The founding of the SAS is brought up in Hu's introductory essay in this volume.

11. Released on July 12, 1997, *Princess Mononoke* had a long run until spring 1998 and was ranked No. 1 to date in the history of Japanese film by earning 11.3 billion yen through distribution and 19.3 billion at the box office. In 2009, *Spirited Away* was ranked No. 1 (30.4 billion yen); *Howl's Moving Castle*, No. 2 (19.6 billion yen); and *Princess Mononoke*, No. 3 in terms of box-office record.

References

Ikeda, Hiroshi. "Pokémon jiken" to sono taiou [Pokémon incident and its responses]. *Anime-shon kenkyu* [Japanese Journal of Animation Studies] 1, no. 1 (1999): 23–29.

Ishiguro Yoshiko, Takada Hiroyuki, Watanabe Kazuyoshi, Okumura Akihisa, Aso Kosaburo, and Ishikawa Tatsuya. "A follow-up survey on seizures induced by animated cartoon TV program Pocket Monster." *Epilepsia* 45, no. 4 (2004): 377–83.

Morishita, Misako. "Kyarakuta- jyuyou ni miru 'otona/kodomo': Pokémon panikku wo megutte" [Receptivity to television characters by children and adults: A study of the difference of opinion between the two over the Pokémon Panic]. *Sekigauin daigaku ronnsou* [Journal of Sekigakuin University] 20, no. 1 (2007): 17–32.

Otsuki Takahiro and an urgent group of reporters of Pokémon incident. *Pokémon no Maryoku: Kodomo tachi wo miryousita 'Pokémon' toha nanika* [The magic of *Pokémon*: What is *Pokémon* by which children were mesmerized]. Tokyo: Mainichi-shinbun-sha, 1998.

Takahashi, Takeo. *Terebi eizo to hikarikanjyuse hossa; sono sinndann to boushi saku* [Television images and photo-sensitive induced seizures: Its diagnosis by EEG and prevention]. Tokyo: Shinko-igaku-shuppansha, 1999.

More on the History of the Japan Society for Animation Studies

Historic Essentials of Animation Studies

—Hiroshi Ikeda

Translated by Masao Yokota and Tze-yue G. Hu

Introduction

The establishment of scholarly organizations often includes the aims of facilitating study exchanges among scholars in areas such as knowledge and friendship with the main intention of pursuing progressive research. However, the activity of "research" gets entangled in the world of self-promotion, one's institutional expectations and other demands and distractions. Basically, to research is to search for the truth, and it requires the hard work of investigation and exploration and rigorous arrangement of facts and details.

The Japan Society for Animation Studies was founded to promote the pristine intention of research. However, like all academic studies organizations, it, too, faces some of the problems mentioned above. My chapter is written in response to my younger colleague Koide Masashi's exposition on the historical background of the society; it wishes to address further the past and present of the society's activities and, in particular, to reflect upon and provide more background knowledge of the founding of the society.

To do so, I will cover the past research animation activities within the Japanese animation industry itself; the research activities that were happening then within the research framework of universities and academic institutions; and the research activities of the Japan Society of Image Arts

and Sciences. The birth of the Japan Society for Animation Studies was a result of specific circumstances and relationships that need to be highlighted. I advocate the view that the society must chart its waters carefully given the limitations of animation studies research in universities and even in other media and cinema research groups. Relating to social developments and happenings is important, and it is one of the main reasons why the society was formed in the first place.

Research within the Industry

In 1959, Ikeda Hiroshi was offered a job in Toei Doga Inc. He contributed to the production of the "Give-and-Take Relationship" *(Motitsu motaretsu* in Japanese) that the American Embassy commissioned Toei Doga Inc. to create.[1] Ikeda took part in the meetings in the American Embassy not only as an assistant producer but also as an assistant director. A staff member of the American Embassy learned that Ikeda had studied *neoriarismo* (neorealism) in his university days and became friendly to him by giving him raw materials and information about animation making. The staff member also emphasized the necessity of creating a storyboard rather than a scenario, and taught Ikeda animation techniques such as space construction.[2]

This latter was Ikeda's starting point into research about the theorization of constructing a frame and obtaining a coherent construction system. Later, results of this research were reported at the conferences of the Japan Society of Image Arts and Sciences (Ikeda, 1978).

Early in 1962, Ikeda wrote the animation section for the publication, "Ten-Year History of Toei." Before writing the paper, he had already begun research on the history of animation in Japan. He interviewed experienced animators like Yamamoto Sanae, Masaoka Kenzō, Kumakawa Masao, Hurusawa Hideo, Daikubara Akira, Yabushita Taiji, Ōfuji Noburō and so on, and many primary research materials of animation were handed to him. These interviews and materials were very helpful for him to write the paper. During the writing process and from the research materials he had amassed, Ikeda discovered an industrial problem related to the establishment of Toei Animation Studio (in Japanese, Toei Doga). To confirm his finding, he and Oshiyama Hiroharu, Imada Chiaki, and the others who were members of a preparation committee established for the founding of Toei Doga Inc.

concluded that the establishment of an animation industry was fundamentally defective due to the presence of certain issues not fully examined.

Years later, the animation industry became the theme of a paper that Ikeda presented at the Japan Society for Animation Studies seminar meeting, which was held at the Takarazuka Zokei Art University on October 10, 2007. The title of the presentation was "The animation industry after the World War II: Before and after the founding of Toei Doga Inc.," and it pointed out the sloppy planning of management and incomplete research of income and expenditure that resulted in the harmful effects on the present TV animation industry in Japan today.

Ikeda had written a draft copy of the animation section, when a student of Waseda University, Yamaguchi Katsunori, visited him in 1960.[3] Ikeda gave him a copy of his article and advised him to collect documents from the Ministry of Education and so on. (Yamaguchi later wrote articles for *Eiga Hyōron* (Critic in Cinema)[4] and together with Watanabe Yasushi cowrote and published *The History of Japanese Animation* (1977), a book cited in several articles printed in this collection.

During that time, all departments within Toei Animation Studio tried to improve methods and techniques of animation making. For example, well-known products like paints for celluloid (which is known as a vinyl-paint) were developed at Toei Animation Studio and a camera stand for XEROX was invented. (For this, the Motion Picture and Television Engineering Society of Japan, Inc., later honored XEROX with an award in recognition of its technical achievements.)

Ikeda himself conducted a research on how to create a natural scene by drawing; a part of this research was published in the journal of Japan Society of Image Arts and Sciences (Ikeda, 1978). This paper shows how an object size on a picture is determined based on a distance from an object. At the industry level, one can say that it was Toei Doga Inc. (Toei Animation Co., Ltd.) that first started to conduct systematic research on advancing techniques of animation. The company section for this kind of development was first established in 1972, almost one year after a significant labor dispute was solved.

The labor dispute in Toei Doga Inc. refers to a series of recurring labor lockouts that lasted for six months in 1972.[5] After the end of the lockout, in order to avoid management failure due to the low productivity of animation artists, rationalization of management administration was instituted. Ikeda, who was an animation director then, was transferred to this research and development section. He was not only a member but also a chief in this one-man section.

One of the aims of the section was to introduce antistatic spray into celluloid; that is, to develop celluloid with high conductivity in cooperation with a laboratory of Toray Industries Inc.. Later this section started to be involved in EVR, which was a mix media of chemistry and electronics. In 1975, Ikeda became interested in a frame-by-frame digital system and started to take part in a project to develop a computer game (interactive animation). He devoted himself to studying game theory and playfulness via reading the works of Johan Huizinga and Roger Caillois. During that time, when Ikeda learned that a system to copy a colored picture into celluloid was delivered to a laboratory of Kanebo Ltd., he rushed to the laboratory to see it. In 1976, he also visited Dainihon-screen Ltd., and inspected a system that showed that a space surrounded by lines could be colored by a computer and it was very similar to the coloring process of animation. Thus, he knew that it would be possible to develop a computer system for animation production in Toei and proceeded to seek cooperation and research partnerships with computer companies, universities, institutes, and others.

From 1977, Ikeda became a committee member of technical development at Toei, and he also became the chief of a second section for development. From 1980 onward, his main task was to focus on the development of a new computer-aided animation production system. The microcomputer had already been launched earlier, and the era of the personal computer soon began after Intel Corporation put the 4004 chip on the market in 1971. The computer content Simulation of Hand and Face (a half-tone animation), which was a forerunner of CG animation, was released in 1972, and the Scanimate System run by an analog computer was made available to the public the same year. Ohio State University and New York Institute of Technology developed ANIMA II in 1977 and the NYIT system in 1979, respectively. Thus, an era of computer graphics began.

Ikeda, who took part in a project for developing a computer animation production system aided by a research grant from NHK,[6] began traveling often to the United States from 1978 onward. The objectives were to collect information on computer graphics and to conduct interviews with researchers residing in America. He visited research institutes of General Electric Company (GE), Evans & Shutherland (E & S), Computer Image Corporation (CI), and several universities including Utah University, Ohio State University, Illinois University, MIT, Harvard University, NYIT, and

Nebraska University. Not only did he constantly attend SIGGRAPH conferences[7] to get information, but also frequently visited venture companies supported by Sumitomo Corporation and other Japanese companies in USA. He, of course, did not forget to visit animation production companies like Hanna-Barbera Productions and exchanged views on animation computer production systems with American animators and producers.

In 1977, besides Toei Doga, other companies like Mitsubishi Electric Corporation, Hitachi Ltd., Fujitsu Ltd., Matsushita Electric Industrial Co. Ltd., NEC Corporation, Universal Automatic Corporation, Yokokawa Electric Corporation, and IBM in Japan faced a similar issue; namely, that of balancing cost and effect rather than placing the utmost attention to technological possibilities. This was also seen not only in Japan but also in other countries where the focus on technological possibilities unfortunately led to the neglect of the balance of cost and effect and eventually caused enterprises to face financial dangers. For example, Japan Computer Graphic Lab (JCGL) and other companies that introduced the NYIT system and ANTICS consequently failed financially in Japan.

Finally in 1985, in cooperation with Toshiba Corporation, Toei Doga met specifications for computer animation production. With the resignation of Ikeda, Yoshimura Jiro became the successor and the chief of this section of development. By then, it was predicted that it was only a matter of time before a low-priced computer system with high quality would be introduced to the mass market.

By the end of the 1990s, Toei Animation Studio started a computer system that introduced low-priced techniques of computer graphics, and this led to a reduction in animation production costs. Now, Toei Animation Studio produces over 70 percent of TV animation series via the computer system at a local subsidiary in a foreign country (in the Republic of the Philippines).

Research within Academic Organizations

The first university faculty in Japan that offered an annual instructional course on animation (from 1971) was the Art College of Nihon University. A professor Ushihara Kiyohiko (who was Ikeda's former teacher) requested Ikeda to design and teach the course. A few years before, Ikeda guided two Nihon University students who wanted to create animation for their graduation papers. At that time, there was no animation stand for film shooting in the university; they had to use an animation stand in a detached room of the home of a professor, Watanabe Shunpei, who was also the dean of the Art College of Nihon University. He was a prominent member of the physics and chemistry laboratory and a founding researcher of the competitive photographic system. It was Watanabe who keenly recognized the necessity of nurturing talents for the TV animation industry that had largely developed and produced a huge amount of animation since the initial screening of *Astro Boy* in 1963.

Eventually, at the request of dean Watanabe, Ikeda became a part-time lecturer of animation at Nihon University. As Ikeda was an employee of Toei Doga, which strictly prohibited external employment outside of the company, an official letter was first sent to Toei's president and after, with the organization's approval, Ikeda began to teach animation as part of the business of Toei Doga.[8]

Soon after the first instructional course of animation started, the dean Watanabe Shunpei informed Ikeda of an idea to create a new department of animation. Ikeda had just finished directing the animated feature film, *Animal Treasure Island*, which was designated as a special film project celebrating the twentieth anniversary of Toei (released in March 1971). He became busy designing the curriculum and making out a list of suitable candidates for teaching staff. If the department of animation were established, he thought that staff would take on active roles in animation research and there would be good conditions for furthering the education and research fields of Animation Studies.

However, faculty members of the Art College of Nihon University were not only indifferent to the idea of establishing an animation department but they also sabotaged it. The reason for this was that among the potential instructors recommended, there was one who possessed only high-school qualification. The candidate was one of the most talented animators contributing to the high-quality animation work of Toei Doga. He might have become an extremely excellent professor of animation.

The project was canceled before being discussed at a faculty meeting. The dean Watanabe later regretted this. Ikeda was deeply discouraged and became isolated in the chaos. Meanwhile at Toei, many talented staff quit one after another. After the *Animal Treasure Island* feature animated film was made, the next animation film project was not realized. The labor dispute at Toei became worse and the studio was locked out in 1972 (as noted earlier). Ikeda was afraid that the studio might close down. In the midst of this situation, the chair of the Cinema Department,

Toru Otake, gave Ikeda information to apply for an associate professor position at Kyushu Institute of Design. Ikeda sent his curriculum vitae to the university. Otake discussed with the chairman of Kyushu Institute of Design and they were determined to appoint him as an associate professor. Ikeda was very pleased to hear the decision and told the president of Toei Doga, Toishi Eiichi, of his decision to quit. However, professor Ushihara Kiyohiko advised that there was no need for Ikeda to hurry, and so stopped Ikeda from handing in his resignation notice to Nihon University and Toei Doga.

Somehow, the associate professor post "decayed" and disappeared in the end. Ikeda narrowly escaped unemployment at Toei. Later, Ikeda found out that his position as an animation director, as opposed to an artist or a research scholar, had raised fury and discontent among the academic staff at Kyushu Institute of Design. Moreover, animation was considered as a subject of low value. Staff members also subscribed to a petition that opposed adopting an associate professor of animation. In hindsight, Ikeda believes that perhaps it was for the best. The advancements of video and computer mentioned above were being realized at that time, and they changed image technology completely. If Ikeda had become an associate professor and stayed in Fukuoka (the location of the institute), he would have ended up teaching animation in the classrooms, without having experienced firsthand the advent of video and digital technology in the industry.

The above shows the unfavorable conditions of animation teaching and research in academic institutions during that time. The complete failure of the establishment of a new department of animation in Nihon University Art College and Ikeda's failed attempt in becoming an associate professor of animation studies at Kyushu Institute of Design demonstrated the immature state of affairs of animation research. Ikeda kept thinking of the idea of establishing an animation department until in 2003 when an animation department was established in Tokyo Polytechnic University (Tokyo Kogei University in Japanese). Tokyo Polytechnic University became the first tertiary institution to establish an animation department in Japan.

At Nihon University Art College, with the progress of the semesters, the lectures that Ikeda had to teach gradually included compulsory animation subjects, graduation theses, and supervision of animated works. Ikeda developed his research of animism to explain animation. He introduced the theory of animism in his lectures and included the cultural anthropological works of E. B. Tylor, R. R. Marett, and Huruno Kiyoto and the developmental psychology of J. Piaget.

He was also much more interested in the concept of perception based on the expression and construction of animation. There was no material for teaching the perception of animation so he started to explore the concept of perception within his lecture by focusing on the dimension of apparent movement in animation. Ikeda's animation course encouraged his students to write animation graduation theses with themes based on cultural anthropology and psychology.

Ikeda wanted to encourage researchers of several universities to do research on animation studies. According to this common universal law of tertiary education, "to teach a theory and its application and to make research," the law enforces teaching staff to do research work. The aim of the master's degree education is to cultivate the abilities of students to undertake research by themselves and to acquire enormous knowledge and, consequently, become a specialist in their field. This means that if there are students who want to develop their abilities to do research then the faculty staff of the university should at least respond to their requests. Even in the artistic field, the same situation was expected. The doctoral degree would have even higher expectations.

In reality, however, there were only teaching staff who taught how to produce animation to graduate students (who simply wanted to learn just that) and there was almost no university teaching staff who taught animation theory in master's degree courses. Graduate students were sometimes called the fifth- and sixth-graders of the university. It was enough for students who wanted to be animators to enter a special vocational school of animation. Furthermore, some students who entered into graduate school of animation had not studied animation in their college days at all. Unfortunately, some graduate schools of animation only cared about their admission figures and were not interested in the students' educational background or what they had studied before.

In Ikeda's opinion, it was not necessary for an animator to get an academic tertiary degree. Animators with master's and doctoral degrees would be nonsensical. It was necessary to reconstruct the curriculum of the graduate course of animation. A majority of graduate students who submitted grant applications to organizations misunderstood the meaning of research activity, and a few students of doctoral courses did not even know what research was. They could not present an appropriate research plan to the organization. This indicated that the professor who guided the students might have done nothing. Or, the professor had not known what research was and might have had no experience of doing research.

It would be easy to understand the reason why there was no animation research specialist in Japan presently.

Research in the Japan Society of Image Arts and Sciences

In 1971, Ikeda made an appeal to the staff members of Nihon University Art College to develop animation research. A few members came together. However, it became apparent that it was sufficient for them to upkeep technical knowledge of cinema that they already had. They did not wish to broaden their research activities to acquire new knowledge. As a result, the research project was dissolved after a few meetings. The dean of Nihon University Art College, Togawa Naoki, was an exception. He was interested in psychology from his university days and participated in another research group of another university with Ikeda. One member of the group was Yamamoto Kikuo a professor at Waseda University. (Kenji Iwamoto, who later became the president of Japan Image Arts and Sciences, had been a graduate student of Waseda University.)

However, they were members of cinema research who were not interested in the electronics media that Ikeda wanted to pursue research in. The group developed into the Japan Cinema Society, but Ikeda left this group. In 1974, Ikeda participated in a preparation committee of the Japan Society of Image Arts and Sciences and wrote the regulations of the society and an operation plan. The society was established in September 1974.

After its establishment, Ikeda first became a manager and later a director of the society. The regulations of the society stipulated that even a creator had to be a researcher as well as a research specialist. However, in fact there were many members who had not done and did not do any research work. This is true of the present Japan Society for Animation Studies as well.

In fact, the first society for animation study ("Animation Research Society") was established in 1975 by Yabushita Taiji, who was the director of the animated film *Hakujaden* (White Snake Tale, 1958) and Ikeda's superior at Toei Doga. He made an appeal to the members of the Japan Society of Image Arts and Sciences to support and participate in the society's activities. Only Uchiyama Shotaro, who later became a professor at the Tokyo University of the Arts, participated in the first society for animation study meeting at the Tokyo Designer College in Ochanomizu. However, both Yabushita and Uchiyama were not researchers and theoreticians at heart but rather pragmatists interested in the practical side of animation. Consequently, the activities of the society came to a halt.

The activities of the society not only included the goal of conducting research within the society but also making available the results of this research to the public. However, the end result of the society's activity was most disappointing. Ikeda left the society and started to do research alone, again. In 1979, Ikeda became highly disillusioned of undertaking research in the society and planned to publish a series of animation as teaching materials for animation education with Bijyutu Shuppann Sha. He asked his friends to join his publishing project, and he organized an editorial committee. His project consisted of six volumes of "A Course of Animation." They were as follows:

Volume One: *An Introduction.* (Editor in charge: the late Manabe Shinsei, professor at Nihon University, unpublished)

Volume Two: *Creators in the World.* (Editor in charge: the late Togawa Naoki, former dean of Nihon University Art College, published in 1987)

Volume Three: *Construction of Images.* (Editor in charge: Hiroshi Ikeda, former professor at Tokyo Polytechnic University, published in 1986)

Volume Four: *Making Movement.* (Editor in charge: Tukioka Sadao, professor at Takarazuka University, published in 1983)

Volume Five: *Techniques of Animation.* (Editor in charge: Yagi Nobutada, former professor at Nihon University Art College, unpublished)

Volume Six: *A New Trend of Animation.* (Editor in charge: Hayama Komei, former professor at Tohoku University of Art & Design, published in 1982)

In volume 3, the contributors were Takahata Isao, Kuroda Shoro, and Miyazaki Hayao. In those days it would have been considered a good textbook. A complete set of the series would have been published in the 1980s from Bijyutsu Shuppan sha in Tokyo. In the end, two volumes were not published. The editors in charge were irresponsible. The case in general symbolized the situation surrounding the subject of animation.

Conclusion

As mentioned above, it is necessary for us to understand the historical background of animation research in Japan. This chapter first notes that there were existing research activities within the animation industry from the early 1960s but that it was necessary for academic and nontechnical researchers to broaden the research field. It also highlighted that there was little or hardly any academic or theoretical research of animation, and there was also no researcher specializing in animation at the university level. Furthermore, it indicated that it is necessary for both researchers from the industry and university to share similar educational goals and concerns. In addition, I also describe how a specific researcher interested in doing animation research in an academic society or an especially formed research group had encountered despair and problems in the past, and recurrently faced a situation whereby researchers who came together in the first place were not interested in studying the subject of animation in-depth.

It was believed that it would be very useful to establish a society for animation studies and departments of animation teaching in the universities, and that consequently, the field of animation research would be developed much more. As demonstrated above, in Japan, there were many restrictions on conducting research in the industry, in universities, and even in the prestigious Japan Society of Image Arts and Sciences. These enforced restrictions eventually led to the establishment of the Japan Society for Animation Studies. Even now, the aspirations and the original aims of the society, taking into account the context in which it was created, should be understood clearly.

Notes

1. This is a short propaganda education animation film that describes economic cooperation between Japan and the United States. The film promotes the idea that the "give-and-take relationship" is common in everyday life and that helping each other produces mutual advantages.

2. Editors' note: The author has chosen to write the article in the third-person perspective.

3. This is an earlier draft of the "Toei Junenshi" (Ten-Year History of Toei), which was later published in 1962.

4. Editors' note: *Eiga Hyōron* is also translated as "Movie Review" in Sano's essay.

5. To cut down on production cost, Toei Doga, Inc., tried to reduce the workforce. Toei Doga asked employees to resign voluntarily. Almost one hundred employees resigned and nineteen employees were fired. After the end of the lockout, Toei Doga reshuffled the personnel to decrease the number of artists employed and those who remained at Toei were forced to work harder.

6. Editors' note: NHK's official English name is Japan Broadcasting Corporation; it is Japan's national public broadcasting organization.

7. Editors' note: SIGGRAPH is the name of the annual conference on computer graphics (CG) and the first conference was held in 1974.

8. A salary of a lecturer was not 4,000 yen a day but 4,000 yen a month at that time. Editors' note: Today, the salary for part-time lecturing in Japan varies from place to place; full-time lecturing ensures not only a monthly salary but status as well.

Reference

Ikeda, H. "Animation no giho: kūkan kōsei ni tsuite [An animation technique: About space construction]. *Kikan-Eizo* [Japanese Journal of Image Arts and Sciences, also known as ICONICS in Japan] (1978): 34.

SECTION TWO

Pioneers of Japanese Animation

Chiyogami, Cartoon, Silhouette

The Transitions of Ōfuji Noburō

—**Akiko Sano**

Introduction

Ōfuji Noburō (1900–1961) is one of the most important artists in the history of Japanese animation. In 1962, the Mainichi Film Awards began offering the Ōfuji Noburō Prize to commemorate his accomplishments. His famous work *Kujira* (The Whale, 1952) was shown in the short film category at the Cannes International Film Festival and *Yūreisen* (The Phantom Ship, 1956) received the Special Prize at the Venice International Film Festival. These works of animation used silhouettes together with colored cellophane; however, until this point, Ōfuji had been creating works of animation in completely different styles. From the 1920s to the 1940s, Ōfuji changed direction twice, from *chiyogami* animation (cutout animation style by using traditional Japanese paper colored patterns, fig. 1) to cartoon-style animation (fig. 2), and then to silhouette animation (fig. 3). This article will examine the historical background that influenced the transitions in Ōfuji's works from the perspectives of both the visual discourse and the narrative text of his works.

Ōfuji Noburō's Chiyogami Animation

Following his apprenticeship with Kōuchi Sumikazu, one of the originators of Japanese animation, Ōfuji Noburō created his first work, *Baguda-jō no tōzoku* (Burglars of Baghdad Castle, 1926), and then went on to release a total of fifty-three works (including three trial pieces), most of them short pieces. Today thirty of the fifty-three are still in existence. To begin with, I will examine *chiyogami* animation, Ōfuji's original animation technique.

Chiyogami animation is a unique form of animation that may be considered a Ōfuji trademark. The process of creating it involves cutting *chiyogami* or paper in the shape of various elements such as a *kimono, hakama*, arms, legs, head, and so forth, and assembling them to form a human figure, and then moving each part bit by bit while capturing this with stop-motion photography.[1] In addition to the embellished nature of the vividly colored *chiyogami*, overlap techniques resembling the avant-garde cinema of the 1920s have also been recognized in *Kogane no hana* (The Golden Flower, 1929) and *Muramatsuri* (The Village Festival, 1930). This animation technique was highly regarded during the silent (film) period. For instance, it received admiration such as, "the beautiful and precise technique of paper cutting is uniquely Japanese, and its elegance is sufficient for us to boast of it abroad."[2] *Chiyogami* animation was in fact shown abroad. *Chinsetsu yoshida goten* (The Fantastic Castle of Yoshida, 1928) was shown in Paris on February 6, 1929, along with Kinugasa Teinosuke's experimental film *Jūjiro* (Crossroads, 1928).[3] Likewise, the film journal *Kinema junpō* ranked *Songokū monogatari* (The Story of Sun Wukong, 1926) eighteenth and *Baguda-jō no tōzoku* fortieth in its poll of the best films of 1926.[4] While the placement was not particularly high, at the time works of animation were regarded as supplements to feature films, and it is noteworthy that Ōfuji's works received such rankings alongside feature-length films.

Chiyogami animation was also frequently shown at Japanese schools and public facilities. Five works of *chiyogami* animation were included in the list of educational films in the educational film journal *Eiga kyōiku*.[5] With the recognition of the Ministry of Education, the first Best Film Medal was awarded to *Kogane no hana*. In addition, *Kokoro no chikara* (The Power of the Heart, 1931) was commissioned by the Ministry of Education.[6] In this way, the entertainment world, the cinema world, and the educational world, widely embraced by both adults and children, welcomed *chiyogami* animation. Why then did Ōfuji suddenly stop creating the highly praised *chiyogami* animation?

American Cartoon Animation: A New Standard

One of the important factors that led Ōfuji to stop creating *chiyogami* animation was the fact that during the transition to talkies around 1930,

American talkie animation dominated the global market. It could be said that American talkie animation had become the world standard, so much so that Hitler had Disney-style works made during World War II. It is likely that the release of *Ye Olde Melodies* (1929) by the Fleischer brothers at the Shinjuku Musashino Kan (Shinjuku Musashino Theater) on September 5, 1929, marked the first time that imported talkie animation was ever shown in Japan.[7] Among the talkies, Mickey Mouse and Betty Boop became so popular and a part of everyday life to such an extent that cafés were named after them and they appeared on the covers of magazines.[8]

In Japanese movie theaters, it was popular to screen *manga taikai* (cartoon animation program) composed of several American animated shorts together with feature films. Although *manga taikai* had been screened intermittently before this time, they were soundly established as profit-producing programs around 1933 during the talkie period. Promoters felt that *manga taikai* were "the safest bet for theaters that specialize in foreign films"[9] and some theaters found that they produced "the first box-office profit since the theater was opened"[10] or that screening a *manga taikai* once a month under a "family week" led to "a month's worth of debt being canceled out."[11] There was also a *"10 sen manga gekijō"* (10-cent cartoon theater) program in which cartoons only were shown at low prices.[12] The popularity of these programs in which multiple short works of cartoon animation were screened together indicates that cartoon animation was no longer viewed as a "supplement" but instead as a "featured product" whose value in the entertainment industry was increasingly recognized.

It is also interesting to note that not only promoters and general audiences, but also the intellectual class at the time, including critics and educators, began to show great interest in cartoon animation. The film journal *Eiga hyōron* devoted its July and August 1932 issues exclusively to animation for the first time since the launch of its publication, while *Eiga kyōiku* did the same with its August 1933 issue. Moreover, Disney's "Silly Symphonies" series was selected as number four in the list of the top-ten foreign films of 1933 by *Kinema junpō*. The tastes of the general public and the intellectual class often diverged; however, when it came to cartoon animation, they coincided.

The contemporary Japanese view of cartoon animation was formed in such a way that American cartoon animation became the "standard." An advertising statement of Seo Mitsuyo's *Genroku koi moyō: Sankichi to osayo* (Love in the Genroku Era: Sankichi and Osayo, 1934), "It is clear that the era when Japanese cartoon animation was inferior to foreign ones has passed!!"[13] indicates that Japanese cartoon animation was in fact seen as second rate in comparison to American-made animation. The tendency of the Japanese to look down on their own Japanese cinema has been observed from the 1910s onward,[14] but in the case of cartoon animation—a genre that was looked down on during the silent period—this tendency became especially marked from the time of the transition to talkies. Most critics viewed the attraction of cartoon animation as primarily in its "three-dimensional space" and "smooth movements." They praised the free and smooth movements of the characters within three-dimensional space, while negating the "two-dimensional space" and the "awkward movement" of Japanese cartoon animation.

One of the reasons Japanese cartoon animation was criticized as two-dimensional has to do with production methods. The cutout technique generally used in the production of Japanese animation consisted of filming the movements of cutouts against a background frame by frame and allowed "flat" movements of characters in upward, downward, left, and right directions. To give the movement of a character from the foreground to the background a three-dimensional feel, a number of individual pictures had to be drawn and this was extremely time consuming, thus the cutout technique was used more than 70 percent of the time in the composition of any particular work.[15] As the characters moved in a flat way, the audience came away with the two-dimensional impression even when spatial expansion was attempted through editing and manipulation of the background.

Paralleling this tendency, reviews that took *chiyogami* animation lightly began to stand out. The "awkward movements" occurring in "two dimensions" of *chiyogami* animation were taken as a sign that the technique remained at an "immature" stage. A review belittled *chiyogami* animation by going as far as to state that the reason it was praised during the silent period was simply "because of its rarity."[16] The contemporary tendency at that time was to view American cartoon animation as of a high standard while Japanese was viewed as of a low one. Even Ōfuji himself subscribed to this opinion. So Ōfuji began to switch to a form of cartoon animation production that incorporated American methods. For example, he made line drawings on top of the celluloid. In other words, Ōfuji works retained the *chiyogami* style while incorporating the American cartoon animation style.

Ōfuji Noburō's Cartoon Animation

What form did Ōfuji's animation take when it incorporated American methods yet exhibited a certain Japanese tradition? For example, in *Kaeru san-yūshi* (The Three Frog Heroes, 1933), *Numa no taishō* (The Swamp General, 1933), *Tengu taiji* (Wiping Out the Tengu, 1934), and *Chinkoro Heibei tamatebako* (Chinkoro Heibei's Casket, 1936) *chiyogami* patterns were used for the background; these give us a glimpse of the embellished nature of *chiyogami*. These characteristics exhibit Ōfuji's uniqueness as an artist. In addition, popular songs at the time—namely, "Ginza no yanagi (The Willows of Ginza)" and "Nikudan sanyūshi no uta (The Song of the Three Human Bombs)"—were inserted into *Kaeru san-yūshi* so that it could take the form of a *kouta eiga*[17] of the sort, which was popular in Japan at the time. A protagonist closely resembling Betty Boop appeared in *Tengu taiji* to meet the demand of an audience that favored American cartoon animation. In addition to the animation, Ōfuji's storytelling approach is also mixed. For example, *Baguda-jō no tōzoku* is a parody of the Hollywood feature film *The Thief of Bagdad* (1924) and it has two main elements, adventure and love; however, the main characters and situation resemble the Edo period in Japan.

The approach that Ōfuji took in trying to realize an ideal hybrid space of "Japan" and "America," coincided with the contemporary trend in Japanese cartoon animation. For instance, Ōishi Ikuo's *Ugoki-e kori no tatehiki* (Moving Picture: Fox vs. Raccoon Dog, 1933), Masaoka Kenzō's *Chagama ondo* (The Teakettle Dancing Song, 1934), and Kataoka Yoshitarō's *Shōjōji no Tanuki-bayashi: Ban Dan'emon* (Raccoon Dog Song of Shōjōji Temple: Ban Dan'emon, 1935) all demonstrated mastery over American-style smooth movements.

However, Japanese cartoon animation, which continued searching for such a compromise, was seen as having "reached a dead end" and efforts toward correcting this were undertaken. One such effort was the Manga Eiga Zadankai (Cartoon Animation Symposium) of 1936 in which animation artists including Ōfuji, Tokyo government officials, and educators participated. Film critics were also added to the mixture of personages from industry, government, and academia, which likely made this the first symposium where such a wide range of individuals associated with the medium of animation gathered in one place. The question of how to realize a "uniquely Japanese form of cartoon animation" was one of the central topics of discussion and although no concrete proposal took shape at the conclusion of the symposium, the Chief Clerk of Culture at the Tokyo Social Education Division indicated to attendees that "the uniqueness of Japanese cartoon animation for children" should be designated as the "correct path."[18] This can possibly be interpreted as the Japanese government authority giving animators who were caught between American and Japanese styles a directive of sorts to aim toward "Japanization."

At the same time, this also highlights the extent to which American cartoon animation penetrated Japan at that time and how strong its influence was on the country. However, it also shows the conflicting view that the authority had at that time in relation to reality for that matter. It was reaffirmed that cartoon animation was expected to be produced in the American vein and that "because it relies upon a certain narrow, so-called 'cartoon-like' effect, both the creators and the audience are unable to escape from these bizarre pre-conceived notions."[19] Ōfuji himself said the following:

> I think that there are storylines in Japan that use uniquely Japanese gags, but since we watch American cartoons, there are constant feelings of sadness in Japanese cartoons, so I have gotten stuck in a rut and haven't made any animation for just about a year now.[20]

Amid the standardization of American cartoon animation, Ōfuji had become stuck in a "rut." Moreover, in 1937, with the outbreak of the Second Sino-Japanese War and rising antiforeign/imperialistic nationalist sentiment, voices emphasizing "Japanese-ness" were growing ever louder in the discourse space for cartoon animation. The authority's directives toward "Japanization" helped create voices of Japanese "tradition" to be displayed in cartoon animation. For instance, in 1938 the film critic Imamura Taihei proposed the use of the tradition of "pictures designed to show temporality," like those of Heian-period picture scrolls, in cartoon animation. Since "religious fantasies" were the subject matter for most picture scrolls, Imamura says that "picture scrolls, as artistic fantasies, are a remote historical prefiguring of the fantastic nature of modern animated films," putting forward the view that picture scrolls are the origin of cartoon animation.[21] The view that cartoon animation can be placed among traditional Japanese arts is one that can be observed frequently during the war. A rise in nationalist sentiments appears in discourse regarding cartoon animation. These tendencies are also reflected in (re-)appraisals of Ōfuji's works; for example, *Chinkoro Heibei tamatebako* was praised unrestrainedly in 1936 as "telling a story that makes use of the unique beauty of *chiyogami*."[22] Indeed, there were reevaluations of *chiyogami* motifs that had been so harshly disparaged in the early 1930s.

Conversion/Regression to Silhouette Animation

However, regardless of the opportunity for reassessment, Ōfuji's *Sora no arawashi* (Eagles in the Sky, 1938) represented the end of his association with cartoon animation (though he resumed its production after the war), and in the 1940s he switched to silhouette animation. For instance, *Marē-oki kaisen* (Sea Battle off Malaya, 1943) was presented as a "kage-e senki eiga (silhouette military history film)" with narration in the style of a news movie using silhouettes and cellophane cutouts to depict the attack of the British Eastern fleet and the sinking of the "unsinkable battleship," the Prince of Wales on December 10, 1941, by the Japanese navy flying corps.

Ōfuji was already creating such silhouette animation in the 1920s (*Kujira* [The Whale, 1927] and *Kokka Kimigayo* [National Anthem: Kimigayo, 1931]). *Kujira*, in particular, was advertised as a "zenei kage-e eiga (avant-garde silhouette animation)."[23] Silhouette animation had originally risen to prominence in Germany in the 1920s and in Japan too such films were produced, with the majority designed to realize a form of avant-garde expression.[24]

Why did Ōfuji, who had already attempted silhouette animation in 1927 with *Kujira*, convert/regress to twenties-style silhouette animation in the 1940s? It is likely that amid the reports that Disney Studios had mobilized a workforce of seven hundred to complete *Snow White and the Seven Dwarfs* (1937)—the first full-length animated feature in the world—Ōfuji, an artist who in contrast would spend his whole life producing works of a personal scale, sensed that there were limits on the production of American-style cartoon animation. At that time, *Sora no arawashi*, a work of cartoon animation depicting animal characters in an air battle, was labeled as a "film unsuitable for general audiences"[25]—meaning children under fourteen years of age were restricted from viewing it—as the characters were seen as too caricaturized and the war was depicted as comical. This could be another reason for the change in direction. It is also possible to hold up the fact that shadow play is an entertainment culture beloved in Japanese-occupied territories since long ago, and that silhouette animation had been regarded as the "film for export."[26] Ōfuji's *Kodomo to kōsaku* (Children and Handicraft, 1941) was in fact shown in Korea.[27] Other works of silhouette animation were also exported: Arai Kazugorō's *Ochō fujin no gensō* (The Fantasy of Madame Butterfly, 1940) to Southeast Asia[28] and *Jakku to mame no ki* (Jack and the Beanstalk, 1941) to Taiwan and Korea.[29]

1. *Kokoro no chikara.*

In any case, Ōfuji's repeated changes in direction clearly demonstrate that Japanese animation continued to grope for a sense of direction while floating in limbo between American- and Japanese-centric orientations. That said, certain things can be consistently recognized in Ōfuji's works: through the production of one-of-a-kind *chiyogami* animation, the compromising processes between *chiyogami* animation and cartoon animation, and the avant-garde techniques in the military history films, we can see Ōfuji's response to the demands of the times, while constantly searching for alternatives.

A final word regarding *chiyogami* animation: although the production of *chiyogami* animation ceased in 1931 with *Kokoro no chikara* as the final such work, the name *chiyogami* continued to exist as a studio name. Ōfuji used three different names for his studio: Chiyogami Eigasha (Chiyogami Film Company), Jiyū Eiga Kenkyūsho (Freedom Film Laboratory), and Ōfuji Purodakusyon (Ōfuji Production). Particularly, he used the name

2. *Kaeru san-yūshi.*

3. *Marē-oki kaisen.*

Chiyogami Eigasha for his studio from 1929 to 1938 and again from 1947 to 1956 for a total of twenty years, and from that studio name, works of cartoon and silhouette animation were released. From this too we can see Ōfuji's affection for and pride in *chiyogami* animation.

Notes

1. Ōfuji Noburō, "Chiyogami eiga to shikisai eiga ni tsuite" [About *chiyogami* film and color film], *Eiga hyōron* [Movie review], July 1934: 65–66.

2. Matsudaira Kakuyoshi, "Kirigami zaiku eiga Baguda-jō no Tōzoku o sansu" [Words of praise for cutout animation film baguda-jō no tōzoku], *Eiga kyōiku* [Film education], August 1926: 17.

3. Okada Shinkichi, "Furansu ni okeru nihon eiga no shinsyutsu" [The advance of Japanese film in France], *Eiga ōrai* [Cinema traffic], September–October 1929: 30.

4. "Taishō 15 nendo yūsyū eiga tōhyō tokuten happyō" [An announcement of the score of excellent cinema voting at the Taishō 15th year], *Kinema junpō* [Film bulletin], March 11, 1927: 25.

5. "Saikin kyōiku eiga mokuroku" [A catalog of the latest education film], *Eiga kyōiku* [Film education], August 1929: 32–35.

6. "Yūsyū eiga syōhai kōfu" [The promulgation of a cup of excellent film], *Monbushō kyōiku eiga jihō* 8 [The news of the education films of the Ministry of Education, Culture, Sports, Science and Technology 8], 1931: 46.

7. *Musashino Weekly*, 9.37 (1929): page not available.

8. Shigeno Tatsuhiko, "Shirī shimufonī" [Silly Symphony], *Eiga hyōron* [Cinema review], April 1933: 91.

9. "Eigakan keikyō chōsa" [The research of economic conditions of movie theaters], *Kinema junpō* [Film bulletin], October 21, 1933: 33.

10. "Tōto eigakan bangumi oyobi keikyō chōsa" [The program and the research of economic conditions of Tōto movie theaters], *Kinema junpō* [Film bulletin], June 1, 1933: 19.

11. "Eigakan keikyō chōsa" [The research of economic conditions of movie theaters], *Kinema junpō* [Film bulletin], August 11, 1933: 21.

12. "Chihō keikyō" [The research of economic conditions of movie theaters in the country], *Kinema junpō* [Film bulletin], May 21, 1933: 25.

13. *Kinema junpō* [Film bulletin], June 11, 1934: 16.

14. Aaron Gerow, "Tatakafu kankyaku—daitōa kyōeiken no nihon eiga to juyō no mondai" [Fighting audience—the problem of Japanese film and demand in daitōa kyōeiken], *Gendai shisō* [The contemporary philosophy], July 2002: 141.

15. Yamaguchi Katsunori and Watanabe Yasushi, *Nihon animēshon eigashi* [The history of Japanese animation] (Osaka: Yūbunsha [Yubun Publishing], 1977), 20.

16. Saitō Kōji, "Chiyogami eigasha sakuhin" [The works of Chiyogami film production company], *Eiga hyōron* [Movie Review], June 1934: 68.

17. *Kouta eiga* are films that incorporate popular songs from music records or film themes. Lyrics appear in the form of subtitles on one portion of the screen, which resembles modern *karaoke. Kouta eiga* attained temporary popularity in the Taishō era and formed a prominent subgenre beginning with the introduction of talkies in 1929.

18. "Manga eiga zadankai (zoku)" [A meeting about cartoon animation (Part II)], *Eiga kyōiku* [Film Education], December 1936: 23.

19. Ibid., 18.

20. "Manga eiga zadankai (1)" [A meeting about cartoon animation (Part I)], *Eiga kyōiku* [Film Education], November 1936: 19.

21. According to Imamura, "pictures designed to show temporality are in fact perhaps the oldest and highest form of art. Like modern *manga*, the story unfolds through pictures. In some cases, the temporal techniques of film resemble this to a shocking extent." This is because picture scrolls depict diverging temporal spaces continuously in one picture as in motion pictures, and do not depict normalized versions of each individual component as in Western art, instead hiding the important parts with clouds by a method of omission corresponding to fadeouts and overlaps. In Imamura Taihei, *Eiga geijutsu no seikaku* [A nature of film aesthetics] (Kyoto: Daiichi geibunsha [Daiichi geibun Publishing], 1939). Reprinted in *Imamura Taihei eizōhyōron* [Imamura Taihei's Image Review], vol. 2 (Tokyo: Yumani shobō, 1991), 150–52.

22. "Amachua eiga" [Amateur film], *Kinema junpō* [Film bulletin], August 11, 1936: 68.

23. *Kogata eiga* (8mm film), June 1930: page not available.

24. See Makino Mamoru, "Sōsōki no nihon animēshon eiga ni okeru zeneisei ni tsuite—shiruetto animēshon no yonin no shineasuto" [Avant-gardism in early Japanese animation—Four cinema artists' silhouette animation], *Animēshon kenkyū* [Animation education], 3(2)A (2002): 53–61.

25. "Monbushō suisen nintei geppō" [A monthly report recommended by the Ministry of Education, Culture, Sports, Science and Technology], *Eiga kyōiku* [Film education], April 1942: 25.

26. "Kōhaku ōrai" [The red and white traffic], *Eiga junpō* [Film bulletin], June 11, 1942: 50.

27. "Jihō" [Current news], *Eiga kyōiku* [Film education], May 1942: 59.

28. *Eiga nenkan* [Film yearbook], 1943: 714.

29. "Jihō" [Current news], *Eiga kyōiku* [Film Education], May 1942: 59, and *Eiga nenkan* [Film yearbook], 1942: 7–6.

The Japanese Walt Disney

Masaoka Kenzo

—Yasushi Watanabe
Translated by Sheuo Hui Gan

Introduction

In recent years, Japanese animation, often regarded as "anime," has gained an international reputation. In 2003, *Spirited Away* directed by Miyazaki Hayao, was honored as the first Japanese animation to win the best animated feature film at the Academy Awards. In 2009, Kato Kunio's *Tsumiki no ie* (La Maison en Petits Cubes) triumphed as the best animated short film in the same prestigious film competition. Besides Miyazaki Hayao, Oshii Mamoru (*Ghost in the Shell*, 1996) and Otomo Katsuhiro (*Akira*, 1988) have also made their names as world-famous Japanese animation directors.

Japanese animation has over ninety years of history since it first emerged in 1917 when the three pioneers Shimokawa Oten (1892–1973), Kitayama Seitaro (1888–1945), and Kouchi Junichi (1886–1970) sought out different opportunities to make the first animation in Japan without acknowledging the existence of each other. The three of them are considered to be the first generation of pioneers in Japanese animation, followed by Yamamoto Sanae (1898–1981), Ofuji Noburo (1908–1961), and Murata Yasuji (1896–1966) as the second generation.

Oishi Ikuo (1901–1944), Masaoka Kenzo (1898–1988), and Seo Mitsuyo (1911–2010) are the third generation of pioneers. Excluding Masaoka, most of them had gathered around Tokyo to make animation. Even today, most production companies are still centered in the Tokyo area.

Among the third generation, *Ugokie kori no tatehiki* (Moving Picture: Raccoon Dog versus Fox) directed by Oishi in 1933 has been highly regarded as comparable to gag animations produced in America at that time. Unfortunately, Oishi was killed during the Pacific War and did not have an opportunity to further exercise his talent. In contrast, Masaoka's career was blessed with good luck, which enabled him to continue making animation in Kyoto until the outbreak of the war in 1941.

Masaoka's distinguished contributions to the technical developments in Japanese animation have earned him the honorary title, "father of animation in Japan." The following sections delineate his roles in the development of the Japanese animation.

Masaoka Kenzo's Background

Masaoka Kenzo was born in Osaka in 1898 as the eldest son to Masaoka Kasaburo (1867–1950). For generations, Masaoka family members were wealthy landlords and Kenzo was raised in a very comfortable environment. Masaoka's father handed over their family business to his eldest daughter and retired early. Following his retirement, he built a huge villa on Awaji Island facing the Seto Inland Sea in order to pursue his interest in Japanese painting.

Masaoka's father lived a quiet life as an amateur Japanese painter in the villa, while Masaoka went to school on the island and spent his boyhood surrounded by this charming natural environment. Throughout these years, Masaoka was slowly exposed to painting through his father's interests. Indeed, even though his father had given up any hope of becoming a professional Japanese painter, he had secretly wished Masaoka would pursue this dream one day.

Masaoka's father sent him to *Kyoto Shiritsu Bijutsu Kogei Gakko* (Kyoto Municipal School of Arts and Crafts) to learn Japanese painting. Upon his graduation, he went to an art institute that specialized in Western painting operated by Kuroda Kiyoteru in Tokyo.[1] A year later, Masaoka returned to Kyoto and enrolled in *Kyoto Kaiga Senmon Gakko* (Kyoto City Specialist School of Painting, now Kyoto City University of Arts) in order to learn traditional Japanese painting. Masaoka spent about ten years in three different schools acquiring his education in painting. The tuition and the lodging fees for those ten years must have been very expensive. Masaoka was considered lucky to have had such a distinctive education and valuable school life thanks to his rich family's background.

Upon his graduation from art school in 1924, Masaoka did not pursue his career in Japanese painting. Instead, he turned to cinema after foreseeing the potential of cinema as a new medium. In fact, Masaoka was already passionate about cinema and theater in his younger years and had participated in quite a few theatrical performances at school.

Masaoka joined Makino Film Productions in Kyoto founded by Makino Shozo (1828–1929), a prominent pioneer figure in Japanese cinema. Masaoka's first assignment in the studio was designing sets and film props in *Nichirin* (The Sun, 1924) directed by Kinugasa Teinosuke (1896–1982).[2] In 1926, Masaoka left Makino Film Productions and set up his own studio called Nonbei Productions in Kyoto. With the financial support of his father, Masaoka quickly made his debut as an independent filmmaker by starting his first project, *Umi no kyuden* (Palace in the Sea), a children's oriental fantasy film that loosely resembled the legend of Urashima Taro, a Japanese legend about a fisherman who is rewarded for his generosity with a visit to the palace under the sea. Despite the film not existing any longer, the remaining still photographs suggest that part of the set design was inspired by the Renaissance artist Sandro Botticelli's "The Birth of Venus."[3]

Umi no kyuden was screened at Nikkatsu theaters. However, the film did not manage to break even and Masaoka returned to Makino Film Productions. The owner of Makino Film Productions, Makino Shozo, was attracted to Masaoka's handsome appearance and recommended he consider becoming an actor. Adopting Segawa Rurinosuke as his stage name, Masaoka acted in a period drama *Hitojichi* (The Hostage, 1927) directed by Hitomi Kichinosuke. Regrettably, Masaoka's prospect of becoming an actor burst like a bubble due to his lack of skill in acting, and once again he left the company.

In 1929, Masaoka joined Nikkatsu Uzumasa Studio. He became the director for educational films and was also in charge of filming. However, the department closed down because there was not much work available. From then on, Masaoka set up his own studio at home with a financial loan from Nikkatsu with the goal of making animation. It is unclear why Masaoka had this sudden interest in animation. It is possible that his experiences in film inspired him to animate the static paintings he had been familiar with at home and in school.

His Animation Career and Other Film Contributions

His first animation, *Nansensu monogatari daiippen sarugashima* (Nonsense Story: First Episode—The Monkey Island, 1930), is a smoothly animated cutout animation. This adventurous narrative was probably inspired by *Tarzan*. The narrative is about a baby boy who was put into a wooden box by his parents right before their shipwreck. The wooden box finally lands on a deserted island inhibited only by monkeys. The head of the monkeys decides that a female monkey will take care of this baby boy. Time flies and the baby boy grew up to be a healthy young man. However, he is often bullied by the monkeys due to his fairer skin color and lack of a tail. Nonetheless, he is very intelligent and has good athletic skills. One day, the young boy is exiled from the group after he threw coconuts at the female monkeys who were enjoying themselves dancing by the beach on the night of a full moon. The film ends with the young boy escaping from the island by making himself a raft from a coconut tree.

In the film's unique opening sequence, sand is used to animate the movement of the waves.[4] This scene was created by Kimura Kakuzan, who was also a graduate from Kyoto Bijutsu Kogei Gakko. Even though it was his very first assignment, Kimura created interesting movements and visual designs with these waves. However, Kimura did not desire to continue his career as an animator and remained as a cameraman in Masaoka's studio.

In 1931, Masaoka made *Kaizokusen* (Pirate Ship) as the sequel to *Sarugashima. Kaizokusen* continues the previous episode where the boy was adrift in the sea after his escape from the monkey island. The young boy was finally rescued by a ship but not long afterward this unfortunate ship was hijacked by pirates. In this film, the narrative focuses on how the young boy tries to free the ship crew from these pirates.

During that time, Masaoka also had contract jobs such as filming the special effects for live-action cinema. Indeed, Masaoka's talents were not limited to making animation but also extended to live-action cinema.

In 1927, Warner Brothers produced the *Jazz Singer*, a feature-length musical film with the first synchronized dialogue sequences. The film was a huge success and heralded the start of the talkie era worldwide. *Madamu to nyobo* directed by Gosho Heinosuke and produced by Shochiku in 1931 is considered to be the first talkie film in Japan. This film was created using the Tsuchihashi-shiki recording system. Many movie companies in Japan were inspired by Shochiku and vigorously developed their own talkies, which led to the gradual demise of the silent film era in Japan.

Masaoka also foresaw the future of the talkie, and in 1932 he set up *Masaoka Eiga Seisakusho* (Masaoka Film Productions) in Kyoto. At that time, the good reception of *Steamboat Willie* (1928) by Walt Disney and other talkie animations imported from America inspired Kido Shiro, the head of the Shochiku's Kamata Studio in Tokyo to produce a talkie animation. Setting aside the geographical distance, Kido approached Masaoka in Kyoto to make a talkie animation. Masaoka decided to take up the challenge and at the same time, Seo Mitsuyo, a young man from Tokyo, called upon Masaoka and expressed his intention to become an animator. Masaoka took Seo into his studio. Seo was quick in drawing and later became another prominent figure in Japanese animation.

The first talkie animation in Japan, *Chikara to onna no yo no naka* (Power and Women in Society, 1932), was oriented toward adults. The story is about a salary man who is having a love affair with his typist. After learning of the fact, the wife confronts the typist with wife and typist ending up boxing each other. In the beginning, the typist is too weak to fight the wife. However, she manages to defeat the wife by spraying her with a water hose and thus winning the fight unexpectedly. Though the animation was mainly made using the cutout method, for the first time, celluloid was used for some sections of the film; for example, the water hose scene.

The film was produced by Kido Shiro from the Shochiku Kamata Studio, which also produced *Madamu to nyobo* (1931), the first feature-length sound film in Japan. The success of *Madamu to nyobo* had stimulated Kido to search for the same potential in animation, especially to attract a broader audience including adults as well as children. Kido was a talented producer and later became the head of Shochiku. Since no print of *Chikara to onna no yo no naka* has survived, the exact length of the film remains unknown. Knowledge of its narrative is based on the description found in the movie magazines of the time. Nonetheless, *Chikara to onna no yo no naka* is said to have been produced in two cans, which suggests that it was about fifteen minutes long. The director Masaoka and his eight team members spent six months completing this talkie animated film; it was released on April 15, 1933. This highly acclaimed adult-oriented nonsensical animation depicted a family conflict where the husband is afraid of his hysteric yet strong, wife. Unfortunately the film is no longer in existence.[5]

Celluloid was first used in animation in 1914 and popularized by Earl Hurd (1880–1940), who also patented the rights to it. In America, celluloid animation was steadily becoming established but this was not the case in Japan. Masaoka had to search for celluloid, and finally managed to get a supply from Dainihon Celluloid Corporation. However, the celluloid from Dainihon was slightly yellowish and thicker compared to the thinner and more transparent variety available in America. Nonetheless, after many trials and errors, Masaoka successfully produced this first animation talkie. His pioneering use of celluloid marks a significant contribution to the technological development of Japanese animation.

In 1933, Shochiku commissioned another talkie from Masaoka. As a result, two animated stories, *Adauchi karasu* (Vengeful Crow) and *Gyangu to odoriko* (Gang and the Dancer), were produced. *Adauchi* and *Gyangu* were initially two different stories. However, due to their similarities, the two films were combined and screened as two parts of a whole. Since both films no longer exist, the details of their narratives remain unknown. However, according to the twenty-four existing photographs, there are some sort of dancing scenes taking place between the leader of the gang and a female dancer, who resembles Betty Boop, the famous character created by the Fleischer brothers. The narrative seems to be connected to a group of gang members who were arrested after their attempt to rob a bank safe. However, the relationship between the dancer and the gang remains unclear. *Adauchi* and *Gyangu* were screened before the main feature film following the mainstream prewar screening pattern in the United States, a time when news reels and short animated films were often shown before the feature. This screening pattern did not generate enough attention, and the film did not manage to break even. This unfortunate outcome stopped Shochiku from making further investments in talkie animation. Nonetheless, Masaoka's spirited belief in continuing the challenge of making talkie animation inspired others to look into this possibility. In this regard, his accomplishment is significant.

In December of the same year, Masaoka received more financial aid from his family, and he built a new studio, *Masaoka Eiga Bijutsu Kenkyusho* (Masaoka Cinematic Art Research Center), in Kyoto. It had two stories and occupied two hundred and ninety square meters. This impressive studio was capable of creating special-effects filming besides making animation. The total number of staff reached forty people, including those required for special-effects filming.

In this new studio, the animation production switched completely from conventional cutout animation to celluloid animation. This was made possible after Dainihon Celluloid Corporation set up their subsidiary company Fuji Film in January 1934, which started to mass produce film stock locally. Until then the majority of film stock used in Japan was imported from Eastman Kodak Company based in America. Besides film, Fuji Film also produced celluloid. This made it comparatively easy to get access to celluloid suitable for making animation.

Chagama ondo (Tune of the Tea Kettle) and *Mori no yakyudan* (Baseball Team of the Forest) from 1934 were fully animated using celluloid due to Masaoka's insistence. These two works were smoothly animated, but the cost of maintaining such a high quality was not cheap. Yet, Masaoka stood by this expensive production process, even with the payments to additional staff members. In 1935, however, Masaoka was not able to get any more financial aid from his father and was forced to close his studio. He had to sell his new studio in order to pay off his debts. Masaoka is no doubt a great pioneer who inaugurated the use of celluloid and the production of talkie animations. However, he was not good at managing his studio financially.

After his studio was dissolved, Masaoka did not withdraw from animation. He joined the J.O recording company, which had been newly set up in Kyoto. Ichikawa Kon (1915–2008), who later became one of the famous directors of Japanese cinema, was also there. Masaoka subcontracted work from J.O Studio and distributed it to his ex-staff.

In 1941, Shochiku approached Masaoka to join them to produce animation in their Tokyo studio. Masaoka and many of his ex-staff agreed and departed for Tokyo. Kimura Kakuzan, who had been in charge of filming in Masaoka's studio, remained in Kyoto.

Animation Made during the Pacific War

The Japanese navy's surprise attack on Pearl Harbor on December 8, 1941, triggered the start of the Pacific War. The Japanese navy commissioned Seo Mitsuyo to work on an animation project including ex-staff member Masaoka. The purpose of this animation was to impress children in Japan and glorify the attack on Pearl Harbor. A thirty-seven-minute propaganda animation, *Momotaro no umiwashi* (Momotaro's Sea Eagles), was made and screened as a result of this project.

After moving to Tokyo, Masaoka adapted a fairy tale by the female author Yokoyama Michiko, *Kumo to churippu* (Spider and Tulip, 1942), into animation. The story is about a young female ladybug that seeks shelter in a tulip from a spider who wants to eat her. The spider becomes really angry and makes a web surrounding the flower in order to prevent the ladybug from escaping. At night, a sudden storm blows the spider away into a pond unexpectedly. All the flowers are scattered around by the storm, but the spiderweb that is woven around the tulip by the spider eventually saved the young ladybug.

Most of the animation made during the war tended to be full of propaganda to raise the nation's spirit for the war. In contrast to Seo's *Momotaro no umiwashi*, *Kumo to churippu* directed by Masaoka was an exceptional work set in a garden filled with flowers and in the author's personal opinion, not colored by any wartime atmosphere.[6] This work has been highly regarded in the history of Japanese animation and is also one of Masaoka's most representative works.

The character design of the spider, especially the pipe and how the boater hat is worn, resembles the appearance of Harold Lloyd, an American actor famous for his silent comedies. The face of the spider resembles the blackface character played by Al Jolson in *Jazz Singer* (1927). From the prewar period until during the war itself, a screening system by the Ministry of Home Affairs was put in place that considered the suitability of all films, including fiction, documentary, and animation produced in Japan, as well as the original film scenarios that were submitted, before releasing them to the general public. Therefore, even though there were complaints from the Ministry of Education, Science and Culture that *Kumo to churippu* lacked the desired fighting spirit, it was not rejected since Shochiku had secured prior permission for its production.

The production of *Momotaro no umiwashi* was commissioned by the Ministry of Navy in Japan and due to that, the director Seo Mitsuyo had ample access to the film stock, celluloid, and paper needed for production. Seo used to work with Masaoka in his studio in Kyoto and had learned how to produce animated films and talkies from him. The two of them had a sort of student and teacher relationship. It is possible that the reason Masaoka created *Kumo to churippu* was to counter *Momotaro no umiwashi*, which was heavily colored with wartime propaganda. In the historical development of Japanese animation, *Kumo to churippu* has been highly regarded for its excellent depiction of nature and poetic sentimentalism. In many aspects, Seo's *Momotaro no umiwashi* and Masaoka's *Kumo to churippu* form an interesting opposition that depicts "war and peace" in animation.

Later, Seo, too, joined Shochiku and once again worked with Masaoka. The result of their collaboration was *Momotaro umi no shinpei* (Divine Sea Warriors), another animation commissioned by the navy to depict the activity of the parachute unit. Seo was the director, and Masaoka was in charge of the silhouette animation for this film. The film was screened in April 1945, toward the end of the war. Shochiku's animation studio was bombarded by American B29 bombers in May 1945 and all the filming equipment was destroyed.

After the Pacific War

Japan returned to peace in 1946. That year, Masaoka made a new animation film *Sakura* (Cherry Blossoms), to depict spring in Kyoto. He selected Weber's *Invitation to the Waltz* (conducted by Leopold Anthony Stokowski [1882–1977]) to accompany the image of two anthropomorphic butterflies dancing in a sky filled with *sakura* petals in Kyoto.[7] Even though this work was beautifully animated, it did not reach the screen or the general public because the initial distribution company Toho judged the work to lack economic value.

After the disappointment of *Sakura*, Masaoka directed *Suteneko tora-chan* (Tora-chan the Abandoned Kitten) in 1947. *Suteneko tora-chan* was well received, especially the cute character design of the cat, Tora-chan. The narrative is about an abandoned male kitten that is fortunate enough to be adopted by a mother cat that treats him like her own child. However, one of the other kittens of the mother cat becomes jealous of Tora-chan and often bullies him. At the end of the story, Tora-chan is able to become friends with this other kitten after it is brought back home following her attempt to run away. Masaoka felt sorry for the children who became orphaned due to the war and the inspiration of this film came from seeing many children who lost their parents during the air raids of the war. The unselfish love of the mother cat made this animation a touching one. The dialogue of the film, too, is uniquely delivered in an opera-like manner worthy of attention.

Following this success, Masaoka directed another two Tora-chan films, *Tora-chan to hanayome* (Tora-chan and Wife) in 1948 and *Tora-chan no kankan mushi* (Tora-chan, the Ship-painter) in 1950. Later, these three films came to be known as the Tora-chan series. Despite their good reception, Nichido Film Company was having financial trouble and was not able to pay its staff. Such incidents affected Masaoka badly, as at that time, his wife was severely ill and admitted to a hospital. The pressure of hospital costs and expenses for medical care forced Masaoka to quit work on animation and shift to magazine work for children, drawing manga and illustrations. This new income from the magazine helped him to pay for his wife's medical fees and their living expenses. It was extremely regrettable that Masaoka, who was so deeply dedicated to animation, had to leave the animation industry. Even so, Masaoka did not abandon his dream of making animation. He continued to produce storyboards and often thought of coming back to make animation once his situation would allow it.

His final storyboard was Hans Christian Anderson's *The Little Mermaid.* Some of the remaining storyboards were carefully colored and may have expressed Masaoka's intention to make this particular work in color, despite his other works all being in monochrome. Masaoka's version of *The Little Mermaid* is significantly different from the original novel, as well as Walt Disney's animation of the same title. It is regrettable that this project was never completed.

In 1987, Masaoka moved to Osaka from Tokyo. He spent the rest of his life surrounded by his favorite cats. He passed away in 1988, at the age of ninety.

Conclusion

Masaoka was raised with the intention that he would become a Japanese painter after his father's dream. Instead, he went into the film profession and achieved acclaim making animation. Masaoka's father was passionate about the quiet world of Japanese painting; on the contrary, Masaoka was attracted to bringing the static into motion via animating images frame by frame. Although what Masaoka did was different from what his father had wished for him, Masaoka shone in his chosen profession of animation.

The key accomplishments (and contributions) of Masaoka for the Japanese animation industry are the production of the first talkie animation in Japan and the popularization of the use of celluloid in animation. Due to these technical achievements, animation scholars, critics, and fans alike have honored him with the title, "father of Japanese animation." The adventurous spirit of Masaoka in challenging the unknown world of animation is quite similar to that of Walt Disney in his early days. Animation was imported to Japan and had been screened in theaters since the prewar period. *Opry House* of the Mickey Mouse series by Walt Disney first opened in Musashino-kan in Tokyo on September 12, 1929, under the Japanese title *Mikki no opera kenbutsu.* The Mickey Mouse and the color *Silly Symphony* series by Disney as well as the *Betty Boop* and *Popeye* series by

Fleischer brothers were popular in Japan. Nevertheless, the *Mickey Mouse* series was the most popular, as demonstrated by the illegal publication of the Mickey Mouse comic books.[8] Against this background, Masaoka was well aware of the fact that many children in Japan preferred foreign-produced celluloid animation to locally produced cutout animation.

The cutout animation technique had been used to produce animation since the prewar period. Compared to the celluloid animation technique, cutout animation was cheaper; however, the process, such as using scissors and knives to do the cutout, was extremely time consuming. Moreover, very often the movement produced in cutout animation was less smooth than the movement generated in celluloid animation. In order to improve the quality of his animation, Masaoka insisted on shifting to the celluloid system despite the costly production fees. In many ways, Masaoka ushered in a technological revolution in animation production in Japan.

Besides animation, Masaoka was also involved in the production of visual effects for live-action film; however, unfortunately this is not well known. He was also one of the pioneers involved in puppet animation in Japan. In 1935, J.O Studio in Kyoto adapted the famous Japanese legend *Taketori monogatari* (Tale of the Bamboo Cutter) into a musical that tells the narrative of Kaguya-hime, who was found as a baby inside a bamboo but who was supposed to be the princess of the *Tsukino miyako* (Capital of the Moon). The directors of this film are Tanaka Yoshitsugu and Aoyagi Nobuo. The cameraman was Tsuburaya Eiji (1901–1970), who later became famous for his special-effects science-fiction films including the *Godzilla* film series.

In the film production of *Taketori monogatari*, Masaoka was responsible for the section where the bullock cart came down to earth from the moon to pick up Kaguya-hime, who had grown up to become a young lady. Masaoka used the puppet animation technique to animate the bullock; each bullock was custom made and individually carved. The technique that Masaoka used resembled the "puppetoons" technique developed by George Pal (1908–1980), an American animator and film producer. It is unclear how Masaoka learned this technique but he can certainly be considered as a pioneer in puppet animation in Japan.

The accomplishments of Masaoka include technical developments, such as the development of the talkie animation and the popularization of celluloid animation. In addition, his contributions to puppet animation and his experimentation with visual effects were also significant for the Japanese animation industry. In many respects, Masaoka's work resembles Disney's daring spirit in challenging the boundaries of his time through technical innovation, such as the development of talkie animation, color animation, and feature-length animated films. For these reasons, the author would like to strongly honor Masaoka as the "Waltz Disney of Japan."

1. *Nonsense Story: First Episode—The Monkey Island.*

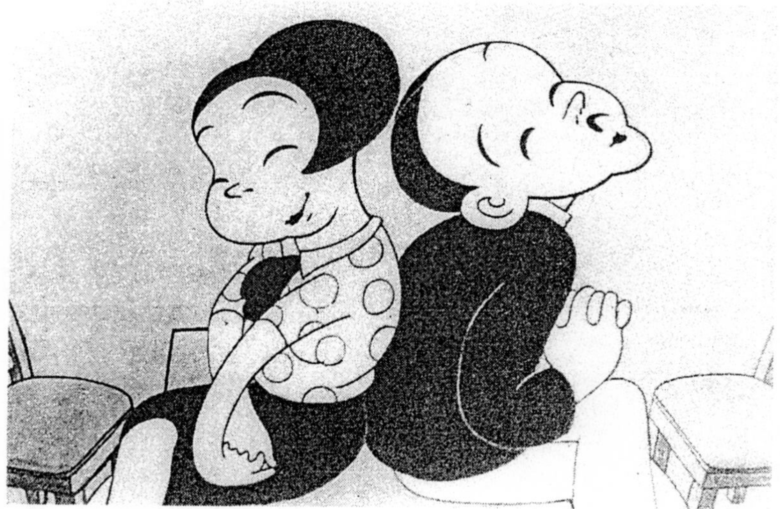

2. *Power and Women in Society.*

3. *Gang and the Dancer.*

4. *Spider and Tulip.*

5. *Cherry Blossoms.*

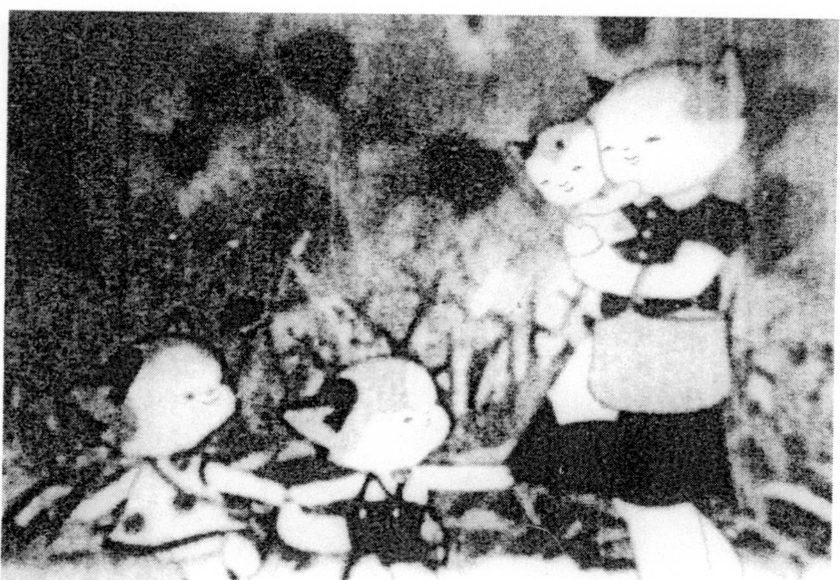

6. Tora-chan the abandoned kitten.

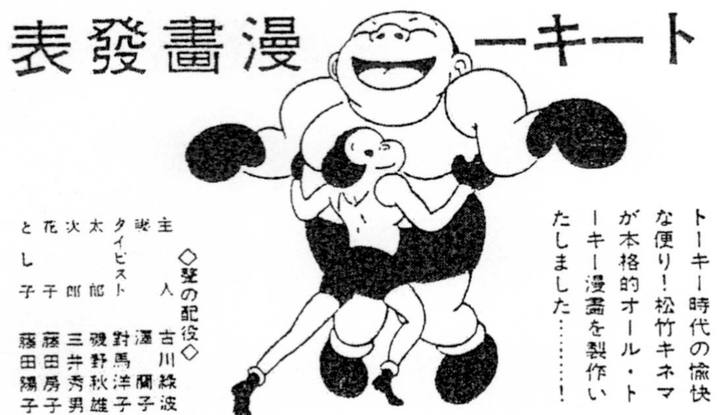

7. Publicity material for the film *Power and Women in Society.*

8. Masaoka Kenzo (seventy-two years old) in front of Osaka train station on June 28, 1970. Photo by Watanabe Yasushi.

Notes

1. Kuroda Seiki (1866–1924) was born in Kagoshima prefecture. A representative Western-style painter in the Meiji and Taisho periods, his given name was Kuroda Kiyoteru. Kuroda went to France to study law in 1884, but soon abandoned it after realizing he liked painting more than anything else. Kuroda studied under Raphael Collin, a French academic painter. The main characteristic of Kuroda's paintings is its mixture of French academism and the impressionism represented by Manet. Kuroda excelled in portraying nature in soft colors. His realistic painting style became the core of modern Japanese oil painting. Kuroda returned to Japan in 1893 and was appointed professor at the Department of Western Art at Tokyo Bijutsu Gakko (now Tokyo University of the Arts). He inspired a whole new generation of Western-style painters in Japan.

2. Kinugasa Teinosuke was born in Mie prefecture. His given name was Ogura Teinosuke. Kinugasa joined Nikkatsu Mukojima Studio in 1917 as an actor specializing in female roles (*oyama*). He later became a film director. In 1924, Kinugasa adapted Yokomitsu Riichi's novel *Nichirin* (The Sun), and Masaoka was hired to design the sets and props. Kinugasa is best known for his *Kurutta ippeji* (A Page of Madness, 1926), an avant-garde experimental film, and *Jujiro* (Crossroad, 1928), a unique period drama. During his stay in Europe, Kinugasa also interacted with Sergei Eisenstein, the famous Russian director. Kinugasa's *Jigokumon* (Gate of Hell), the first Japanese feature-length color film (Eastmancolor), won the prestigious Golden Palm award at the Cannes Film Festival in 1954.

3. Film stills that closely resembled the "Birth of Venus" scene appeared in the *Umi no kyuden* (Palace in the Sea) and were printed in the 1978 special issue on Masaoka Kenzo in *Film 1/24*. *Film 1/24* is more of an animation fan magazine (*dojinshi*).

4. Lotte Reiniger (1899–1981), a German silhouette animator and film director, was the first to animate using sand in *Die Abenteuer des Prinzen Achmed* (Adventures of Prince Achmed, 1926). However, *The Owl Who Married the Goose* (1974) directed by Caroline Leaf (1946–) for the National Film Board of Canada was considered as one of the most famous and excellent works to use sand as a medium. Reiniger's film was screened in Japan in June 1929 at Tokyo Musashino Theater. It is believed that the film was also screened in Osaka and Kyoto.

5. *Chikara to onna no yo no naka* reflects the remnants of feudalism in prewar Japan, especially the tendency of male domination of women even within the family. It was common for the wife to obey the husband. However, there were also men who had a lower status at home and were afraid of their wives; they were often teased as henpecked husbands. After the war, Japan became a democratic society. Among many aspects, the women's liberation movement and growing power of gender equality in America led to a rise in women's status in Japan. The production of *Chikara to onna no yo no naka* was intended to provide courage to women who had been treated lowly in the feudal society. Though this film has a nonsensical comic touch, it depicts a wife standing up to fight her husband who has an extramarital affair.

6. Editors' note: Hu's essay in this collection gives a different view and provides a critical analysis of Masaoka's works and readers may cross-reference the various interpretations.

7. Stokowski also conducted the music for Disney's *Fantasia* (1940).

8. Editors' note: Due to rising war tensions and international disagreements with Western nations, Japan's turn against the West included the United States of America. Hence, Anglo-American media works were increasingly banned in Japan from the late 1920s onward.

References

Film 1/24. *Masaoka Kenzo Tokusyu* [Special Issue on Masaoka Kenzo]. Tokyo: Anido, issue 23+24, 1978.

Hagihara, Yukari. *Masaoka Kenzo*. [A thought on the relation between art and the early animated movies (manga eiga)]. Master's dissertation. Ritsumeikan Asia Pacific University, 2008.

Kinema Junpo. *Nihon eiga kantoku zenshu* [Complete works of Japanese movie directors] Tokyo: Kinema Junpo, 1977.

Tomono, Takashi, and Mochizuki Nobuo. *Sekai anime-shon eigashi* [History of world animation]. Tokyo: Parupu, 1986.

Yamaguchi, Katsunori, and Watanabe Yasushi. *Nihon anime-shon eiga shi* [The history of Japanese Animation]. Osaka: Yubunsha, 1977.

Animating for "Whom" in the Aftermath of a World War

—Tze-yue G. Hu

In this chapter I will focus on the development of animation in postwar Japan, with emphasis on the period of the Allied Forces Occupation from 1945 to 1952. Hirano Kyōko's (1992) groundbreaking work about the state of the Japanese cinema during that period should have been the most direct reference for this research. However, like other similar publications, it does not cover the animating medium, giving the overall impression that Japan had stopped producing animation after the end of the Second World War. Among the notable publications in English that have appeared so far and have given due emphasis to Japanese animation, especially in relation to the first half of the twentieth-century cinema, are Komatsuzawa Hajime's articles in the book, *The Japan/American Film Wars* (1994). In it, he introduces the well-known wartime *Momotarō* film series made in 1942 and 1945.

So did Japanese animators go into hiding after the war, or simply drop their art altogether till the founding of Toei Animation Studio in 1956 and the rise of manga-artist Tezuka Osamu as an animation director in the early 1960s? Or, did the making of the *Momotarō* film series and other numerous short animated films with its fantastical features on the war front exhaust the imagination of the animation artists involved? This paper aims to fill the gap in Japanese animation history and, for that matter, the history of Japanese film and cinema as a whole. By singling out two animated films made by two separate animation artists after the surrender of Japan, it seeks to present and also speculate on the postwar context of their making. On another level, it will also self-question the interpretative position of the viewer in appreciating and theorizing an artistic creation, asking whether it is appropriate to speculate on the intention of the artist and whether an appropriate reading of a film should be affected more or less by some informed knowledge of the social context in which it is made.

I do not intend here to disregard other animated films made during the Occupation period (1945–1952). For example, Yamaguchi and Watanabe (1977: 233) wrote that "the very animated work made after the war was *Konchu tengoku* (1945) [Insect Kingdom]," a nine-minute film directed by Ashida Iwao and produced by the film company Sankō Eiga Sha. In 1946, five other animated films were made besides the two films discussed in this chapter. By 1947, more than a dozen more had been produced. Due to limited time and space, and scarce opportunities to view more of such films made during this period, here only two animated films that were made immediately following the war will be specifically examined.

Throughout the chapter are references to the issues that surrounded Japan's path to modernization. Without attempting to delve philosophically into the origin and development of the Japanese response to modernity, the animation works that are highlighted and their analyses provided below aim to give a sense of *how* the nation and the animation artists (thus the nation) responded to a new political era while working via a mass medium. In the face of great challenges and during a time of survival, Japanese animators remodeled their fantastical storytelling in a way that may seem new, progressive, and forward-looking, yet in reality, embedded within are prenotions of geopolitical communicative fantasies and visual representations.

Animation Artist Masaoka Kenzō (1898–1988)

The first film in discussion is *Sakura* (1946) directed by Masaoka Kenzō. Most of the published writing in Japanese relating to the growth of Japanese animation has hailed Masaoka as the "father of Japanese animation." This honorary title was given to him in respect to his artistic contributions to Japanese animation but more important, is the trail of successful apprentice animators he trained. Within this collective group is not only the younger Kumakawa Masao, who will be discussed later, but also early Toei Animation Studio teacher-animators and directors such as Yabushita Taiji (1903–1986) and Mori Yasuji (1925–1992).

Like most of the animators working in wartime Japan, Masaoka directed and participated in other capacities in the making of a number of animated short films sponsored by the military. Such films often featured anthropomorphic characters acting child-like to express the underlying themes of nationalism and imperialism. But given the creative background of Masaoka and the steadfast passion with which he upheld his animation art, he would occasionally produce animated works that were artistic and innovative in addition to attending to the propagandistic elements that were required. For example, in the second sequel of the *Momotarō* series, *Momotarō and His Divine Army* ("Momotarō umi no shinpei," 1945), which was directed by his younger colleague Seo Mitsuyo (1911–2010), Masaoka was credited for introducing some artistic sequences into the film. Though designated as a photography supervisor in that production, he inserted a series of innovative segments that carried a dream-like *avant-garde* appeal, breaking up the straightforward narrative about war and nationalism.

Earlier in 1943, Masaoka had already directed an animated film, *Kumo to chūrippu* (Spider and Tulip), which demonstrated his artistic inclination and individualistic interpretation of a well-known literary work. Coming from a wealthy family and a graduate of the renowned Kyoto City University of Arts, Masaoka was exposed to both Eastern and Western forms of art at a young age. In his early student days, he was attracted to theatrical works from Russia. For example, he was inspired by the work of Russian artist Léon Bakst (1866–1924), who designed scenes and costumes for the theater and the revolutionary productions of Russian ballet impresario, Sergei Diaghilev (1872–1929). Masaoka was also drawn to the innovative musical compositions of Igor F. Stravinsky (1882–1971) (Matsunomoto and Ostuka, 2004: 28–29).

His ability to see and appreciate such art forms was also due to the more open cultural and political environment of the earlier Taisho period (1912–1925) during which a number of Western art forms continued to be introduced into the country.[1] Though the literary work originated from the Japanese female writer Yokoyama Michiko, in animation, Masaoka seems to have transformed the narrative into a neo-romanticist tale with traits of European black theater influence and a sense of a mask-like marionette spectacle, as exemplified by the animating movements of the Spider character. Both Bakst and Diaghilev were influential members of the Mir Iskusstva art movement at the turn of the twentieth century, a movement which advocated individualistic artistic expression and the return to folklore and previous European art traditions (for example, eighteenth-century rococo). The movement's artistic aegis included elements of self-parody, carnivalistic art, and marionette and puppet theater (see

Read, 1994: 28, 379). The artists of the movement were known for their excellence in line drawing, "contouring each form and shape by means of a firmly stencilled line, and dividing them into a number of juxtaposed planes" (see Petrov, 1997: 116). A reading of *Kumo to chūrippu* is guided by the stage-like and theatrical spectacle of the animated frames presented. The juxtaposed characterization is reflected in their animated actions and character designs alluding to the influence of the movement's stylistic elements Masaoka was inspired by.

On a side note, based on a reading of the theatrical spectacle, the performative aspects make one recall Czech theater. The suspense and the juxtaposed characterization of the two main protagonists as represented by their movements and oral renditions show a rather East European influence with tinges of Czech black theater play of light and darkness in terms of the audiovisual effects and the stage-spectacle presentations. Coincidently, in European theater history, there was a famous theatrical production called *The Insect Comedy* (1922) created by one of Czechoslovakia's greatest twentieth-century dramatists, Karel Hugo Hilar (1885–1935). The production was also about the grotesque and the sensual using aspects of insect life depicting the fallibilities of human society. According to Czech theater studies scholar Jarka M. Burian, Hilar's theatrical play was "less a matter of arbitrary 'effect' or self-indulgence than an appropriate reflection of wartime stress and horror" (Burian, 2002: 8) in Eastern Europe. *Kumo to chūrippu* also reflects that wartime tension although the geographical backdrop differs.

SCAP and Animating a New "Dawn": *Haru no gensō*

During the Allied Forces Occupation of Japan, filmmaking activities did not come to a halt. Rather, the administration encouraged freedom of speech and repudiated the feudalistic way of thinking; instructions were handed down demanding the film industry to discard its past militaristic inclinations. Thompson and Bordwell (1994: 462) have reported that right from the beginning, the new administration "took a keen interest in the film industry." To broaden the variety of filmmaking content, opportunities to experiment with new filmmaking techniques were also encouraged. Led by the Americans and presided over by General Douglas MacArthur, the Occupation was also termed as the Supreme Commander of the Allied Powers (SCAP). By November 1945, a total of 236 Japanese films considered to be "feudal and militaristic" were ordered to be banned and destroyed (Dower, 1999: 426). Film historian Isolde Standish in her work in English about the history of Japanese cinema (2005: 158) writes that "many of these films were destroyed by the studios themselves, and the Occupation Forces were also active in destroying many negatives." Not all of the master copies were destroyed, however; some were sent to the Library of Congress in Washington.

Policies to consolidate the film industry personnel were carried out by SCAP, and at one point a list of war criminals working in the industry was drawn up. According to Satō Tadao (1982: 104) and his later work, *Nihon eigashi 1941–1959* (1995 vol. II: 186, Tokyo: Iwanami Shoten) cited in Standish (2005: 175), the list consisted of merely film company executives who were involved in the business and decision-making process of the film production. Directors and scriptwriters were excluded. It is not known whether any animation producer was listed. Writing about that "unrest period," Yamaguchi and Watanabe (1977: 46) reasoned that Japanese animators decided to "stand united" rather than to work independently. Hence, about a hundred animators led by Yamanoto Sanae, Yasuji Murata, and Masaoka Kenzō made the critical decision to group themselves into an organization called Shin Nihon Dōga Sha in August 1945 (later renamed Nihon Manga Eiga Kabushiki Kaisha in October 1945). According to Taiwanese film studies specialist and director Fan Jian-you, its formation was also probably due to the presence of pressure from SCAP (which the animators might have anticipated) that it might want to police their creative activities (Fan, 1997: 125).[2] To put it succinctly, this unusual organization was set up for "survival reasons." Moreover, the SCAP's censorship policy also extended to other forms of media like magazines, journals, and even children's books.[3] Another probable reason for the formation of the organization might be due to the participation SCAP was expecting from the film industry screenwriters and film critics etc. for the listing of film personnel who were in active support of the war ideology. For example, the screenplay writers' group, the critics' association and the newly formed All Japan Film Employees Association were asked to compile a list of such war criminals (Standish, 2005: 175, cites Iwasaki Akira's work, *Gendai Nihon no eiga: sono shisō to fūzoku* [Tokyo: Chuō Kōronsha, 1958], 112, as a source).

One significant film made under this umbrella grouping was *Sakura* (also known as *Haru no gensō*, 1946) directed by Masaoka Kenzō. With his experience in making war propaganda animated films, one might expect something faintly similar from his next film project. Contrarily, *Sakura* showed no traces of any militaristic sentiments; rather, it expressed the familiar Japanese spring feeling: the natural rays of sunshine, rhythmic raindrops, girl clad in kimono and clogs, the awakening of nature as depicted by lively butterflies, insects, beetles, and so on and the overflowing cherry blossoms as German composer Carl Maria von Weber's romantic music (*Invitation to the Waltz*) was played in the background. Eight minutes in length, the film was not so much propelled by the animated figures as by the rhythmic atmospheric changes. In keeping with the black and white presentation, there are no cluttered images or central narrative characters that call for attention but merely the fragmentary frames of an early spring, as if its aim was to pique any disgruntled soul for not acknowledging the arrival of the renewing delightful season. However, records show that this poetic art-piece was considered out of place in a defeated Japan, was unwelcome generally by the distribution network because it lacked much "commercial value," and was "buried" and hardly screened during those years (Tsugata, 2004: 116).

In the period immediately after the war, it was difficult and possibly unimaginable for the average Japanese to appreciate a "new dawn" era, much less to savor highly artistic work in the cinema. Food was scarce especially in the cities and the SCAP gave conflicting political directions. For example, while over-nationalistic and feudalistic practices were frowned upon, extensive criticisms of past militaristic activities and ideology were not duly encouraged, as the Occupation was also wary of leftwing sentiment and its rising popular appeal given the dismal devastated state of the country (Thompson and Bordwell, 1994: 462). Thus, "democracy" was implemented the SCAP way with the view of keeping the previous imperial emperor system with some convenient changes. It was hoped that retaining the emperor as the head of the state would stabilize the alien democratic path on which Japan would embark. In other words, Emperor Hirohito's wartime responsibility and his presiding role in the entire militarization of Japan, including the Imperial Army's systematic inhumane militarist actions abroad, were never questioned thoroughly, examined, and tried by his own people.[4] His postwar symbolic head-of-state status and, in a way, that historical/ancestral sense of godly aura, was more or less pristinely preserved, paradoxically by a democratic liberator intending to engineer a less problematic and turbulent path in "modernizing" Japan.

Hence, a combination of the "old" and the "new" was what postwar Japan was to become, and what remained viable, and in a survival sense applicable, was the drive to pursue economic growth for the country, to acquire material comforts and personal wealth, and to relive an old familiar "Meiji dream," which was to further acquire technology and science but this time from a newer Pacific western land, the United States of America. In an abstract sense, the animated film *Sakura* is an indication of a new dawn, a symbolic portrayal of a utopian postwar era. Quintessentially, the inner "soul" of Japan lives on since the cherry blossom is the national flower and an aesthetic symbol of Japanese culture. In animated terms, the country's ancient *anima* still preexists and the inspiriting nature proves it to be so.

What makes the film intriguingly appealing and at the same time odd and fantastically romantic is the overwhelming representation of a festive, celebratory Japan embracing a cheerful spring season. Till today, the animated piece has been regarded as a spectacular artwork denoting a new sense of freedom and a milestone in Japanese animation development after the Second World War. Pioneer animation writers Yamaguchi and Watanabe (1977) and contemporary animation historian Tsugata Nobuyuki (2004) attribute the overly artistic nature of the work as the reason that Toho's distribution network did not show the film in cinemas. Retired animation producer Yamaguchi Yasuo (2003: 64) also points out that the "GHQ"—namely, the Allied Forces military administrative center—did not show much enthusiasm toward the completed film.

The gist of the matter is, did both the Toho management and the GHQ recognize the symbolism of cherry blossom images found in the film? Hirano (1992: 52–53) notes that during the occupational period, the American administrators were particularly suspicious of the images of Mount Fuji, regarding it as "a powerful symbol of Japanese nationalism," and it was one of the tabooed subjects prohibited by the censors. But it is not sure that the image of cherry blossoms was considered as such then. However, to a number of East Asians and Southeast Asians who suffered and experienced the brutality of the Japanese military during the war, somehow the fragile feminine flower carries deadly traces and memories of an invading force; so are the emblems of a chrysanthemum (a flower, representative of the Japan's Imperial House) and Japan's scenic Mount Fuji.

Is it valid for a contemporary viewer and one who has substantial knowledge of Japan's immediate postwar conditions to be made curious by the harmonious, peaceful, and lively representations found in the film? Is he or she overly reacting or interpreting the film? The concern is, despite the presence of light-hearted images found in *Sakura* and a profuse sense of feminine touch that resulted, some doubts of the film remain. This is so, as it is precisely the collection of nature-based "harmless" images that arouses suggestion and further interpretation. A cat lazing leisurely in the sun, the momentary focus of a demure female face clad in traditional clothing, and the fluttering lively butterflies, and so forth, suggested a vaguely familiar "floating world," a world of sensuality, relaxation, and subtle eroticism. For it was common knowledge that in the period immediately after the war, a number of Japanese women also assumed the role of "comfort women"[5] for the GIs who arrived at the island country in great numbers, particularly in the city areas. The ruling authorities, including the higher Japanese administration and the police, were aware of such "romantic liaisons." The subtle policy of using the "feminine" to serve and stabilize the confused situation had been covered in the works of Dower (1999) and Tanaka (2002), for example.

Thus, the animated film *Sakura* could be seen to fulfill a dual objective; nationalistically, the spring images were representative of a newly dawned Japan, but *orientalizingly*, such images were enticingly feminine, sensual, and innocent. Perhaps the dainty and delicate images were seen as too close to home, making it controversial even for the main film distributor Toho to publicly release the film at its commercial chain of cinemas, although its animator-director Masaoka knew better. Upon obtaining a print copy of the film from Toho, the film was later pirated abroad under another title, *Haru no gensō*. When viewed today, the film is just as appealing and entertaining given the dreamlike setting and the lingering mother-nature feminine feeling, if one does not inquire about the historical context of its production.[6]

Psychoanalysis scholars Laplanche and Pontalis (1986), in analyzing fantasy and sexual consciousness, find that expressions of fantasy are results of instinctive drives and defenses and they can be auto-erotic in nature as the subject self-addresses its own negations and prohibitions. Knowing how militaristic and ultraconservative the Japanese society had become since the early 1930s, Masaoka's animated film *Sakura* could be read as his postwar filmmaking right to touch on the natural and sexual aspects of everyday living. From the fields of civic and military education and family life to economy, leisure, and entertainment, the harsh imperialistic ideology had literally permeated the so-called reformed society since the Meiji era (1868–1911). The images of the flighty "female butterflies" with long slender human legs (as seen in the film) give forth a sense of liberated eroticism and depict a physical life that the biological earth possesses. Moreover, given the natural playfulness of the animating medium and its innate ability to unleash fantastical thoughts (conscious or unconscious) via any mode or form of expression, the film *Sakura* demonstrates not only the artistic skill of Masaoka but also the psychological dimension of his animating world, which hitherto had been restricted to the strict regiments of militaristic control and austere authoritarianism.

Analyzing from a geo-cultural perspective, however, the implicit eroticism of the ultrafeminine figure, the kimono-clad geisha girl, raises another plane of intriguing interpretation. It is as if Masaoka with his status as one of the leading animation artists and together with his community of animation staff members sought playfully yet objectively to present and stage a totally opposite image of their past animating selves; that is, to dabble in a world of passion, nature, and pure leisure entertainment. For the animation that they had produced in the past often contained images of kids and animals dressed in military attire or school uniforms engaged in nationalistic-like heroic adventures.[7] It has also been said that the film *Sakura* is Masaoka's answer to the earlier Disney-made *Fantasia* (1940). Moreover, as stated above, the background music is of Western classical origins expressing a perfect pro-West harmonious setting.

Having examined the animation community's survival circumstances and Masaoka's past corpus of authorial works, the animated film *Sakura* is open to multilevel dialectic interpretations. Completed in May 1946 and made in a period with an acute sense of the new censorship demands and film confiscation activities of the Allied Forces administrators, it is difficult to appreciate and analyze this animated work purely on an artistic basis. For that matter, the Toho management decision and that of the GHQ might have faced the same complex reactions and dilemmas. In an interview given years later, Masaoka revealed that he subsequently renamed the film *Haru no gensō* (Spring Fantasy) in order to distribute and pirate the film abroad. So all is not lost; to whom or where he had sold his animated short film remains to be speculated upon or researched given its romanticist and orientalistic aura.

Animation Artist Kumakawa Masao and his film, *Mahō no pen*

An eleven-minute black and white animated film directed by Kumakawa Masao (1916–2008), a younger colleague of Masaoka Kenzō, was completed at almost the same time as the film *Sakura*. It features an orphan boy and his dream-story (*yume monogatari*). The film began with the orphan boy who picked up a Western-looking doll. Later at home, in the midst of studying the English language, he fell asleep. He then dreamed that the doll gave him a pen to draw anything he liked, in return for his earlier compassionate act of mending her broken body.[8] He first drew a small tree but later ran to a nearby street and drew such images on the empty space: skyscrapers, houses, apartment buildings, a sports car, highways, and expressways. To juxtapose these infrastructural prosperous-looking images, other animated segments featuring desolated parts of the city where the boy lived were also illustrated. They then spent some time together driving through the countryside of Japan while a background song was played hailing a new Japan to be built. Later, the doll then bid good-bye to the boy as she reentered the chic convertible car. She gave the shy boy a handshake before they parted. Later, the orphan boy woke up and realized it was a dream.

The storyline is created by Susukida Rokuhei (1899–1960), who was a renowned scriptwriter known for his creations of action-packed period-dramas influenced by the American style of filmmaking. Susukida's way of scriptwriting often paid attention to the hero-character, particularly his psychological outlook and pose, and his realistic surroundings and actions. For example, in previous kabuki-influenced film stories made in the 1910s, the swashbuckling heroes' acting and actions tended to be theatrical and ballet-like. But in the early 1920s, Susukida revolutionized the Japanese period-dramas into a kind of American action genre where there were fast movements and editing and more filmic angles were used to focus on the protagonist's acting including his facial expressions.[9] More important is that Susukida's screenplays are often about *rōnin* ("samurai without a master"), the outlaws and their alienation from society.

It is not known how many other animation scripts that Susukida had worked on but his participation in this short animation film raises some speculation and ways of reading the film. Compared to *Sakura, Mahō no pen* ["Magic Pen," 1946] is not so well known or much highlighted in Japanese animation history. This may perhaps be due to the overwhelming fatherly figure of Masaoka Kenzō and his esteemed status in Japanese animation development. As mentioned before, authorially, Masaoka had made a collection of animated works that left distinctive marks in Japanese animation. Kumakawa, on the contrary, was indeed a junior apprentice when he asked Masaoka to grant him the opportunity to work and study under his supervision. Like Masaoka's other trainees (for example, Seo

Mitsuyo, who went on to direct the much publicized wartime *Momotarō* film series), Kumakawa also eventually directed or co-directed animation films, too, mainly sponsored by the military. After the war, his contribution status in Japanese animation history tends to be associated with Toei Animation Studio as he was employed as a senior trainer and supervisor nurturing the younger talents working at the studio. But Kumakawa did make two unusual animation films during the immediate postwar years. One is *Mahō no pen* and the another is *Poppoyasan no nonki ekichō no maki* (meaning "A railway man: An episode of an optimistic stationmaster," 1948).

The latter is a thirteen-minute film featuring the anxiety and suspense of a train driver when he faced the imminent danger of a train accident. His earlier film, *Mahō no pen*, is centrally discussed in this chapter because it was made soon after the arrival of the Allied Forces and the country's knowledge of its war defeat. Unlike the film *Sakura*, which had often been valued for its artistic value, *Mahō no pen* tends to be less regarded and little had been written about it until recently. Yet, the filmic images are no less fantastical than those found in *Sakura*, and it also carries subliminal geopolitical messages despite its simple, innocent storyline and animated illustrations.

While *Sakura* paints a demure, soft, feminine image of Japan, a stark contrast to its previous aggressive, warmonger, military, image, *Mahō no pen* portrays the country metaphorically as a "parentless child" in search of comfort, educational guidance, and maternal belonging. This is so as in reality, the "stuff" of the orphan boy's "dream" was not an illusion; it was almost a direct listing of national redevelopment items and material acquisition requesting the help of a Western colonist. It exudes an awkward and disquieted feeling because the Western-looking doll was metaphorically illustrated as a benevolent savior and a life-giver, and although her show of generosity might seem comforting and consoling, it was condescending in a manner indicating an oriental lost child's search for a fairy godmother's blessing and fulfillment of wishes. In early 1946, SCAP set up a unit within the Civil Information and Education Section, and its central role was to view all completed films and give the seal of approval for theatrical release (Anderson and Richie, 1982: 162). It is very likely that *Mahō no pen* passed the approval test; moreover, the outward expressions of affection like kissing and hugging as seen in *Mahō no pen* were in tune with the democratic guidelines stipulated by the administration presided by the Americans. For example, bowing was disliked by SCAP as it was considered to be a feudalistic behavior, but kissing was encouraged as a liberal show of affection.[10]

In comparison, while the animated film *Sakura* narrates on an adult basis as one Japanese anime fan critic has commented,[11] *Mahō no pen* has a conspicuous child character sustaining the flow of the narrative, a kind of a mesmerizing antihero as designed by Susukita. However, he is not an ordinary child. From a gender perspective, he may appear powerless and tend to daydream but from a deeper psychoanalytical perspective, he can be seen as someone who is capable of communicating seductively and charmingly his innermost desires and wants. Aesthetically, the orphan-boy character has a cute face design plus pretty eyes with long eyelashes, and he "blushes" easily in front of the camera. His counterpart addressee featured in the film is a chic young lady with an American actress-like coiffure fashionable in those times, and she is also someone who can drive a luxurious convertible sports car. Ultimately, the animation film can be seen more like a realist communal ongoing people's project made to communicate subtly to the new foreign administration via the deft use of fantastical images. Or, the magic pen can be addressed as the hidden invincible "General MacArthur's pen" calling forth his political power and abilities to transform Japan materially.

Director Kumakawa was also ingenious in not directly referring to the dismal conditions of Japan after the air raid and the deadly atomic bombings. Instead, he subtly included images of the dilapidated and burnt-out state of the city streets. Rather than dwelling on the negative aspects of the streetscape, the "stuff" that the orphan child later fantasized in his dream was illustrated as desired "replenishments," which clearly presented an air of positive, optimistic attitude and vision. In keeping with this constructive portrayal, the orphan is also illustrated as having a healthy normal appearance. Though realistically, the underlying inexpressible lurking imagery were the countless numbers of starving orphans and poverty-stricken children who roamed the streets of Japan immediately after the war. Strangely in the film, the energetic child-boy befriends and brings home a Western lady doll, which he has picked up from a dilapidated street. At home, he is illustrated as having an above-average life as he is seen studying the English language before he sleeps soundly by his study table and dreams. In the film, he is depicted as a newspaper delivery boy, and the film ends with him carrying the doll as he optimistically works on his daily job. Toward the end of the film, he and the doll warmly exchange "good-bye" greetings in English. Kumakawa's collaboration with the savvy

1. Image of *Mahō no pen* (1946).

screenwriter Susukita also points to the film's pro-American approach of narrating and its allusive ideological stance. While the child-boy does not appear unruly in acting or samurai-like dressed in a historic-period outfit, in reality, he is an orphan boy and can be considered as an alienated figure devoid of belonging and kin.

Given the political circumstances of that time and knowing the new administrative conditions that existed during the Allied Forces Occupation of Japan, particularly the period immediately after the surrender, it is difficult to ignore and not to speculate on the ways with which animator-artists tried to create and animate subjects that would relate to the new social cultural environment, including adhering to new and existing censorship constraints then. Furthermore, these two animation artists were also prolific directors of animation war films supported by the previous military government, which made their immediate postwar animation projects all the more open to intriguing observations.

Conclusion

To conclude, I would argue that it is more fruitful and polemical to apply the knowledge of Japan's sociopolitical conditions in analyzing the two animated films as highlighted. It helps to enrich and broaden our interpretations of the animated films made. The further application of psychoanalysis, gender theories, and historical industrial research in interpretation are also prompted mainly by the motifs presented and the creative animating energies that were expressed.

Based on what has been analyzed above, it is not quite adequate to classify Masaoka's highly acclaimed animated film *Sakura* as simply an artistic film and then lament its lack of official recognition and public exhibition during the time of its completion. Nor is it satisfactory to basically regard Kumakawa's *Mahō no pen* film as purely a child-boy's dream of material gifts or a wish for a future construction career. Layered within the two animated projects were other influential factors affecting the directors' visionary creations.

It was only a few years ago, in 2004, more than fifty years after the end of the Second World War, that the Japanese people had the better opportunity to view or review more of the animated films made before and shortly after the war. Earlier in 1978, a Japanese animated film retrospective event was organized by the National Film Center where films made in the period of 1924–1958 were shown publicly. However, the recent major exhibition film event organized by the center in 2004 screened a staggering number of 230 animated films and *Sakura* and *Mahō no pen* were among those shown.[12] Interestingly, the 2004 program was also presented according to each animation artist's corpus of works (*NFC Calendar*, 2004). A thorough comprehensive research still needs to be conducted in order to review and see a wider collection of animated films made during the immediate postwar years. One consistent underlying fact remains, and it is that the legacy of the Allied Forces Occupation of Japan as led by the Americans has not only influenced the development of live-action films in Japan but also films made via the animating medium.

As animation has the power to stretch fantastical imagination further and beyond, and even achieve transnational and inter-geopolitical communication—Japanese animation artists (as discussed in this chapter) working in the immediate postwar period understood the medium's potential intimately. In order to continue practicing and self-protecting their animation work, some also subconsciously co-participated and helped achieve the dual nationalistic goal of reconstructing new images, even though these images have orientalistic and self-psychoanalytical tendencies. Combining aesthetics with realist thinking, the result is a form of social-cultural imaginary that charms and entices. It not only assists to allay the clash of the foreign and the local but even gently veils and erases a much-darkened past. The Japanese experience of modernity is imbued with imagination and fantastical thinking, and the country's past animation artists have had their share of contributions. The "stuff' of what the orphan-boy had drawn *is* exactly what urban Japan is today; fantasizing can materialize and the ageless *sakura* trees continue to blossom in every spring.

Notes

This paper was first published in Japanese of the same title. In *Senryō-ka no eiga: kaihō to ken'etsu* [Films Under Occupation: Liberation and Censorship], 243–68, edited by Iwamoto Kenji (Tokyo: Shinwasha, 2009). Printed in English by permission from Shinwasha.

1. The Taisho period has been regarded as a "renaissance age" in all aspects of Japanese society. See Hu (2010): 64–65.

2. It is not known how much notice the SCAP had paid to the filmmakers involved in animation making. For example, it was reported that Ichikawa Kon's animated puppet film, *A Girl at Dojo Temple* ("Musume Dojoji") was banned because the film script was not submitted for review in the first place (Anderson and Richie, 1982: 162).

3. See the article, "Prange exhibit recalls Occupation's censorship," in *The Japan Times*, May 31, 1999. The article is about the Prange Collection of censored print materials amassed by the SCAP authorities during the Occupation.

4. The Tokyo War Crimes Trials were presided over by SCAP and lasted from April 1946 to November 1948. The trials simplified the whole issue of war responsibility and placed the blame on a few individuals who were later sentenced and executed. See Hirano (1992), particularly chapter 3, "The Depiction of the Emperor," where the author details the American policy on Emperor Hirohito in face of pressure from the rightist postwar Japanese government.

It is interesting to note that just as in the *Momotarō* film (1945) where the "natives and the oppressed" were absent at the negotiation table (a segment in the film featuring Momotarō facing the British colonists), at the Tokyo Trials, the direct victims of the war and their representatives were missing, too. In other words, the rest of Asia (particularly regions of Southeast Asia and East Asia) also became a "third party" observing the trials. See Tanaka (2002), who questioned the missing Asian voice in Japanese wartime trials.

5. In Japanese, "comfort women" means *ianfu*, a term used by the Japanese military forces to highlight the "maternal feminine" role played by groups of women enlisted to serve the Japanese military during the war. In reality, they were sexual slaves abducted and forced to give sexual services to the military personnel. See also Yoshimi Yoshiaki, *Comfort Women: Sexual Slavery in the Japanese Military during World War Two*, translated by Suzanne O'Brien (New York: Columbia University Press, 2000).

6. In an interview, the late director Masaoka explained that the background scenery was based on a certain scenic spot in Kyoto, and the kimono-clad female figure was modeled after a Kyoto geisha dancer including her hair, make-up, and accessories. The interview was originally published in a magazine, *Film 1/24*, numbers 23 and 24 in October 1, 1978, under the title, "Masaoka Kenzō Interview." It was reprinted in a commemorative exhibition book (Matsunomoto and Otsuka, 2004: 20–33).

7. Here I clarify that Masaoka's works tended to be stylistically different from such pro-nationalistic animated stories. For example, even though his name was credited for this film, *Manguwa shin saru kani gassen* (1939, in English, translated directly as "Manguwa New Monkeys Crabs Collective War"), in reality the director was Kumakawa Masao. See *NFC Calendar* (2004).

8. At the beginning, the doll drew him lots of presents in the form of nicely packaged boxes; in display were also cakes, sweets, and fruits, and she also drew him a big house where he could live in.

9. See Standish (2005: 84–88), where she gave a detailed account of Susukida's screenplay's *The Serpent* ("Orochi," 1925) and the filmic techniques involved.

10. The physical show of affection as seen in film was not intended to be sexual as the orphan boy appreciated the doll's friendship and comfort after he woke up from his dream. One oddity is that it is uncommon to find a young boy showering such kind of affection to a toy doll as compared to a relationship between a girl and a doll.

11. See http://2.csx.jp/users/sinkan/eigahyou26/sakuraharunogensou.html (Accessed on June 26, 2008).

12. I am not sure whether the above two films were shown at the 1978 screening event; the printed materials that I have did not show the film titles.

References

Anderson, I. Joseph, and Donald Richie. *The Japanese Film: Art and Industry.* Princeton, NJ: Princeton University Press, 1982.

Burian, Jarka M. *Leading Creators of Twentieth-Century Czech Theatre.* London: Routledge, 2002.

Dower, John W. *Embracing Defeat: Japan in the Wake of World War Two Defeat.* New York: W. W. Norton, 1999.

Fan, Jian-you. "Riben donghua de lailong qumai" [Origin and development of Japanese animation]. In *Donghua dianying tanshu* [Explorations of animation cinema], edited by Wong Yu-shan and Yu Wei-zheng, 114–52. Taipei: Yuan Liu, 1997.

FC Film Center: Nihon no anime-shon eiga (1924–1958). Tokyo: The National Museum of Modern Art Film Center, No. 46, February 24, 1978.

Hirano, Kyōko. *Mr. Smith Goes to Tokyo: Japanese Cinema under the American Occupation, 1945–1952.* Washington, DC: Smithsonian Institution Press, 1992.

Komatsuzawa, Hajime. "Toybox Series 3: Picture Book 1936 (Momotarō vs. Mickey Mouse)." In *The Japan/America Film Wars: World War II Propaganda and Its Cultural Contexts*, edited by Abe Nornes M. and Yukio Fukushima, 198–200. Chur, Switzerland: Harwood Academic Publishers, 1994.

Laplanche, Jean, and Jean-Bertrand Pontalis. "Fantasy and the Origins of Sexuality." In *Formations of Fantasy*, edited by Victor Burgin, James Donald, and Cora Kaplan, 5–34. London: Routledge, 1986.

Matsunomoto, Kazuhiro, and Otsuka Yasuo, eds. *Nihon manga eiga no zenbō* [Japanese animated films: A complete view from their birth to *Spirited Away* and beyond]. Tokyo: Nihon manga eiga no zenbōten jikō iinkai, 2004.

NFC Calendar: A History of Japanese Animation. Tokyo: National Film Center, National Museum of Modern Art, Tokyo, July–August, 2004.

Petrov, Vsevolod. *Russian Art Nouveau: The World of Art and Diaghiliev's Painters.* Bournemouth, England: Partstone Press, 1997.

Read, Herbert, ed. *The Thames and Hudson Dictionary of Art and Artists*. Revised, expanded, and updated edition. London: Thames and Hudson, 1994.

Satō, Tadao. *Currents in Japanese Cinema*. Translated by Gregory Barrett. Tokyo: Kodansha, 1982.

Standish, Isolde. *A New History of Japanese Cinema: A Century of Narrative Film*. New York: Continuum International Publishing, 2005.

Tanaka, Yuri. *Japan's Comfort Women: Sexual Slavery and Prostitution during World War II and the US Occupation*. London: Routledge, 2002.

Thompson, Kristin, and David Bordwell. *Film History: An Introduction*. New York: McGraw-Hill, 1994.

Tsugata, Nobuyuki. *Nihon anime-shon no chikara* [Power of Japan animation]. Tokyo: NTT Shuppan, 2004.

Yamaguchi, Katsunori, and Watanabe Yasushi. *Nihon anime-shon eiga shi* [The history of Japanese animation]. Osaka: Yubunsha, 1977.

Yamaguchi, Yasuo, ed. *Nihon no anime zenshi* [A whole history of Japanese animation]. Tokyo: Ten-Books, 2004.

Section Three

Popular Culture, East-West Expressions, and Tezuka Osamu

Tezuka and Takarazuka

Intertwined Roots of Japanese Popular Culture

—Makiko Yamanashi

Introduction

For anyone who teaches and researches Japanese comics and animation, particularly of the manga and anime kinds, Tezuka Osamu (1928–1989) is one of the most important artists. He has written about seven hundred titles of manga and produced about seventy titles of anime. Today, in Japan, as well as in the rest of the world, he has been credited with elevating the status of manga and anime, which in the past was regarded as an unrespectable form of art suitable only for children. His work is now acknowledged for its artistic expressions that can be appreciated by an adult audience as well. In this respect, Tezuka Osamu made a significant accomplishment by elevating the recognition, if not the status, of manga and anime to a distinctive form of "popular art."

From 2008 to 2009, there has been a growth in the numbers of celebratory events to mark the eightieth anniversary of the birth of the most prolific Japanese manga-anime artist in twentieth century. Despite his fame and continuing popularity, the roots of his vigorous creative life are little known outside Japan; that is, where and how he cultivated his creativity, as well as the development of his talents in the city of Takarazuka where he once lived. Takarazuka City, a renowned suburban center for leisure and entertainment, besides the presence of hot springs, a botanic garden, a theme park, and more is also the home of the Takarazuka Revue Company (in short, Takarazuka). For Tezuka Osamu, it meant more than a town; to him, it was a fantasy land, a source of inspiration and dreams. By bringing his formative years into light, my main aim is to examine how integral

1. and 2. The exterior and the entrance hall of the Edo Tokyo Museum, announcing the anniversary exhibition of Osamu Tezuka. Photograph by Makiko Yamanashi in May 2009.

Takarazuka was to this Japanese pioneer manga-anime artist's early creative development and inspiration. Additionally, the chapter also highlights how the roots of Japanese popular culture in the later half of the twentieth century can be traced back to Tezuka Osamu's relation to Takarazuka and his subsequent prolific production of manga and anime work.

A special commemorative exhibition, *Tezuka Osamu—Message for the Future* took place at Edo-Tokyo Museum from April 18 to June 21 in 2009. It was supervised by his son, Tezuka Makoto, who now works as an anime director, adapting his father's manga to animation, such as the TV series of *Black Jack*. This extensive story about an unlicensed doctor called Black Jack is partly autobiographical and reflective of Tezuka Osamu's own medical career (this will be discussed in more detail in the following sections). While his enthusiasm for manga was steadily growing in his teens, he was planning on going to medical college to become a doctor. Eventually, he did obtain a Doctor of Philosophy in medicine. However, various wartime experiences during the Second World War led him to make the decision to become a manga artist as a career. It can be argued that Tezuka's background in medicine raised the status of manga as it served as proof that manga could be proudly produced by a man of high and respectable education. In addition to manga, Tezuka Osamu was very interested in producing animation as well. During his time, however, it was expensive and technically difficult to create animation—as such, his son working in this medium with advanced digital tools can be seen in this light as further continuing and realizing his father's dream.

Tezuka Makoto supervised this exhibition and designed it in a way that reveals more about his father's private life, especially in relation to his hometown of Takarazuka City where he spent his childhood and student years right through the Second World War. The photos and 8mm home video on display underline his most formative years in this small suburbia city, about half an hour away from Osaka.

Takarazuka City and Tezuka Osamu Memorial Museum

It is important to know how Tezuka Osamu is commemorated locally. The Tezuka Osamu Memorial Museum is in the cultural area of Takarazuka City, a minute from the famous Takarazuka Grand Theatre. It was built following the wishes of his wife, Tezuka Etsuko, attesting to the view that it was here where his most crucial formative years were spent between the

3. The mall of Takarazuka station decorated by large illustrations of Tezuka's representative characters: Atom, Black Jack, and Sapphire. Photograph by Makiko Yamanashi in May 2009.

age of five and twenty-four and where his talents and ideas were nourished (Kawauchi, 1996: 12). Visited by an annual average of one hundred thousand people (June 2009), it is a kind of pilgrimage place for manga-anime lovers not only from Japan, but increasingly from abroad as well. Run by the city's municipality as a public institution, this museum stands within the premise of Takarazuka Family Land (then still called Shin Onsen and Luna Park, which was closed in 2004; however, the quarter remains as Garden Fields) by the old garden pond, across from the Takarazuka Grand Theatre.

A year after its completion, in January 1995, the devastating Great Hanshin Earthquake struck the city. Having survived with relatively little damage, Hyogo Prefecture selected the statue of *Hinotori* (The Phoenix) to be placed at the gate of the museum as a symbolic monument of peace and rebirth in hope of the city's redevelopment.[1] Since the earthquake, while the townscape has considerably changed, Tezuka's popularity has remained constant. The anniversary exhibition presented at the local museum in 2008, titled "Towards the New World," was aimed at inspiring visitors' reconsideration of Tezuka's legacy in Japanese popular culture.

4. Entrance of Tezuka Osamu Memorial Museum in Takarazuka. Photograph by Makiko Yamanashi in May 2009.

In the museum, the visitor can see cartoons and sketches Tezuka had made since his elementary school days, and how the local environment drew the young boy's attention to music, theater, and cinema, especially animated films. The exhibition highlights that his father was fond of music and movies (hence the music player and 8mm video at home that allowed him to enjoy Walt Disney or Hollywood MGM musicals from an early age), while his mother was a great fan of the Takarazuka Girls Opera.[2] Within the exhibition, a small in-house cinema named Atom Vision and an anime laboratory were set up for visitors to gain a better understanding of Tezuka's biographical background. For the small high-vision cinema accommodating about an audience of fifty-two people, a few original short animations of fictionalized biographical content were produced by Tezuka Makoto. The first production is *Osamu to Musashi* (Osamu and Musashi, 1994), a story about a boy called Osamu who befriends an insect called Musashi in the wartime rural town and comes to understand the meaning of life and peace. The second production is *Tezuka Osamu den* (Tezuka Osamu Story, 1994) followed by *Tokai no bucchi* (City Boy Bucchi, 1995), stories of a poor artist resembling Osamu himself who encounters a popular revue girl.

5. The anime laboratory. Photograph by Makiko Yamanashi in May 2009.

Besides becoming successful as a manga artist and the high demand for adaptations of his manga work into TV anime series, notably, for example, in the case of *Atom Boy* (1963–), Tezuka Osamu was serious about producing animation films, especially experimental ones driven by his artistic desire. For example, the film *Arumachikadono Monogatari* (Story of a City Corner, 1962) addresses antitotalitarianism with humor and an experimental style.[3] *Onboro Film* (meaning "Worn-Out Film," or its better known English title, Broken Down Film, 1985) is an adorable homage to silent film comedy using contemporary sound and animation techniques. This latter was awarded the Grand Prize at the first International Animation Festival in Hiroshima in 1985.

Tezuka Osamu and Takarazuka

In Japan and internationally, however, Tezuka Osamu is remembered for his contribution to world animation via the unique adaptation of manga into animation. As such, it is hard not to mention the late manga-artist

Tezuka Osamu when discussing the history of manga and anime in Japan. When manga still stood for caricature and humorous comics, Tezuka Osamu advanced the content of Japanese manga by including serious drama elements. He is acclaimed not only as "the god of comics" in Japan, but he is also respected as the founder of *shōjo manga* (girl comics) and as one of the early pioneers of popular graphic narrative (called "story manga," in general). Even today, his story comics have the most innovative influence on aspiring manga artists in Japan.

His best-known work is *Tetsuwan Atom* (1952), called *Mighty Atom* or *Astro Boy* in English. Given its success as the first TV manga animation series (1963), he is also known as the pioneer of such TV animation series.[4] Despite his enduring popularity as well as his prominent position in the history of Japanese manga and anime,[5] his covert yet important relation to Takarazuka is rarely mentioned and little known. It is meaningful, therefore, to show the formulation of his characteristic manga style, including his important contribution to the creation of the new manga genre of *shōjo manga* (those mainly targeted at girls).

It was not by coincidence that Tezuka grew up in the small spa town of Takarazuka. In 1933, a little before he became five, his family moved from industrial Osaka to rural Takarazuka. The town of Takarazuka had by then established an image of utopian suburbia for well-off middle-class families, as well as of an international residential province, conveniently close to Osaka and Kobe. Osamu's mother, who was a piano teacher and a longstanding fan of the Takarazuka revue, would often take her little son to the theater, and even more frequently after they moved to the neighborhood and befriended Takarasiennes.[6]

In reading and researching Tezuka's manga and his anime work, it is important to recognize that the author gathered considerable inspiration from Takarazuka. Here and there in comic strips, one finds the local townscapes he inscribed; Hankyu trains, stations, bourgeois houses along the Hankyu line, Takarazuka Hotel,[7] and Takarazuka Music School and the theater. Even after he moved to Tokyo in 1952, Takarazuka remained as a special place for him: "Takarazuka is a city of memories as well as the starting point of my work, where my philosophy was born" (Kawauchi, 1996: 208). He spent his formative twenty years from the age of five to twenty-four that fostered his sensibility in Takarazuka, a culturally affluent environment surrounded both by peaceful nature and the unique culture that emerged from the juxtaposition of Japanese tradition and Western influence. The theater, the zoo, the Green House garden, and the insect museum in Takarazuka Family Land[8] would have stimulated his curiosity and creativity, providing him numerous fascinating subjects to illustrate in manga. Takarazuka theater in particular was for him an inspiring fantasy sphere where he encountered an unknown world presented in impressive, lavish sets and costumes. He said:

> In Takarazuka, everything is "fake/kistch," but it shows things international. At any rate, from the pre-war to the post-war period when we had no means to go abroad and it was like a dream to go abroad, it showed us the feel of London, Paris or New York. No matter how momentary the satisfaction might have been, it was full of romance. There was adolescence. I think of adolescence in many ways, but it is a "dream of dream / unfinished dream." That kind of thing certainly existed in Takarazuka. Very amateur-like, and adequately gorgeous, the dream-like world as if in the crowd somewhere there—that is dominating all my early works.[9]

Takarazuka's theatrical production is a "Fantasy Adventure" that is made possible by faith in fake as in the term used by Italian writer Umberto Eco (1998) to describe the hype-reality in such fabricated worlds of imitation like Disneyland. When we take that faith as positive, the degree of dream where one explores creative imagination can be made stronger when the degree of fantasy intensifies.

Takarazuka both as the theater and the town, nevertheless, had a great impact on the little boy and provided him with unforgettable childhood memories.[10] He became interested in comic writing in which he could play with the characters he wanted to "stage" on paper. When the new theater movement was instigating amateur students' performing circles nationwide, he belonged to a college theater group called Gakuyūza that influenced his use of dramatic method for story manga.[11] The unique method used by Tezuka was to construct manga stories as "acts" and select his manga characters like theater performers. Akin to the star system of theater and film, Tezuka's comic stars are divided into teams and given roles even with the guaranteed fee indicated.[12] In Tezuka's manga, none of the individual characters are downplayed because of their narrative roles. Even tiny supporting players are presented valuably, akin to the Takarazuka students practicing and performing at their full strength. Further, his manga is described as *mukokuseki manga*.[13] *Mukokuseki* means nonnationality and it can also carry meanings of hybridism and, ideally, it can mean peaceful coexistence. This characteristic has become a coherent ethos that we can find throughout his works common to the theme of utopia often advocated in Takarazuka theater productions.

There is a reason why his manga tended seriously to such philanthropic direction. When he was undecided about whether to become a doctor or a professional manga writer, what drastically affected him was the Second World War. Many acts of cruelty, injustice, and inequality he himself experienced in the Takarazuka region left unforgettable scars in his heart and motivated him to write manga for the future to come. He said, "In the air raid, I had the biggest shock in my life, which wouldn't leave me. That was such a strong impact. This is how I thought this shall be the theme for all my life."[14] On making up his mind to become a professional manga artist, he said, "a doctor saves the life of man, but it is also an important profession to save the heart of man, especially the hearts of children who are seriously hurt by the war."[15]

He became estranged from his beloved Takarazuka theater during the war, regretting that the military control came in to manipulate theatrical productions.[16] Inevitably, his works have reflected his wartime experience. His most significant work in relation to Takarazuka is *Kami no Toride* (Paper Fortress 1974). It depicts the tragedy of war through first love and friendship between a schoolboy modeled on Tezuka himself and a student of Takarazuka Music School. The schoolboy is Ōsamu Tetsurō, an art club member who dreams of becoming a manga author but is discouraged by the loss of freedom in the war. The Takarasienne is Okamoto Kyōko, who has no chance to act, dance, play music, or any of the theatrical activities due to the wartime restriction. Forced to work in a military factory, she laments and tells Tetsurō, "I'm in charge of storage . . . it's merciless to do this kind of thing after entering Takarazuka Music School. So, the only fun is the chorus at lunch time." They exchange their future dreams. Tetsurō, working for another military factory, expresses his determination, "when the war is over, the time shall allow me to write manga freely. I will become a manga artist!" Kyōko wishes, "I will be an opera singer!" At the end of the story, the war ends and Tetsurō is about to go into writing manga but cannot find Kyōko. She has disappeared from his life because her face was burnt by the bombing and she must give up her dream. This fictional work can be seen as a convincing recollection of Tezuka Osamu himself and written in memory of his neighboring Takarasiennes; for example, Itoi Shidare, who died in the war.

So did Tezuka Osamu begin writing manga soon after the war ended in 1945? He made his debut with a series for a children's newspaper. Crucially,

Takarazuka publications were one of the early media to present his comic writing skills. He would draw portraits of stars—for example, of Kasugano Yachiyo—and illustrate dramas such as *Manon Rescou* (Kageki, April 1947) as well as writing comic strips in *Kageki* and *Takarazuka Graph* magazines. For instance, he wrote sixteen amusing strips titled *Takarazuka in 100 Years* in *Takarazuka Graph*, imagining the future of Takarazuka.

Working so closely to the Takarazuka theater, it can been seen how he was inspired and influenced by the all-female revues. *Ribon no Kishi* (Princess Knight, 1953) is the most prominent outcome with which he is widely acknowledged as the pioneer of *shōjo manga*. It was as engagingly dramatic, flowery, and romantic as the theatrical narrative that captured the fascination of girls. He himself remarked that this first Japanese *shōjo manga* was his homage to Takarazuka. He affirmed, "Takarazuka is my hometown. That place was left burnt in the war. Even when the nation was lost, the mountains and rivers remained the same. *Princess Knight* is a complete nostalgia for Takarazuka."[17] What kind of nostalgia did he inscribe in *Princess Knight*, and what was the reason for the popularity it obtained?

Princess Knight is an eventful story of conspiracy, adventure, and love. Princess Sapphire was born with the heart of a boy, due to the mischief of angel Chink. She was an only child of the ruling family of a kingdom called Silverland in medieval times. In that kingdom, the rule was that the heir to the throne must be a man. Thus, the king decided to bring up his daughter as a boy pretending that she was a prince. In living such a falsified life, for Sapphire, there was little time to be her natural self, a girl in a dress—to be exact, only one hour in the early morning. To appreciate the precious time of girl-hood, she is depicted in the garden picking fresh flowers and singing *Sumire no hana saku koro*, the famous Takarazuka song. One day, she goes to a ball disguised in a dress and falls in love with the prince of a neighboring country. When she realizes both the duty as a prince and the love as a princess, the story ends happily with a marriage and union of the two countries.

The influence of Takarazuka can be observed both in the graphical execution and the narrative content of this manga work. Its graphical impact is theatrical: settings and costumes are gorgeous and exotic and scene developments are speedy, full of dynamic movements as in dancing and singing where the players' motions and speeches are exaggerated like stage choreography. There are many musical scenes (e.g., achieved through the insertion of music notes) and group arrangements as on stage. *Katen wa kon'yamo aoi* (The Curtain Is Blue Again Tonight, 1958) is another good example where he inserted the stage behind the famous silver bridge and the orchestra pit singing "beloved memory, a girl of Paris, Parisiennes," evoking the great hit production of *Mon Paris*. His nostalgia for Takarazuka kept appearing again and again and created a stream of postwar popular subculture influenced by *shōjo manga*. The method of dramatic comic strips invented by Tezuka Osamu was to become a structural method for future *shōjo manga* to convey delicate feelings of characters, as expressive and romanticized as on the Takarazuka stage.

Artless innocent Sapphire in impersonating a prince may immediately evoke the charm of Takarazuka's *otokoyaku* (male impersonators). Heroes such as the prince are also represented as slender and feminine as if to be played by *otokoyaku*.[18] Like Takarazuka stage characters, Tezuka's manga characters sometimes appear sexually neutral. Iwai Shunji, a film director renowned for depicting girls' sentiments, says "the sexual ambiguity is the real thrill of Tezuka Osamu, and this charm can be understood when one passes adolescence."[19] Robots such as Atom (initially planned as a girl) and Michy in *Metropolis* (who can transfer into either a boy or a girl by switching the button in her throat) are by their mechanical nature sexually neutral, however it is worth noticing that Tezuka accords a female gender for these superhuman characters. Katherine Mezur in writing about Takarazuka revues uses a term "costumed gender." She regards it as "a new technology of gender, a hybrid art form, combining physical manipulation with cyborg-like constructions that are partially 'machine-like' and partially 'human.'"[20] This ambiguous identity precisely explains what Tezuka and Takarazuka have in common; that is, what Tezuka fundamentally inherited from Takarazuka. Patently obvious since *Princess Knight* was created in the early 1950s, this seems to be one of the ongoing common features between them, and furthermore among *shōjo manga* in general as well as their adaptation to animation.

Furthermore, the visual significance of this manga genre derived from Takarazuka is the facial features depicted like stage makeup, especially the big eyes. Takarazuka performers including *otokoyaku* would wear big false eyelashes and very thick eye shadow so that their eyes shine reflecting the spotlight, and their expressions reach the furthest seat in the upper gallery. This is where the famous big sparkling eye depiction of Japanese *shōjo manga* came from. Tezuka confirmed that his characters' makeup is influenced by Takarazuka.[21] This means that Takarazuka's elaborate makeup that influenced the way characters are depicted created the stereotype of Japanese *shōjo manga*. From the heroine with big eyes to dramatic treatments found in the story of love and adventure in foreign settings that were inspired to a large extent by Takarazuka productions, these characteristics laid the foundations for typical *shōjo manga* features that combined to establish a genre in Japanese popular culture.

It is not only the visual features but also the narrative content that provide an understanding of the interrelated popularity of *shōjo manga* initiated by Tezuka Osamu and Takarazuka. Tezuka Osamu was aware that "my work was so-to-speak *shōjo* taste, sweet and that is most obviously expressed in *Princess Knight*. . . . if my work is romantic, that romanticism was born out of Takarazuka."[22] *Princess Knight*, however, is not at all a sheer sweet romance with a happy end. Sapphire is a woman, but possesses the soul of both a man and a woman. As the title indicates, she is a knight, a fighter like Jeanne d'Arc, who is not only heroic with the sword but possesses a strong-willed persona in suffering and asserting her own way. She fights to defeat evil, to obtain liberty and love as a wife, a mother of twins, a woman, but above all as an independent human being.

It may be that Tezuka Osamu reflected the images of women with courage and strong spirit such as his mother, who survived the war alone without his father when he was called for military service, and the Takarasiennes, who made a petition and directly submitted it to the American Occupation Force to get the theater back.[23] Sapphire's cleverness and challenging spirit, bravery, feminine compassion, and naivety formed an adorable character of the princess-prince and captured the hearts of millions of Japanese girls who became his fan-readers. He would receive one hundred fan letters from girls per day when the series was in the magazine, and commented that "they must have been really hungry for that kind of thing . . . girls of that time had a wish to dress like boys. I guess there were still many families who expected their daughters to be apron-stringed gentle, polite."[24] It was in any case a revolutionary *shōjo manga* that depicted not only the active exterior of the girl but also the delicate interior of her love, rejoicing, lament, and her strong independent spirit. Sapphire was the archetype of a *shōjo manga* heroine—active, clever, positive, righteous, gentle and delicate, but also courageous, combining physical and intellectual accomplishments that are conventionally attributed more to men.

It indicates that both *shōjo-manga* as represented by such titles like *Princess Knight* and the spectacular-theatrical Takarazuka are enlightening as well as entertaining media for girls, but also likely grown-up women as well who would continue to cherish their cross-appealing elements. In the fantasy adventure, Sapphire shows what girls aspire to do: like boys, girls want adventures, to fight against unjust people, to express opinions and feelings, including saying "I love you" to the man they really love, to choose how they spend their own lives and endeavor to realize ideals, as well as to dress in boy's clothes and even to rage about it once in a while. Tezuka Osamu addressed young women as follows:

> I want to talk about female models in my work. There are two types. These two merged into one woman in *Princess Knight*. One is the Jeanne D'Arc type whose strong spirit is enough to defeat men. Another type is the woman of gentleness and noble grace who would live for love and dedicate her life for love. The heroine of *Princess Knight*, Sapphire has both of them. This *guyūsei* (double characteristic) is my ideal image of women. . . . ladies who can maintain strong belief and passion for work, and who possess at the same time a broad mind to give their love to the whole world . . . this is what I wish.[25]

Here, the double characteristic he idealizes is different from *ryōsei-guyū* (androgyny). It is better referred to as *ryōshitsu-guyū* (holding both temperaments). Unlike the strict gender criteria that we are accustomed to, this characteristic could be something culturally determined and thus subtle and ideologically manipulated; however, that is the very element that makes the subject interesting and exploratory. In the case of Sapphire, as the title shows, she is a girl-knight; however, she is not only heroic through her use of the sword but also because of her strong-willed persona. In other words, she is an adorable prince-princess, a woman by birth, but possessing the merits of both (gender) souls. Through *Princess Knight*, Tezuka Osamu would encourage women to fight against injustice and not to give up anything they believed to be desirable.[26] Those girls who wrote fan letters were, therefore, cheering for Sapphire's fighting spirit and adoring her, just like Takarazuka fans who cheer for their favorite students "fighting" to develop themselves and realize their dreams. Sapphire obtained happiness out of her own will and effort with which the female readers sympathize. This message was further emphasized and strengthened in subsequent *shōjo-manga* titles such as *Berusaiyu no bara* [The Rose of Versailles (1972), popularly shortened as *Berubara*] created by Ikeda Riyoko, an admirer of Tezuka Osamu's *shōjo-manga*.[27] Ikeda's *Berubara*, a female manga-artist, shows the Takarazuka-Tezuka manga influences in terms of the story contents and its stylistic representations.

6. Exhibition leaflet (2007).

7. *Black Jack* poster.

8. Tezuka-Takarazuka tie: *Hinotori* flyer and *Black Jack* by Anju Mira (*right*).

In 2007, the Tezuka Osamu Memorial Museum presented a retrospective exhibition about their ties called *Takarazuka, eien no rondo ten* (Takarazuka Forever Rondo Exhibition). Motivated by Tezuka's Takarazuka-inspired graphics, Ikeda's style is instantly recognizable as seen in Takarazuka theater where the principal characters are presented as tall and svelte figures, and their appearances are aesthetically controlled stylistically rather than realistically. The dramatic pages of her manga contain images that are full of flowing hair, sparkly eyes and tears, as well as symbolic shots of flowers in the background—indeed, similar to Takarazuka's ornamentations with frills, flowers, and feathers.

Given the epoch marking the success of the adaptation of *Berubara* for the Takarazuka stage in 1974, the relation between manga and Takarazuka became intimate, and adapting manga to the stage and vice versa became a popular tendency. Ironically, before *Berubara* Takarazuka theater first thought it would degrade their reputation to use manga, which was then regarded as a form of low culture.[28] However, throughout his life, Tezuka strived to elevate the status of comics and animation in Japan, even if his manga works including *Princess Knight*[29] were not adapted for stage until recently. *Juju* (1974) was a show inspired by *Hinotori* (Phoenix), but it was not until the eightieth anniversary of Takarazuka in 1994, in conjunction with the opening of the Tezuka Osamu Memorial Museum, that his manga was effectively "performed" on their stage. The most engaging works of his life were chosen for this event: *Black Jack* (Black Jack: A Great Bet) was produced as a serious musical to accompany the remake of *Hinotori* as a joyful show. The anniversary year coincided with the opening of the memorial museum and together created a celebration fever for this icon of Japanese popular culture. Since then, the Tezuka-Takarazuka relation has become more revealed and acknowledged, and it is possible that the historical as well as cultural significance of their mutual influences will become even more widely recognized in the future.

Conclusion

It is not easy to imagine what would have happened to Japanese popular culture without Tezuka Osamu, and how different his work would have been if he had not been related to Takarazuka City and the theater. In Japan, the roots of manga and anime (and their generic characteristics) are inseparably integral to Tezuka Ozamu and accordingly, Takarazuka. Given the wartime experiences he encountered, the cruel side of human nature inspired him to pave a way to work with manga and anime, through which he wished to relieve the anguish and helplessness felt by the people as well as to make an appeal for love and peace.[30] The futuristic vision depicted in his life work of *Hinotori* expresses a hope that all of humanity, and of nature, may find redemption to live in harmony.[31] With this message, he will remain the tour de force in the world of Japanese popular culture and beyond. Media Studies scholar John Fiske (1994) considers consumption as a way of negotiating identity, and through the increasingly regional production and worldwide consumption of manga and anime, it is no wonder that Japanese popular culture is spreading, as is the notion of Japanese identity transcending its origins to incorporate more of a global identity.

Tezuka Osamu formulated a unique manga style that is reflected in his manga-adapted anime works. Starting from *Atomu* in 1963, his manga works, like *Princess Knight* and others, were all made into TV anime series, feature animated films, and even live-action films. In the growing trend of the use of mix-media in Japanese popular culture, Tezuka's manga, which employed both theatrical and cinematographic storytelling skills, continues to be reproduced using other media. For teachers and students researching on Japanese comics and animation especially of the manga and anime kinds, it is essential to pay heed to the significance of Takarazuka's influence in the works created by Tezuka Osamu and to develop discussions that are more steeped in an intercultural and intergenre context. This kind of interdisciplinary approach will eventually broaden the scope of understanding of the roots of Japanese popular culture and of the phenomena of "Japan-Pop" and "Japan-Cool," their excessive global popularity, and how sometimes they are not explained historically but rather uncritically in the media and cultural study of Tezuka's contributions to manga and anime in general.

Notes

1. The Phoenix inscribed the hope that "any human being, and all of humanity, can find such redemption and live to love another day." See W. M. MacWilliams, "Revisioning Japanese Religion: Osamu Tezuka's *Hi no Tori* (The Phoenix)," in *Global Goes Local: Popular Culture in Asia*, ed. Timothy J. Craig and R. King (Vancouver: UBC Press, 2002), 177–207.

2. Now officially called Takarazuka Revue Company, it is an all-female theater founded by the Hankyu railway tycoon Kobayashi Ichizō in 1914. This entertainment company has since brought fame to the city.

3. The film won him the Ōfuji Noburō Award sponsored by Mainichi Shinbun in 1962. (Editors' note: See Sano Akiko's chapter in this volume about the artistic background of Ōfuji Noburō.)

4. He founded Mushi Production in 1968. Inspired by Walt Disney films, producing animation had been one of his biggest aspirations. See, for example, Ishiko (2002: 25).

5. Editors' note: While Yamanashi is referring to Tezuka's contributions to the history of Japanese manga and anime per se, especially with the generic characteristics that the world has come to know, in Japan, "manga" and "anime" are simply considered as "comics" and "animation" in general. See Hu's work (2010: 102, 165) where she points out the multilingual terms used in Japan to address the animation medium.

6. Ishiko (2002: 54): For instance, the Takarazuka star Amatsu Otome and her sister Takarasienne Kumono Kayoko were living next door. See an article by his sister, Uno Minako, in the Grand Theatre program of *Black Jack* (1994: 48).

7. One of the leading Western-style hotels built in 1926 where he also later held his wedding.

8. For the history of Family Land, see Yasuno (2003).

9. Quoted from his article in *Akahata* newspaper (January 1974) on display at an exhibition at Tezuka Osamu Memorial Museum (March 1–July 10, 2007).

10. When at an elementary school in Ikeda, his passion for the theater made him produce his own play with friends, and he recklessly went to the Takarazuka company to borrow costumes, although in vain (A. Kawauchi, ed., 1996: 70). In 1940 when he was twelve, he had already written a study of graphic stories named *Shina no yoru* (Night in China) which is said to have been inspired by the Takarazuka production of the same title from that year (Nakano, 1994: 62).

11. Kawauchi, 1996: 81.

12. Tezuka Osamu Exhibition catalogue (2009: 58–59).

13. Kawauchi, 1996: 9.

14. Ibid., 1996: 79 and Nakano, 1994: 214; lectured on October 31, 1988). Also, see Tezuka Production, ed. (2007).

15. Kawauchi, 1996: 83.

16. Ibid., 75.

17. See Ishiko, 2002: 52.

18. Nakano points out that the prince resembles the Takarazuka star Kasugano Yachiyo of that time (1994: 104).

19. *Switch Vol.* 22 (March 2004: 31).

20. Katherine Mezur in Stanca Scholz-Cionca and Samuel L. Leiter ed., 2001: 210.

21. Nakano, 1994: 189.

22. Ishiko, 2002: 53.

23. Kawauchi, 1996: 97. (Editors' note: See also Hu's chapter in this volume, which describes the period of the Allied Forces Occupation in Japan from 1945 to 1952.

24. Ishiko, 2002: 53.

25. Ibid., 147–48. This speech was made on March 1, 1983.

26. After the war, the image of girls like Sapphire became a popular stereotype heroine in *shōjo manga*—active, positive, righteous, gentle, but courageous. The psychoanalyst Saitō Tamaki (2003: 151) describes these fighting girls as "Takarazuka-kei" (Takarazuka-branch as a transvestite genre).

27. Akin to the story of *Princess Knight*, the heroine Oscar is brought up as a boy to serve the royal court.

28. The stage director, Ueda Shinji's statement in Suzuki (1977: 235): "I was dismissive at first. It was absurd to adapt manga for the Takarazuka stage."

29. Takarazuka director Kimura Shinji remade it with the young girl team, Morning Musume, together with a few Takarazuka graduates in 2006.

30. Nakano, 1994: 214.

31. See W. Mark MacWilliams (2002: 177–207), *Revisioning Japanese Religion: Osamu Tezuka's Hi no Tori*.

References

Eco, Umberto. *Faith in Fakes: Travels in Hyper Reality*. Translated by William Weaver. London: Minerva, 1995.

Edo-Tokyo Museum. *The 80th Anniversary of Tezuka Osamu—Massages to the Future*. Tokyo: Edo-Tokyo Museum / Yomiuri Shinbun / NHK, 2009.

Fiske, John. *Understanding Popular Culture*. London: Routledge, 1998.

Ishiko, Jun. *Tezuka Osamu Part 3: Shōjo manga no sekai* [The world of young girl-comic]. Tokyo: Doshin-sha, 2002.

Kawauchi, Atsurō, ed. *Tezuka Osamu no furusato takarazuka* [Tezuka Osamu's hometown, Takarazuka]. Kobe: Kobe Shinbun Sogo Shuppan Center, 1996.

McGray, Douglas. *Japan's Gross National Cool, Foreign Policy* (May 2002) at www.douglasmcgray.com (Accessed on May 2012).

MacWilliams, Mark W., ed. *Japanese Visual Culture: Explorations in the World of Manga and Anime*. New York: M. E. Sharpe, 2008.

Nakano Haruyuki. *Tezuka Osamu no takarazuka* [Tezuka Osamu's Takarazuka]. Tokyo: Chikuma Shobo, 1994.

Saitō, Tamaki. *Sentō bishōjo no seishin bunseki* [Psychological analyses on fighting beauties]. Tokyo: Ōta-shuppan, 2003.

Scholz-Cionca, Stanca, and Samuel L. Leiter, ed. *Japanese Theatre and the International Stage*. Leiden/Boston/Köln: Brill, 2001.

Suzuki, Tazuko. *Zuka fan no kagami: Mon Paris kara berubara made* [The mirror of Takarazuka fans: From Mon Paris to the Rose of Versailles]. Tokyo: Ushio-shuppan, 1977.

Switch vol. 22 no.3. Tokyo: Switch Publishing (March 2004).

Takarazuka Grand Theatre. *Black Jack: A Great Bet / Phoenix*. Takarazuka, 1994.

Tezuka, Osamu. *Kami no toride* [Paper Fortress]. Tokyo: Kodan-sha, 1983.

———. *Ribbon no kishi* ["Princess Knight": Shōjo Club version]. Tokyo: Kodan-sha, 1999.

Tezuka Productions, ed. *Tezuka Osamu no manga no genten: Sensō taiken to egakareta sensō* [The origin of Tezuka Osamu's manga: His experience of the war and the war illustrated]. Tokyo: Showa-kan, 2007.

Yasuno, Akira. "Yūenchi takarazuka shin-onsen ga keiseishita goraku-kūkan no shiteki-rikai" [A personal understanding of the leisure space constructed by the amusement center of Takarazuka new spa]. In *Takarazuka-shishi kenkyū kiyō vol. 20* [Takarazuka City Bulletin], edited by Takarazuka-shi chuō toshokan shiryōtantō [Takarazuka City Central Library archivist], 1–42. Takarazuka City: Takarazuka City Education Committee, November 2003.

Audio Visual Resource

Osamu Tezuka Film Works (DVD GNBA-3036, 2007); Geneon Universal Entertainment Japan, Tokyo.

Web Resource

Tezuka Osamu: Message for the Future took place at Edo-Tokyo Museum, see http://www.edo-tokyo-museum.or.jp/kikaku/page/2009/0418/200904.html (Accessed on June 2009).

Growing Up with *Astro Boy* and *Mazinger Z*

Industrialization, "High-Tech World," and Japanese Animation in the Art and Culture of South Korea

—Dong-Yeon Koh

Introduction: The Return of *Astro Boy*

Astro Boy (2009), the Hollywood remake of Tezuka Osamu's classic *Mighty Atom* (*Tetsuwan Atomu*, originally created as a manga series in 1952 and made into an animated version in black and white in 1963), stirred great nostalgia among the generation of Koreans who were brought up with "Astro Boy Atom" or "Atom Boy from Outer-Space" in Korean.[1] Some parents, seeking to overcome the generation gap, brought their children to theaters to see whether they would share their sympathy toward their childhood hero. These parents often expressed their opinions about the Hollywood remake of *Astro Boy Atom* on their personal blogs, comparing it with what they believed was the original *Astro Boy Atom*. It was not so much the animation per se, but their memories of a long-gone hero from the world of manga and animation once popular in Korea that had attended the recent surge of interest in the "return" of *Astro Boy*.

Understanding this nostalgic reaction toward the "return" of Astro Boy in Korea requires examination of the extensive popularity of postwar Japanese animation characters in Korea during the 1970s and 1980s. These characters served as national icons through which the members of a postwar generation of Koreans could communicate with one another, apart from their various social standings and cultural upbringings. Indeed, the character of "Astro Boy Atom," as renamed by the Korean media, was adopted and imitated for commercials during the 1970s. For instance, the "Rocket Boy" character for battery products of Honam Electronic Corporation in the 1970s has the round face and huge eyes which are the core visual features of the Japanese "Mighty Atom."

During the postwar years in Japan as well as in Korea, Tezuka's *Mighty Atom* symbolized an optimistic vision of science and technology, and the Korean battery commercial appropriating its slightly modified version was largely indebted to the reputation of Astro Boy as a "son of science." The image of *Astro Boy* produced into numerous manga and animation versions over the last five decades and the message he carried in postwar Japan, remains complicated, sometimes convoluted and controversial, to say the least. *Astro Boy* has been often cited with the painful memory of the atomic bombs dropped at Hiroshima and Nagasaki during the Second World War, as Tezuka wrote in *Tetsuwan Atomu* (1999).[2] At the same time, it represented postwar Japan's desire to move forward into the future relying on the power of science and technology. Tezuka initially proposed that an "Atom continent" might exist where atomic power was used for peaceful purposes in "Atom Continent (*Atomu takiku*)," his first episode of "Mighty Atom," better known as "Ambassador Atom (*Atomu Taishi*)," in 1952.[3] In postwar Korea, especially during the 1970s and 1980s, the image of *Astro Boy* also ironically served as an emblem of the futuristic ideals of Korea, a nation trying to recover from its colonial past and economically devastated condition after the Korean War by following in the footsteps of Japan. Toys based on the Astro Boy character were usually associated with scientific and technological innovations. (See later section of this chapter.) In addition to the Honam Rocket Boy commercial, the Astro Boy toys were accompanied by plastic models for complicated vehicles, such as tanks or boats. Advertisements for the Astro Boy Boat were published in magazines such as *Haksaeng Gwahak* (Science for Students).

What follows then is a discussion of the historical context into which Japanese animation was imported into Korea during the 1970s and 1980s. What role did Japanese animation play in Korean society, particularly during the period of Korea's intensive industrialization and modernization? Images of *Astro Boy* and *Mazinger* Z as appropriated by contemporary Korean artists will also be mentioned in an effort to further investigate the cultural and historic significance of the iconic images of Japanese animation among the generation of artists who were brought up with postwar Japanese popular culture.

The popularity of postwar Japanese animation in Korea during the 1970s and 1980s remains controversial; until 1990, importing Japanese popular culture was officially illegal in Korea. The administration of Kim Dae-Jung finally agreed to the gradual opening of the Korean market to Japanese popular culture beginning in 1998.[4] Nonetheless, Korean national policy regarding Japanese popular culture has been far from static, having been sporadically interrupted by territorial disputes over the Dokdo problem and by ongoing debates about the treatment of the Pacific War in Japanese textbooks.[5]

Upon announcing "The Agreement for the Partnership of Korea-Japan in the 21st Century," signed by Korean president Kim and the Japanese ministry in 1998, President Kim made it clear that the plan should be executed without "the fear" of dominance of Japanese popular culture in Korea.[6] However, throughout the 1990s, the Korean government undertook a massive plan to support and protect the domestic manga and animation industry against Japanese animation and manga. The government provided animation companies that produced allegedly "national" manga and animation characters with a 20 percent tax exemption with the aim of transforming domestic productions into a more internationally viable and competitive industry, particularly relative to Japanese production companies. The more publicly conspicuous efforts in support of a domestic industry have included the opening of the Seoul Animation Center and the House for Manwha in Seoul, and the annual Seoul International Cartoon and Animation Festival (SICAF), which began in 1995 and attracted more than 300,000 people in its first year. SICAF is usually held around August 15, Korea's Independence Day from Japanese occupation, called *Kwang-Bok-Jul,* literally "the day when Koreans recovered their Light." This choice of date is significant, as the fair usually includes exhibitions related to the themes of national independence and Japanese occupation.

Despite anti-Japanese sentiment and an extremely nationalistic cultural policy in Korea, Japanese manga and animation had continued to influence the Korean youth and industry throughout the postwar years. The proposal of lifting the ban on Japanese popular culture was also prompted by the growing problem with the illegal import of pirated Japanese CDs, DVDs, and publications in Korea. With Korea joining the World Trade Organization in 1989, the government faced the new challenge of abiding by international standards of copyright law.[7] Considering the history and extent of Japanese manga and animation already circulated in Korea, the cultural and media theorist Han Kyung-Koo claims that the announcement of the "opening" of the Korean market to Japanese popular culture during the 1990s might be a misnomer. Most trendy Japanese manga and animation had already been available in Korea for decades, and the new governmental plan could only provide a legal framework for authorizing and controlling economic transactions.[8]

In explicating the increasing dominance of Japanese popular culture in Korea—from either non-nationalistic or pro-nationalistic perspectives—researchers and theorists in media studies, cultural studies, and education have taken comparative approaches to Korean and Japanese cultures. To summarize a few opinions, Japanese culture, like American popular culture, has robust financial and human resources that facilitate the creation of more sensual and violent, and therefore more marketable and commercially successful, popular-culture products. In 1995, the special division monitoring the influence of Japanese manwha on Korean youth, called "Manwha Monitor" of the Young Women's Christian Association (YWCA), called for the establishment of a more serious review system for Japanese animation and manga. "With an increase of Korean publishers importing Japanese manga and translating them, Korean youths who had already been familiar with Japanese manga became more provoked, and the sensual and violent nature of manga contents reached a level beyond our peril."[9] However, the researchers have also pointed out the similarities between the Korean and Japanese cultures, such as the traditional values of Confucianism, and the authoritarian social and governmental structures during the postwar years.[10] As a result, the researchers argue, Korean audiences have tended to be relatively comfortable and familiar with Japanese TV dramas, music, animation, and manga, especially when compared to American popular culture.[11]

These comparative approaches often have serious limitations, in that they tend to generalize cultures based upon national boundaries; these approaches fail to explain the elements of heterogeneity within each culture. As pointed out by Han Kyung-Gyu, throughout the postwar years, both official and unofficial ways of importing Japanese culture into Korea had been already developed and any protectionist attempt to define the distinctive Japanese and Korean culture might be misleading.[12] Instead, such divided opinions appear to correspond to Koreans' ambivalent attitude toward Japanese popular culture—that is, Japanese animation and manga are perceived as familiar, albeit somewhat advanced in terms of technology, marketing, sophistication of fashion, self-expression, and presentation, and therefore extremely useful to Koreans, at the same time that they are regarded as frightening and grossly violent. This latter perception is also linked to the idea of Japanese "cultural" invasion, which immediately evokes in the minds of most Koreans terrible memories of the Japanese occupation.[13]

I hereby propose a new approach to the historical contexts and social ideals shared by Korea and Japan during the postwar years—namely, their fascination with new technology, the high-tech drive in science education, and the anticommunist ethos, especially under a military dictatorship in Korea during the 1970s and 1980s. This chapter discusses President Park Jung-Hee's rather pragmatic approach of reestablishing diplomatic relationships for economic and diplomatic collaboration but ultimately, the nationalistic and protectionist approach toward culture effectively illustrates both the Korean people's and Korean government's ambiguous attitude toward Japanese popular culture. I see this approach as more of an ongoing alternative account to the predominant attitude toward Korea's relationship with Japanese popular culture, which was reliant more or less on vague interpretations of "national" culture. *Astro Boy* and *Mazinger Z* were introduced in Korea during the 1970s and 1980s, almost a decade after these animated works were made in Japan. This "belatedness" of the animation popularity supports the idea that the period of intense modernization and industrialization coincided with the introduction of iconic Japanese animation characters in Korea.

An examination of the historical significance of Japanese animation and manga during the 1970s and 1980s will be followed by a discussion of Korean pop art. In the mid-1990s, a group of artists loosely dubbed the Korean pop artists began appropriating the images of Astro Boy and Mazinger Z, the two most classic Japanese animations imported into Korea during the 1970s and 1980s. In a 2007 one-person show, Hyun Tae-Jun lined up his replicas of Japanese animation characters along with visual artifacts, including real toys based upon popular characters of the 1970s. Likewise, in 1992, Yi Dong-Gi, the most renowned Korean pop artist, invented his character "Atomous" by combining Astro Boy and Mickey Mouse.

The images of Astro Boy and Mazinger Z pervasive in Korean pop art can be considered as effective illustrations of the iconic meanings that these classic Japanese animation characters can convey among members of the postwar generation in Korea. Their work, as I will argue, sheds a critical light on the legacy of authoritarianism, educational fervor, and obsession with technological innovation, upon which the success of

Korea, Japan, and the greater East Asian economic model was deeply reliant during those decades.

How Did *Astro Boy* Change Korea?

The popularity of Japanese animation in Korea during the 1970s was largely prompted by the nascent television industry in Korea. In 1968, the Korean government announced a five-year plan for the electronics industry, marking a transitional phase of economic development in Korea.[14] The national policy involving the electronics industry became important not only for the economic structuring of the nation, but also for ideological and political purposes as the Park Jung-Hee administration announced the *Yushin* in 1972, meaning "rejuvenated reform," which was no less than a thinly disguised plan for reinforcing and extending Park's authoritarian government and presidency.

Most domestic broadcasting companies in the early 1970s, either public or privately owned, lacked financial and human resources to produce their own programs.[15] During the 1970s and even into the 1980s, the majority of movies aired on TV for adults had been imported from the United States. As for children's programming, however, the number of Japanese cartoons on television far exceeded the number of American cartoons, largely due to lower royalty fees. During the early 1970s, South Korean television stations were still broadcasting black-and-white programs, and therefore Japanese cartoons, such as the first series of *Mighty Atom* (1964), were ideal for South Korean companies with limited budgets. Considering the overall financial difficulty that domestic broadcasting companies experienced in importing foreign animated works, the South Korean government granted an exemption to its ban on the import of Japanese popular culture, especially in the area of animation, as long as the original Japanese names of the characters and locales were omitted.[16]

The first Japanese animation aired in Korea was *Astro Boy Atom*, translated as "Mighty Atom," by Tezuka. *Mighty Atom* was originally published as manga during the early 1950s, and its black-and-white animation was aired between 1963 and 1966 in Japan. Unlike the Japanese *Mighty Atom*, which was more popular as manga in book format during the 1950s, *Astro Boy Atom* in South Korea was primarily known as an animated character. The black-and-white version of *Astro Boy Atom* was first aired by the Tong Yang Broadcasting Company (TBC) in 1971, and the color animation was aired on the second channel of Korean Broadcasting System (KBS) in 1981. When *Astro Boy Atom* was first broadcast in 1971 it became an instant hit, as there were few competitive animations of refined quality available on TV, especially during the 1970s. Koreans watching Japanese animation were also mostly unaware of the origins of *Astro Boy Atom*. The name of the doctor, Tenma, was changed to Doctor *Koh Myung-Whan*, and his deceased son Tobio was changed into *Koh Chul*, meaning "the old (useless) steel" in Korean, while certain exotic locales such as Atlas or planets of Mars remained unchanged.

Japanese animation and manga are also characterized by their lack of specific historical and national references, and the physical features of Astro Boy do not correspond to those of "typical" Japanese. The huge eyes and flat nose of Astro Boy, which were notable features of most of Tezuka's characters as well as of Japanese shōjo-manga characters, appear to combine non-Japanese and even Caucasian physiognomies with Japanese features. According to Iwabuchi Koichi, author of *Recentering Globalization* (2002), postwar Japanese producers and artists deliberately purged any trace of national cultural references in order to expand the appeal of their work to international audiences, including those in Asia who remained very antagonistic toward Japan. The result, in his description, was "odorless" cultural commodities.[17]

The success of *Astro Boy* in Korea, however, as I will argue, was not contributable to the sheer lack of animation programming in Korea during its early phase of industrialization and popular culture, or the lack of the distinctive national traits—what Iwabuchi has called the "odor"—of Japanese animated works. It remains unclear whether the "odorless" nature of Japanese popular cultural products was a phenomenon limited to graphic facial features. One can argue that in both South Korea and the United States, some of the original names, locales, and even themes were modified or omitted, depending on where the Japanese animation was broadcast. This process of adaptation was not necessarily caused by the particular "national" characteristics of Japanese "stateless" popular culture, but rather by the general process of transcultural or transnational adaptation.

This chapter on the contrary looks at the historical context of Korea during the early 1970s, a context that became increasingly susceptible to the national image of Japan as a role model for Korea's high-technological drive. The early 1970s still witnessed a serious level of anti-Japanese sentiment as the majority of Korean people were still uncomfortable with the Korean government's decision to rekindle its relationship with Japan, which came to fruition in 1965 with the reestablishment of an official diplomatic relationship between the two nations. Preceding the 1965 agreement, a major topic of discussion between the two nations concerned economic and military collaboration, particularly how Korea would be able to catch up with Japan's postwar development of technology.[18] In its basic storyline and theme, *Astro Boy* is notable for its positive and futuristic vision of machines and technology, especially compared to the much darker and adult-oriented American animations such as *Batman* and *Superman*.

The primary setting of *Astro Boy* is the futuristic Metro City. Although Astro Boy is initially rejected by his human father who created him as a robot replacement for his deceased son, Tobio, he eventually discovers a way to achieve a harmonious relationship between robots and the human world. In his 1986 interview with the *Journal of the Robotic Society of Japan*, Tezuka explained that he wanted to create Atom to be a reversal of Pinocchio, a nearly perfect robot which remains as "an interface between the two different cultures of man and machine."[19] Frederik Schodt, author of *The Astro Boy Essays* (2007), also claimed that in the postwar years in Japan, Atom became a highly exploitable property. "Atom could represent a new, humanized sort of machine. Atom could represent advanced technology that was nonthreatening and could lead to a better future; a cuddly, warm sort of technology wrapped in scientific optimism."[20] Indeed, the first of the ten principles of "Robot Law," which were outlined by Tezuka himself from the inception of his character, was that "Robots are created to serve mankind."[21]

Tezuka's vision of a robot, which would eventually overcome the conflict between Metro City and Planet Earth below, may have originated from his personal experience with the tragedy created by technological innovation itself. In 1967, Tezuka wrote in the *Tokyo Shimbun* that he had never intended to create a story in the twenty-first century about a glorious scientific civilization.[22] He was instead inspired by his frustrating experience at the end of the Second World War. As aforementioned, his original idea with the "atomic continent" effectively summarized his idea of technology that is not completely positive. According to Schodt, Tezuka developed a policy of not allowing power companies to use *Mighty Atom* imagery to promote atomic energy, and in his new animated series of *Mighty Atom* in color, during the 1980s, he inserted Atom's engine fusion reactor that did not require the dangerous process of atom fission but the relatively harmless isotope deuterium, known as heavy water.[23]

Tezuka's somewhat oblique vision of technology in the context of postwar Japan was neither fully understood nor even considered by his South Korean audience. First, the tragic event of the atomic bomb had a different historical significance for Koreans. Although there were several Korean casualties at Hiroshima and Nagasaki, the atomic bomb had, in the end, liberated the Koreans from Japanese occupation. Second, Tezuka did not give up his utopian vision of technology and scientific civilization. As cited in Schodt, Tezuka remained firm in his desire to create a story about an idealistic future.[24] Finally, most of the South Korean audience for Tezuka's animated version of *Astro Boy Atom* were children, who were not capable of recognizing the complicated historical and political theme of *Astro Boy Atom*. Instead, *Astro Boy Atom* was generally considered to be the epitome of euphoria in response to Western technology. The title song consistently underscores a utopian and futuristic vision: "Through the sky—la la la—to the distant stars / Goes Atom, as far as his jets will take him. The oh-so-gentle—la la la—child of science / With 100.000 horsepower, it is mighty Atom."[25]

If *Astro Boy* represents the Japanese vision of an ideal futuristic robot that serves human civilization, Korean society during the 1970s was equally obsessed with the idea of national progress using technological innovations. Korea established the KAIST (Korean Advanced Institute of Technology), modeled after MIT (Massachusetts Institute of Technology in the United States). Under the Park administration, the "National Economic Development Five-Year Plan" was first established in 1962, then a second plan from 1967 until 1971, shifting its focus from the production of consumer products to technologically based and heavy industry, such as electronics and steel. The restructuring of the nation's focal industry entailed nationwide reeducation through the science curriculum and teaching in Korea. In 1965, the country began adopting new educational methodologies for science developed in the United States under consultation with the Korean Research Institute of Natural Science Education.[26] The project got the attention of UNICEF (United Nations Children's Fund), which subsequently supported the national project of science education in Korea from 1968 until 1970.[27]

In 1969, the Korean government also announced its systematic plan to change math and science education in Korea throughout the next eight years, which was not dissimilar to the economic five-year plan. The first plan began in 1972, followed by the second plan between 1972 and 1974, and the final plan between 1975 and 1977. This series of reform plans resulted in the revision of textbooks for elementary schools in 1971 and for middle and high schools in 1973.[28]

The relationship between scientific education and industrialization in Korea is far from being trivial and tangential. The concentration on a higher level of learning, as pointed out by a number of economists and historians, constituted one of the determining factors that contributed to what has usually been called the economic miracle in East Asian countries, including Japan, Korea, and Taiwan, during the 1970s and 1980s. According to Shin Jang-Sup, author of "High-Tech Industrialization and Local Capability" (2006), it is unlikely that Korean society was equipped with intrinsic learning capabilities before industrialization. Rather, he argues, "Korea's initiative toward high-tech industrialization, which required rapid local capability formation, was facilitated by concurrent expansion in public education."[29] Indeed, the secondary enrollment ratio in Korea expanded from 27 percent in the 1960s to 78 percent in the 1980s, compared to Malaysia, where it rose from 19 percent to 48 percent, and Brazil, where it rose from 11 percent to 33 percent during the same period, and math and science education for high-tech drive of economic policy was underscored throughout higher educational institutions in Korea.[30]

The plastic toys and science magazines for the youth of these decades reflected wide-ranging national endeavors to foster science education in Korea. Local stationeries, selling cheap and small toys and snacks, began introducing youth magazines on miscellaneous topics including science, as well as plastic model toys. There was always a mixture of scientific discovery on the one hand and information associated with animation on the other in most major children's magazines, such as *Sae Sonyun* (New Boys), which began in 1964, and *Sonyun Joongang* (Joongang Magazine for Boys), first published in 1971. Plastic models had been often categorized as educational toys, as they were claimed to enhance children's spatial recognition and construction skills.[31] The name of the company that produced plastic models was the Academic Science Company. This company also established a center for children and other educational facilities that were mostly devoted to the display of small science-related objects and simple mechanical structures.[32]

It was through advertisements for plastic models in youth magazines that Korean children became familiar with trendy Japanese animation characters. A considerable number of these plastic models were based upon Japanese animation characters or variations of these characters. An increasing number of Korean children were living in apartments or in areas surrounded by factories that had once been open fields. According to the artist Hyun Tae-Jun, much of the suburban area in Korea was transformed into construction sites for buildings and factories during the 1970s and 1980s. The rapid process of urbanization changed not only the physical landscape of Seoul and its vicinity, but also how children spent their free time. Children began to use more of their leisure time in watching television and keeping up with the new super-robot characters of animation.[33]

The Cold War ethos that constituted the backdrop of *Astro Boy* may have also helped postwar Japanese animation avoid further censorship in Korea and subsequently gain popularity among Korean audiences. Tezuka used the contrast between the colors red and blue, as well his classical narrative of good punishing evil. In the episode "The Birth of Astroboy," part of a second animated color version broadcast in 1982, Count Walpurgis, who was devising an evil plot to duplicate Doctor Tenma's omega factor, control the robots and rule the world, was depicted in red. Indeed, not only was he wearing a red gown, but his environment and omega factor were also colored red. In direct contrast, the following sequences featuring Doctor Tenma were all colored blue to imply how the same power could be used for different purposes of good (blue) and evil (red).[34] As Astro Boy came under the control of Count Walpurgis, his eyes turned red to indicate that he was under the evil power of Count Walpurgis.

Tezuka's fundamental antiwar beliefs, as Schodt argues, sometimes made him appear anti-American, or even as a communist sympathizer, especially for the duration of the Vietnam War. However, Tezuka resisted any specific ideological leaning: "Frankly, I consider anyone who is thoroughly steeped in the ideology of the left or the right to be an idiot."[35] However, considering the underlying Cold War message of Astro Boy only in relation to the creator's personal political belief might be too limiting. Tezuka was quite adaptable to his targeted audience and market, which was not confined to his home country.

On the contrary, the color red must have been perceived as the unmistakable symbolism of communism to most South Korean viewers, including children, who had been exposed to an array of creative literature, popular culture, and educational material that underscored anticommunist and anti-North themes throughout the 1970s and 1980s.[36] In anticommunist literature for children during this period, the patriotic progenitors expressed their fear or hatred of the "Palgaengi" in Korea, which literally meant "the reddish people" in Korean. There was even a distinct genre of anticommunist animation in Korea. *The Small General Tory* (1979), one of the earliest animated feature films, presents the characters of Red Wolf troops who are in fact the spies from North Korea—not unlike Count Walpurgis in his red gown.[37]

Anticommunism was, indeed, among the pressing issues of national security that Japan and Korea continued to share throughout the postwar years. Although Japan, Korea, and China may not be situated in an identical geopolitical context, the threat of North Korea appears to be one of the most consistently shared concerns in South Korea's diplomatic collaboration with Japan, from the reestablishment of a diplomatic relationship in 1965 to the recent unilateral effort against the nuclear threat of North Korea.[38] Moreover, the Chun Doo-Whan administration of the early 1980s, which signaled the continuation of a military dictatorship in South Korea, maintained the repressive diplomatic and cultural policy. The "democratic uprising" at Gwangju on May 18, 1980, was followed by the highly conservative and anticommunist social atmosphere in the name of national security. Therefore, it is hard to ignore the political implications of the "evil red energy," whether perceived directly or subliminally, by South Korean policymakers and the public.

With respect to the influence of Japanese animation on the ideological underpinnings of children's popular and toy culture in South Korea during the 1970s and 1980s, *Mazinger Z* is another notable example. Nagai Gō's *Mazinger Z* was originally published in *Shōnen Jump* in 1972 and subsequently developed into an animated version in the same year. Unlike *Astro Boy Atom*, which was based upon the "boy" characters, *Mazinger Z* signaled a new form of super-robot character in animation. The fighting scenes of robots became much fiercer and the weapons and techniques, such as eye-fired energy beams, melting rays from the chest plates, and gale-force winds, became more sophisticated. Another innovative element of the *Mazinger Z* character is the relationship between the super robot and the humans; the main progenitor Kouji "piloted" the robot from its head as if he controlled the body of the robot from its brain. Whenever Kouji would move or suffer inside the cockpit, the robot felt the same, a method that would be later adopted by a variety of spin-off robot characters, including *Astroganger* (known as "Zzanga") and *Grendizer*, also aired in South Korea during the 1980s and 1990s.[39]

Mazinger Z, which premiered on Moonwha Broadcasting Corporation (MBC) in 1975 in South Korea, is remembered as the most popular and formidable super-robot character of Japanese animation. The boom in plastic toys also began with *Mazinger Z* during the late 1970s, with the success of *Mazinger Z* interdependent on the sales of its plastic models. To reiterate, *Mazinger Z* introduced a distinctive method of matching the movements of a pilot with those of robots according to a complicated structure that was deconstructed throughout its episodes.

The original concept of *Mazinger Z* was as a demon-god in a continuation of Nagai Go's first creation of *Devilman* (1972). Although also imbued with a mythic and apocalyptic vision of science and civilization, *Mazinger Z* had a more positive and simplistic interpretation of the superhero concepts prevailing within a South Korean context. Unlike Japanese audiences, who had been exposed to various versions of *Mazinger Z*, from manga to animation, most South Korean children became familiar with *Mazinger Z* as a cartoon that they watched as an afterschool children's program.[40] The translations of the main characters and locales, such as "Seo-Do-I" for Kouji, which meant "the boy of steel," underscored the fascination with the technological development of "Super-Alloy Z," a fictitious form of metal that first appeared in *Mazinger Z* and was subsequently used as the name of a new line of die-cast metal robot and character toys in both Japan and Korea. It is no wonder that the reception of *Mazinger Z* in South Korea centered on the new weapons, later incorporated into plastic models from each episode.

Mazinger Z also served as the prototype for *Taekwon V* (1976), the first Korean animation feature film in 1976 that focused on the super-robot character, and the influence of *Mazinger Z* on *Taekwon V* for its character development has been a consistent topic of dispute. The head of Taekwon V resembled the helmet similar to the one worn by Admiral Yi, who fought off Hideyoshi's sixteenth-century invasions, a series of wars that lasted more than a century between Japan and Korea. Taekwon V also used the technique of *taekwondo*, which was believed to originate from the traditional martial arts of Korea and was established as the national sport by the postwar administration under Park in 1971.[41] A number of scholars, however, have provided alternative interpretations of the origins of *Taekwon V*, noting that Taekwon V, when blasting his weapon, is more akin to Mazinger Z than to other precursors of super robots. The idea that the physical reaction of the pilot concurs with that of the robot is also shared by *Taekwon V* and *Mazinger Z*. The establishment of *taekwondo* as a national sport that draws upon purely traditional martial arts is also questionable, as *taekwondo* demonstrates the influence of traditional sports as well as that of *karate*, developed in the Okinawa region, and of Chinese *kungfu*.[42]

The argument over whether *Taekwon V* is the total invention of Korean animators or relies upon Japanese precedents might be unproductive. Instead, one could contend that *Taekwon V* is the result of a range of historical issues and sources, such as traditional history, martial arts, Japanese animation, and even contemporary concern with the steel industry—as much as the imaginary material of "Super Alloy Z" in *Mazinger Z* became the major occupation among Korean children. President Park Jung-Hee made his first announcement about the national policy for the steel industry during his New Year's message on January 27, 1970. Five months later in May, the Committee for Steel Industry was established, followed by the announcement of a special policy designed to foster six major industries—steel, nonmetal products, ship construction, chemistry, machines, and electronic products—in July. As noted earlier, during the late 1960s and early 1970s, Korea entered a different phase of industrialization, shifting its primary focus from "light" industry to "heavy" industry, largely in order to overcome the critical moment of international stagnation immediately after the oil shock of the early 1970s with a more proactive national strategy.[43] As the first major animation film on robots opened in theaters, *Taekwon V* would cope with the national policy regarding the steel industry. During the 1970s, film industry in Korea should undergo the most extreme stage of censorship, and all films should contain the message that can enlighten the shared social ideal, referred to as "sound contents." In *Taekwon V*, all major characters are related to various types of metals. Taekwon V, for instance, is composed of newly invented hard steel; "Can robot," the younger brother of Hun-I, the main character, however, is made of an old form of cheap tin. (In 2006, three decades after the birth of *Taekwon V*, the Department of Industry and Resource [currently the Department of Knowledge and Economy]) announced Taekwon V as its first officially registered robot. Over the last three decades, as the announcement made by the Department of Industry and Resource reads, *Taekwon V* has played a significant role in reinforcing Korean children's positive attitudes toward robots in particular and science and technology in general.[44])

The hybrid nature of *Taekwon V* also indicated the Korean government's basic diplomatic stance and strategy toward Japan during the 1970s. Park Jung-Hee, the dictatorial president of the 1970s, took a much more pragmatic stance toward Japan by trying to expand economic and political interactions and collaborations, although he himself remained deeply nationalistic. Originally trained as an officer under the Japanese military, he adopted Japanese economic and social structures as the role models for his domestic policy in Korea. In 1965, he made the bold move of reestablishing Korea's diplomatic relationship with Japan. In the end, Japan set the prototype for what Rudi Volti, author of *Technology Transfer and East Asian Economic Transformation* (2002), called the "East Asian Model" of foreign technology acquisition and uses in a non-Western context.[45] At the same time, President Park publicly admired General Yi Sun-Shin, who led the final victory of the Korean navy over the Japanese navy during an invasion in the sixteenth century, and he placed a statue of General Yi on the main road of *Gwanghwa Moon* ("gate") in Seoul.[46]

Japanese animation has been, therefore, more than a children's interest in Korea. The popularity of *Astro Boy* and *Mazinger Z* was closely tied to both economic and political conditions in Korea during the 1970s and 1980s. The robot characters and narratives of postwar Japanese animation corresponded to many of Korea's propagandistic ideals over the decades' strong work ethic, overly euphemistic view of technology and futurism, Cold War anxiety, and nationalism. The development of toy culture became part and parcel of the dominant visual culture of the 1970s and 1980s in Korea, a period of intensive industrialization. Moreover, the creation of *Taekwon V* and its relationship with *Mazinger Z* is significant for understanding the postwar reception of Japanese culture in Korea, as *Taekwon V* illustrates the effort of Korean industry to move away from Japanese influence while utilizing what they believe is the "useful role model" that Japanese history and culture provided.

Representing *Astro Boy* in the 1990s: Japanese Animation and "Korean Pop Art"

Astro Boy and *Mazinger Z* exemplify the influence of Japanese animation in the everyday lives of children in Korea during the 1970s and 1980s. In this context, a group of contemporary artists emerged, loosely dubbed the "Korean pop artists" who began appropriating familiar images of animation characters, mostly those associated with *Astro Boy* and *Mazinger Z*.[47] Yi Dong-gi painted "Atomous" as a combination of Japanese Astro Boy and American Mickey Mouse; as mentioned earlier Hyun Tae-Jun also made kitsch replicas of Japanese animation characters that he enjoyed watching on TV during his childhood in the 1970s and 1980s.

From the 1990s onward, the primary purpose of the Korean pop artists was to question the consistency of cultural identity by appropriating imagery from popular culture, mostly imported from Japan or the United States. In a way, their artistic production came to celebrate cultural hybridization—that is, how foreign developments in arts and popular culture were appropriated and copied yet continuously revised to the point of having confused origins. Yi's Atomous, for instance, represents a fluctuation among the influential forces of Japanese and American art and culture in postwar Korea.[48] The consistent transformation of the Atomous character also implies its indeterminate nature. Likewise, Hyun placed Astro Boy's face on top of Superman's body. According to Hyun, the mixed state of his replica follows the typical manner of making children's toys in Korea during the 1970s; toymakers recycled the bodies and faces of superheroes in order to save on production costs.[49]

For Yi and Hyun, *Astro Boy* and *Mazinger Z* represent the state of "old" technology at a time when the process of industrialization and the development of a consumer society were still in their nascent stages in Korea. With its strong moral message of good versus evil and the clumsily drawn images, *Astro Boy* might not seem as refined and sophisticated as *Pokémon* and *Yukio*, the animation and game characters that became international phenomena during the 1990s. In light of the rapid succession of newer animation and games, *Astro Boy* and *Mazinger Z* can no longer serve as symbols of a futuristic vision; they are part of a visual culture of the past that is no longer popular in Korean society. These characters have dual meanings for the generation of Korean artists who grew up with *Astro Boy* and *Mazinger Z*. They are comforting and cuddly robotic characters closely linked to their personal memories. At the same time, these characters are problematic, given their strong association with the history of modernization, industrialization, and nationalistic fervor in Korea during the 1970s and 1980s.

One area that most effectively attests to the nostalgic qualities of these characters is Hyun's toy collection. In addition to being an artist and illustrator, Hyun is known for his huge archive of toys, which has become two separate toy museums. "The Center for the Boys and Girls of the 20th Century," located in Heyri, first opened in 2007; the rest of his collection went to the "Pul-la-la Archive" in the Hongik University area in 2009. In his *Toy Diary of the Middle Aged Man* (2002), Hyun recorded his journey to find rare toys, including toys representing animation characters popular in Korea during his childhood. The images of local stationeries mostly located in the old and less developed neighborhoods of Seoul and its vicinity are juxtaposed with the artist's writings in order to convey a sense of historical accuracy, and, above all, nostalgia. The majority of his collection originated from flea markets or from the owners of the closed stationeries when children were no longer purchasing the character toys of animation that had been popular during the 1970s and 1980s.

The artist also installed a huge glass wall beside a long aisle at his 2006 one-person show, which allowed the viewer to examine visual artifacts from the past—mostly cheap, small toys, magazines, and other ignoble items frequently found in neighborhood stationeries during the 1970s and 1980s. Aligning himself with the American pop artists of the 1960s, Hyun—and, for that matter, the rest of the Korean pop artists—became less interested in devising his own artistic themes or styles than in appropriating visual artifacts borrowed from his childhood memories. He did not believe in the sacred nature of originality in fine arts, not to mention the age-old distinction between high art and low popular culture.

Apart from their nostalgic reaction to long-gone superheroes, Yi and Hyun shared critical insights on typical postwar Japanese animated superheroes. Yi's series of Atomous paintings demonstrates the slight yet consistent transformation of the character; at one point, its overall contour becomes fuzzy, as if the face had begun to melt and disappear.[50] The whole process appears to be a metaphoric emblem, in that his Atomous character begins losing its power and fading into oblivion. In *Brands* (2003), a stark black sky is filled with famous multinational brand logos, and a sense of futility over freedom dominates the painting. While the message remains unclear, the critical theme of "global" economy is unmistakable. Likewise, Kim Seok is known for his treatment of superheroes in religious context; he identifies Mazinger Z, among others, with Jesus Christ hung on the cross. Kim has also depicted Taekwon V as a hero who has run out of energy and can do nothing but sit helplessly at the dinner table. Interestingly enough, he depicted Mazinger Z in unrefined natural wood, defying its original structure made of fictitious and invincible "Super Alloy Z."

Humanized as they seem, these characters are used to challenge the mythic dimension of superheroes. In Hyun's one-person show in 2007, most of the displayed objects are also trivial and intentionally unnatural. Superman's overblown muscles and shoulders of his replica do not match with Astro Boy's face at all. This rather degraded and depreciating way of presenting trivial objects in a museum complicates their artistic intention. Hyun also juxtaposed a poster that he painted as a reminder of the authoritarian culture under the military dictatorships. During the 1970s and 1980s, most schoolchildren in Korea were required to submit posters about various social issues, and one of the most frequently assigned themes was anticommunism. There was a fixed format in which students placed images in the middle and placed short phrases, which functioned as proverbs, at the top or bottom. Hyun revisited this format and cited the famous phrase "report 113," a number specially designed for reporting spying activities of communists or pro-communists in Korea. Beneath this line, he placed the incongruous image of couples kissing in darkness.

Therefore, the characters of Astro Boy and Mazinger Z have contained meanings deeply associated with the visual culture of the 1970s and 1980s; they were indeed the icons of a period when rapid industrialization was at full scale. At the same time, Korean pop artists used the *Astro Boy* and *Mazinger Z* images as tools to convey their oblique perspective toward the extremely authoritarian, repressive social context of the 1970s. The painted and molded copies of *Astro Boy* in the artwork of Yi and Hyun remind viewers of the awkwardness of the naive belief in technological progress; Hyun's poster that makes fun of the fanatical search for North Korean spies evokes the repressive social atmosphere pervasive under the military dictatorship of the 1970s and 1980s in South Korea.

Conclusion: "High-Tech World," Nostalgia, and Science Education in Korea

While most discussions about the reception of Japanese popular culture in Korea have relied on the vague notions of cultural proximity or the violent nature of Japanese popular culture, this paper has attempted to offer historical context that contributes to a better understanding of the cultural exchange between Korea and Japan. The Japanese economic miracle, which was believed to rely on a strong work ethic and education in math and science, served as a feasible role model for the rest of the Asian countries. Without a doubt, Japan was one of the most influential countries for postwar Korea, in that it set high standards for transferring Western economic and technological development into a non-Western context.[51] The widespread influence of the animations *Astro Boy* and *Mazinger Z* in Korea can thus indicate the overlapping economic and ideological concerns shared by Korea and Japan—rather than a mere cultural or market invasion.

As the title "Growing up with *Astro Boy* and *Mazinger Z*" suggests, these characters continue to occupy important places in the memories of Koreans who were brought up with these characters during the 1970s and 1980s. The popularity of *Astro Boy* and *Mazinger Z* in contemporary art proves that Japanese animation offered iconic images, although the underlying message of Korean pop art remains vague and obscure. On the one hand, there was a persistent interest in robots in both nations, illustrating the perpetual legacy of technophilia; namely, a utopian vision of high technology. On the other hand, the martyred heroes (Astro Boy, Mazinger Z, Taekwon V) in Kim's work pushed robot heroes into the past or brought them into the realm of less-than-perfect superheroes.

Considering the dual meanings of Japanese animation characters, should Yi's *Atomous* be interpreted as straightforward criticism of the cultural colonialism of Japanese animation, or should it be seen as making a distanced and neutral reference to the 1970s visual culture in Korea? Korean pop artists' treatment of Japanese animation characters may seem to be parodying the nationalistic obsession with technological advancement through which the popularity of *Astro Boy* emerged in Korea. Their ambiguous attitude toward *Astro Boy* and *Mazinger Z*, however, also evinces their nostalgia for an era known for the simple fascination with science and technology among children in Korea.

Korean pop artists' attitude toward popular Japanese animation characters concurs with the dual policy of math and science education in Korea during the twenty-first century. Educational practitioners in Korea have been emphasizing creativity and methodologies borrowed from nonscientific areas of research as alternatives to traditional education in math and science, but the obsession with a futuristic vision, high technology, and centralized and nationalistic concerns seems to be intact. In 2007, *Chosun Ilbo* (one of the major newspapers) gave special coverage to science education in Korea. The article compared national rankings of PISA (Program for International Student Assessment) scores in science for fifty-seven nations. As the title "Science education falls from 1st to 11th" suggests, Korea scored first place in 2000 but subsequently fell into fourth place in 2003 and eleventh place in 2006.[52] What is interesting in this article is not the seriousness of the predicament that science education is supposedly facing in Korea, but the tone of anxiety with respect to the current state of science education upon which the future of the nation depends.

Finally, the cover image used for The Center for the Boys and Girls of the 20th Century is a pertinent example of this incoherent view toward the optimistic vision of scientific innovation and technological development

1. The commercial "Rocket Boy" for Honam Electronic Company.

2. *Atomous*, acrylic on canvas, 100 x 100 cm, 1993 by Yi Dong-Gi. Reprinted by permission from Yi Dong-Gi.

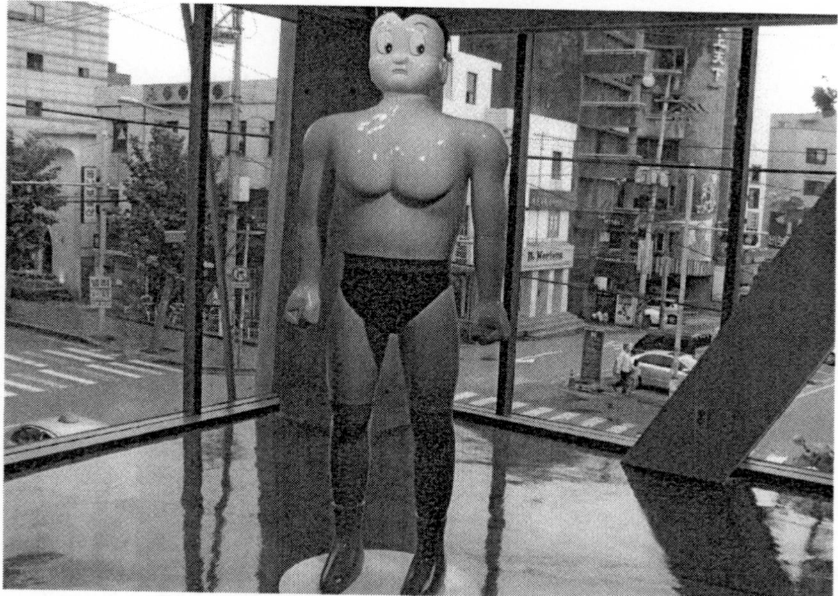

3. *Astro Boy Atom* model by Hyun Tae-Jun at "A Show of the Products Made in Korea," 2008. Photograph by author.

in Korea from the 1990s and onward. On the poster, boys and girls are supposed to symbolize the nation's future, as the dual nature of the title of the twentieth century clearly sets the tone. For members of the postwar generation in Korea who grew up watching *Astro Boy* and *Mazinger Z*, this poster and the classical robot characters in Japanese commercial manga-influenced animation still represent a futuristic vision. The outdated images as brilliantly chosen and displayed by Hyun, however, fluctuate between past and future, between low-tech nostalgia and futuristic hope. The propagandistic traits of the poster reinforce its outdatedness. The young boys and girls gazing in one direction resonate with the propagandistic nature of the poster. The poster image calls the viewer's attention to a futuristic vision of science that can be regarded as something that is deeply nationalistic and outdated yet no longer straightforwardly optimistic. It reminds the viewer of the nostalgic return to the futuristic vision that postwar Korean society continued to teach and to transmit to "future" generations.

Notes

1. Throughout the paper, the country Korea means South Korea. The title of *Ujusonyun Atom*, meaning "Astro Boy Atom," is a combination of the original Japanese title of "Mighty Atom" and the American title of "Astro Boy." The Korean Broadcasting Company might have been reluctant to use the original title in Japanese due to the anti-Japanese sentiment that exists in Korea.

2. Osamu Tezuka, *Tetsuwan Atomu*, Sunday Comics ed., vol. 3 (Tokyo: Akita Shoten, 1999–2000), 213–14; cited in Frederik Schodt, *The Astro Boy Essays: Osamu Tezuka, Mighty Atom, and the Manga/Anime Revolution* (Berkeley, CA: Stone Bridge Press, 2007), 20.

3. Schodt, *The Astro Boy Essays*, 19–20.

4. According to the four stages of opening the Korean market to Japanese popular culture, the official importation of Japanese movies, including animation in 1998, would follow the importation of printed materials in September 1999. Beginning in June 2000, animation films that had won critical acclaim and prizes at international film festivals could be opened in Korean theaters. The entire domestic market for animation would be open to Japanese productions in 2004. For the summary of President Kim's announcement, see Han Bum-Su, "The Opening of Japanese Popular Culture" (2006), a report uploaded at National Archive of Korea, http://contents.archives.go.kr/next/content/listSubjectDescription.do?id=003611&pageFlag=A (Accessed on December 1, 2006) (Korean).

5. While one of the five basic principles of improving cultural interaction between Japan and South Korea, as pronounced in Kim's plan, was to prohibit political conflicts and interests that interfered with the process of cultural interaction, this was hardly realized. In July 2001, with the controversies over the Japanese history, the Korean government temporarily postponed its plan to allow its domestic market to import Japanese popular songs, television shows and dramas, videos, and movies for audiences over eighteen years old. "Government Decision to Revenge for Japanese Distortion of Histories," *Hangyurae* (July 12, 2001); http://www.hani.co.kr/section-003100002/2001/07/003100002200107121739045.html (Accessed on July 12, 2001) (Korean).

6. Cited in Han, "The Opening of Japanese Popular Culture." See note 4.

7. With Japanese popular culture officially imported into Korea, publishers and distributors of media products in Korea were required to fully acknowledge the original Japanese producers by including the artists' names and original titles in their products.

8. Han Kyung-Gyu, "The Assessment Problem of Japanese Culture," in *Report of Public Forum on the Issues of the Opening toward Japanese Popular Culture* (Seoul: Korea Culture and Tourism Institute, Cultural Industry Research Division, 1994), 18–19 (Korean). According to Han, the opening might bring the reform of how Japanese cultural products become circulated in Korea rather than considerably accelerating cultural interactions between the two nations.

9. *Manwha Monitor* YWCA, cited in Noh Su-Een, "Japanese Manga: How Can We Read It?: From Their Culture to Our Culture," a paper presented at "Research Methodology in History of Journalism" (Seoul: Soekang University), http://moongsil.com/study/manga.htm (Accessed on September 5, 1998) (Korean). The notable studies about the influence of Japanese animation in Korea include Jung Mun-Sung's work, "Studies on the Influence of Japanese Popular Culture on Korean Youths," *The Studies on Korean Youth*, 3, no. 4 (1992): 19–33 (Korean).

10. The theory of cultural proximity can be used by those who protest the opening of the Korean market to Japanese popular culture as well as by those who agree with exchange between the two cultures. Those who take the first approach tend to be fearful of the influence of Japanese popular culture on Korean youth, whereas proponents of the second approach, called a "pragmatic approach," tend to have mixed feelings about the influence of Japanese popular culture. For the more informed discussions about the different approaches of protectionist (nationalist) and of pragmatist (industrialist), see Noh, "Japanese Manga: How Can We Read It?" n.p.

11. The popularity of Korean drama (*Hallyu*) in Asian countries (including Japan) during the late 1990s can be seen as a counterexample to the dominant influence of Japanese popular culture in Korea, but Korean scholars still acknowledge a huge influence of Japanese television programs such as dramas and entertainment programs on their Korean counterpart over the last four decades; see Song Do-Young, "The Hybridity of Korean Popular Culture and the Discourse about 'Hallyu,'" *Damron* [Discourses] 9, no. 4 (2007): 40; 58 (Korean).

12. Han, "The Assessment Problem of Japanese Culture," 14–41 (Korean).

13. The efforts to associate the influence of Japanese popular culture in Korea with invasion dominated the media coverage of Japanese manga and animation in Korea. One example is "Cultural Invasion initiated by Manga," in *Joongang Ilbo* (a daily newspaper in Seoul), March 1, 1996 (Korean). Compared to censorship of Japanese manga and animation in other Asian countries, the censorship in Korea was largely led by nongovernmental organizations. John Lent, "Comics Controversies and Codes: Reverberations in Asia," in *Pulp Demons: International Dimensions of the Postwar Anti-Comics Campaign*, edited by John Lent (Teaneck: Fairleigh Dickinson University Press, 1999), 179–214.

14. From 1970 until 1979, the number of houses in South Korea with a television increased more than thirteen times. However, there was a serious imbalance between the production of television monitors and that of domestic programs. Ironically, the *Yushin* regime of the Park administration (1972–1979) applied strict censorship to all artistic and cultural productions in order to limit the mass media as a potential means of propagating critical views toward its domestic and foreign policies while encouraging the importation of foreign popular culture. Kang Jun-Man, *The Roadmap for Our Popular Culture* (Seoul: Gaema Gowon, 1998), 36 (Korean).

15. During the 1970s, the three major networks—TBC, MBC, and KBS—were dominated by imported programs. Between 20 and 30 percent of all movies played

on TV were imported from the United States. Lee Dong-Hoo, "A Local Mode of Programme Adaptation: Korea in the Global Television Format Business," in *Television Across Asia: TV Industries, Programme Formats and Globalisation*, edited by Michael Keane and Albert Moran (London: Routledge, 2004), 38.

16. The original Japanese names and locales were obscured in most imported Japanese animation in the United States and Europe, a practice that was pervasive in South Korea until the late 1990s. For adaptations of Tezuka's animations in South Korea, see Schodt, *The Astro Boy Essays*, 89.

17. Important Japanese audio-visual products—what Iwabuchi calls the three Cs: consumer technologies, comics and cartoons, and computer/video games—are devoid of clear association with what he characterizes as Japanese cultural "odor." Iwabuchi Koichi, *Recentering Globalization: Popular Culture and Japanese Transnationalism* (Durham, NC: Duke University Press, 2002), 24–28.

18. For a study about Park's diplomatic policy as part of his reconstruction plan, see Kim Hyung-A, *Korea's Development under Park Jung Hee: Rapid Industrialization, 1961–79* (London: Routledge, 2004), especially chapter 8.

19. Tezuka Osamu, "Robot Technology and the World of Mighty Atom," *Journal of the Japan Robotics Society* 4, no. 3 (June 1986): 103; cited in Schodt, *The Astro Boy Essays*, 107.

20. Schodt, *The Astro Boy Essays*, 115.

21. Ibid., 108. The optimistic image of human/robots such as Mighty Atom introduced to the postwar generation in Japan had a significant impact on the Japanese fascination with robot phenomena: Honda's "Asimo" and Sony's dancing "QRIO" robots, underscore the friendly, cute, and user-friendly aspects of their creation. Ibid., 116. This overall positive perception of robots in Japan constitutes an important contrast with the linguistic origin of the term "robot" in the 1920s, which first appeared in a Czechoslovakian play entitled *Rossum's Universal Robots*. *Robot*, in Czechoslovakian, denotes a slave, and later became applied to a machine having an anthropomorphic shape but lacking a human soul or destroying human civilization, an image that had already been predicted in Mary Shelley's novel *Frankenstein* in the late nineteenth century.

22. Cited in Schodt, *The Astro Boy Essays*, 121.

23. Ibid., 131; according to Schodt, Tezuka's publishers and readers were eager to have a peaceful version of Atom, sometimes contrary to the author's own intention. Ibid., 115.

24. Tezuka explained that the gloomy depiction of science and technology partly reflected the period of the late 1960s. Cited in ibid., 121–22. Tezuka's treatment of the Mighty Atom's relationship to the atomic bomb during the postwar years may have reflected Japan's ironic relationship with atomic energy in particular and technological development in general.

25. Ibid., 73.

26. Particularly, ESS (Education and Science Society), an educational program of science, social studies, and math developed by EDC (Education Development Center,

Inc.), was accepted as the official framework for further research on the science curriculum and textbooks for kindergarten through eighth grade in Korea.

27. The joint financial support from UNESCO (United Nations Educational, Scientific, and Cultural Organization) and UNICEF was largely initiated by the regional meeting for the reformation of science education in Asia, first held in Thailand in 1968, which made an important announcement about the worldwide effort to change basic educational policy and philosophy regarding science.

28. "Science Education in Korea," in EnCyber & EnCyber.com (on-line encyclopedia), http://100.naver.com/100.nhn?docid=723881. Copyrighted date: October 19, 2010 by Doopedia.

29. Shin Jang-Sup, "High-Tech Industrialization and Local Capability," in *The East Asian High-Tech Drive*, edited by Yun-Peng Chun and Hal Hill (Cornwall, UK: MPG Books, 2006), 112.

30. *Statistical Year Book*, 1995 (World development indicators), cited in ibid., 112.

31. Hyun, interview with author, 2008, n.p.

32. The Center for Children was first opened in 1974. It has now been renovated and is used as a wedding hall.

33. Hyun, interview with author, 2008, n.p.

34. In the 2009 Hollywood remake, the color contrast became more obvious than in the original, as the robot is powered by a blue energy source, while President Stone wants to obtain the dangerous "red core" to achieve full control over the city.

35. Cited in Schodt, *The Astro Boy Essays*, 136. Tezuka's manga episode "The Angel of Vietnam" (1967–69) is the most obvious example of his antiwar position during the late 1960s. His antiwar spirit may shed light upon his ambiguous relationship with the United States and the Cold War ethos.

36. As Sun An-Na, the author of *The Children's Literature and Anti-Communism* states, throughout the postwar literature, anticommunism was the most powerful tool in sustaining commercialism of the media and the publishing industry, on the one hand, and the conservative political ideology of government on the other. Sun An-Na, *The Children's Literature and Anti-Communism* (Seoul: Choengdong Geoul, 2009), especially chapter 3 on anticommunism and children's literature (Korean).

37. During the 1970s, the broadcasting companies were obliged to imbue anticommunist themes in TV programs for children. For a brief introduction to the censorship and legal stipulate for the media and films under *Yushin*, see Kang Jun-Man, *Strolling Modern Korean History: The 1970s*, vol. 2 (Seoul: People and Thoughts, 2002), 23–30 (Korean).

38. The military strategies during the Cold War era in Japan and Korea could not have been identical, as Japan was fundamentally not allowed to have its own military troops due to Article 9 of the Japanese Constitution. In addition, the Japanese people had also learned from the past that military power alone cannot guarantee their security. Thomas Berger, *Culture of Anti-Militarism: National Security in Germany and Japan* (Baltimore: Johns Hopkins University Press, 1998), especially chapter 2.

Nonetheless, both South Korea and Japan shared the similar geopolitical circumstances in East Asia and the post–Cold War era; they both continued to rely heavily on the economic and military power of the United States and to face the consistent militaristic threat of North Korea.

39. The character Mazinger Z opened up a new era of the super-robot character. The anime *Mazinger Z* had a total of ninety-two TV episodes in Japan from 1972 to 1974, and episode 68 broadcast on March 17, 1974, achieved the series' highest rating of 30.4 percent. *Astroganger* is another super-robot animation aired simultaneously with *Mazinger Z* in Japan between 1972 and 1973. Created by Knack Productions, Astroganger is characterized by its human traits of feeling pains and winning the battle with its agile bodily movements and spirit. *UFO Robot Grendizer* or *Grendizer* in short was first broadcasted in Japan between 1975 and 1977. It was Nagai Gō's third entry in the Mazinger trilogy, best remembered as one of the first Japanese animations that won huge success in Europe and Canada.

40. In his animated version, Nagai minimized the violent elements of his original manga and concentrated on the weapons of the super robots and the power of Super Alloy Z. However, after episode 25, *Mazinger* Z was temporarily censored in Korea due to the controversy over the violent fighting between the robots. When the program *Mazinger* Z was resumed in 1977, it gained more popularity.

41. Although *taekwondo* evolved into a modern sport under the first administration of Yi Seung-Man, it was under the Park administration during the 1970s that it became the national sport and highly politicized by the media and sports education in Korea. Yi Ok-Hun, "The Comparative Approach toward the National Sport Policy between the third and fifth Republics in Korea" (Master's thesis, Graduate School of Education, Youngnam University, Daegue, 2002) (Korean).

42. Park Joon Magnan, "Our Toys, Our Selves: Robot *Taekwon V* and South Korean Identity," a talk in conjunction with the exhibition "Toy Stories: Souvenirs from Korean Childhood"; paper presented at The Korean Society, New York, February 7, 2008.

43. During the 1970s, there was also the overall shift of industry in the international economy. Major industrialized countries of the West began focusing on high-tech industries such as semiconductors rather than the steel industry, which required a relatively high concentration of labor and resources to minimize the problems with pollution. Kang, *Strolling Modern Korean History: The 1970s*, 15–22.

44. Team for Robot, Future Life and Industry under The Ministry of Industry and Resource (currently "The Ministry of Knowledge and Economy"), "The New Effort of Ministry of Industry and Resource: The Meeting between Robot Industry and Cultural Industry," a pamphlet, published on July 1, 2006 (Seoul: Korean Development Institute, Center of Economic Information, 2006), n.p. (Korean).

45. Rudi Volti, *Technology Transfer and East Asian Economic Transformation* (Washington, D.C.: American Historical Association/Society for the History of Technology, 2002); booklet.

46. President Park Jung-Hee also embarked on the conservation project of Temple "Bulguksa," located in Gyungju, the old capital of the Shilla dynasty. During the 1970s,

scholars recovered various natural treasures and structures that were on the verge of destruction during the Japanese occupation. Shin Eun-Je, "Making Memories under the Park Administration and General Yi, Sunshin," in *Imagining the Nation in Modern Memories and History* (Seoul: Sejong Publication, 2006), 97–132 (Korean).

47. In Korea, the genre of pop art was given to a group of then-emerging artists who appropriated images from popular culture in graphic and Warholian fashion from the 1990s onward. Unlike American pop artists of the 1960s, whose subject matter reflected the beginning of postwar consumerist culture in the United States, Korean pop artists concentrated on the "borrowed" images of Japanese and American popular cultures. Such choices of subject matter can be also interpreted as a reaction against the preceding generation of artists in Korea, also known as "Minjoong Misool (Art for People)" artists, who were opposed to popular or mass culture imported from America. Considering the extended art historical and cultural theories underlying their appropriation of popular images in a non-Western context, You Kyung-Hee, an art critic, distinguished Yi Dong-Gi from the usual definition of pop art or K-pop, categorizing him instead as a neo-conceptual artist. You Kyung-Hee, "Rethinking Parody and Pastiche," *Art in Culture* (October 2003): 51 (Korean).

48. The shape of Atomous as the combination of the pointy hair of Mighty Atom and circular shapes of Mickey Mouse is consistently evolving from its debut in the art world in 1993. Regarding the extremely nomadic and rootless nature of his character as the emblem of cultural hybridization in Korea, refer to Koh Chung-Hwan, "Contemporary Art through the Lens of Iconic Characters," *Critics' Club* (on-line); http://www.daljin.com/2004/_main/critique/contents/contents.detail.php?code_critique=G01&code=C00330&nPage=4&dal=56c2a1b02302fcbcf0c20f986166f6ee (Accessed on May, 2006) (Korean).

49. These cheap toys were still good companions for Korean children during the country's rapid industrialization. Nonetheless, these plastic models of animation characters were soon replaced by more sophisticated and expensive Japanese originals and games throughout the 1990s in Korea. Hyun Tae-Jun, interview with author, 2008, n.p.

50. Before inventing "Atomous," Yi Dong-Gi had painted numerous media images involved with consumerism, such as a portrait of Shin Chang-Won, a fugitive from prison who became an instant celebrity. Shin's notoriety with vanity and fashion fascinated people while he was on the loose. Yi called his work "non-objective," as its meaning does not arise from the author, arguably the ultimate origin of his creation. Kim Jong-Ho and Ryu Han-Seung, *Young Contemporary Artists in Korea: Interview with 45 Artists (*Seoul: Da Vinci Project, 2006), 145 (Korean).

51. In Japan, this went back to the classic idea that the Japanese spirit should be combined with Western abilities—namely, Western technologies—throughout the Meiji Revolution. Through technology, the Japanese adaptation of Confucianism could be developed into a new form of nationalist philosophy. Morishima Michio, *Why Has Japan "Succeeded"? Western Technology and the Japanese Ethos* (Cambridge: Cambridge University Press, 1984), 18. (Morishima's book, written in the 1980s, appears to be

outdated, given the relatively long economic recession in Japan from the 1990s onward and the serious technological deficiencies in a series of cars produced by Toyota in 2010.)

52. The author added a sense of urgency, arguing that the future of the national economy has been largely dependent upon the level of science and math education. "Science education falls from 1st to 11th," *Chosun Ilbo* (editorial), December 2, 2007 (on-line); http://news.chosun.com/site/data/html_dir/2007/12/02/2007120200628.html (Accessed on December 2, 2007) (Korean).

From Haiku and Handscroll to Tezuka

Refocusing Space and Camera in the Narrative of Animation

—**Kenny K. N. Chow**

Space versus Time in Art

In the Western tradition, the art of discourse reflects the Aristotelian notion of mimesis and diegesis. In Greek, the former literally means "imitation" and the latter "narrative." In a contemporary context, imitation is manifested by "showing" in the visual or performing arts or by description in verbal forms. Narrative is usually related to the act of "telling," or narration. The dichotomy seemingly corresponds to the orthogonal relationship between space and time, in showing a collection of interests over a space and telling a sequence of items along a timeline. This concept prevails in most conventional art forms. For example, we tend to think that paintings are best for depicting spectacles, portraits, or landscapes; sculpture is an effective means of presenting shapes, shades, and textures; written and spoken texts are widely used to recount the happenings of events. It seems that there are certain intrinsic qualities dividing various art forms into "space art" and "time art."

However, some theorists and progressive artists contend with this reductive binary opposition. In his essay about perception of time and movement, the art and film theorist Rudolf Arnheim points out that painting can also be regarded as "time art," because a viewer usually scans the various parts of a painting in succession. The action is very much like reading a written text since neither the eyes nor the mind can process multiple inputs of sense data at the same time (Arnheim, 1974: 376). Sculptures are also looked at from successive points of view determined solely, somehow arbitrarily, by the observer, including those labeled "mobile sculpture," exemplified by Alexander Calder's works, in which the sculptor attempts to "carve" movement in space. The viewer is presented with a continuously changing form that is open not at the viewer's disposal but to chance, as named "work in movement" by the semiotician Umberto Eco (Eco, 1962: ix). Some pioneers challenge the linear temporal domain of verbal arts. The French poet Guillaume Apollinaire is famous for his "calligrammes" in which words were arranged to explore every spot on the printed page, and no definite point of entry is specified. The transgression of the spatial domain influenced the development of later concrete poetry.

Character over Space in Animation

With the advent of motion pictures, two orthogonal domains were ontologically combined by modern technology. The film reel symbolizes the linear timeline, while the silver screen represents the picture frame. However, the screen in its infancy was able to display only a framed stage, because in the early days of cinema the camera was clumsy and had to be fixed on filming. This technological constraint engendered a particular cinematic style, sometimes referred as *tableau vivant*, in which the subjects, mostly human figures, enacted very much like as the theatrical arts. The fixed frame immobilized most of the screen area, submerged it into what we called "background," and highlighted the enacting "figure(s)." The audience was directed to focus on the action or happening surrounding the subject. This phenomenon can be seen as an interesting nostalgia for the figure-ground relationship in visual perception. Even at a later time, after the technology advanced and the camera could move, the convention that prioritizes figure and downplays space had already been firmly established. In today's mainstream cinema, camera movement is subservient to character action. Narratives are mostly character-driven and the camera is just a passive observer.

Regarding animation, which is generally seen as a marginal type of film genre, the triumph of character over space is even more a landslide victory. Beginning with Stuart Blackton's animated films, which successfully demonstrated the use of stop-action filming technique for the illusion of animated cartoons, followed by Winsor McCay's well-known Gertie, Max Fleischer's Betty Boop, Walt Disney's Mickey Mouse, and many others, cartoon characters have been the celebrities in American animation. All of them are comparable to Hollywood's live movie stars. Ironically, we all seem to remember the personality of Donald Duck, but few of us know where he lives, what his place looks like, and what happened there. For instance, Disney animators might be very conscious of creating the illusion of life, but they are prone to overlook the vitality of space. Whether the background or the location is castle, countryside, ranch, family house, or restaurant, the design of space is usually stereotypical (*Monsters Inc.*, [2001] is an exception). Hence, it barely impresses the audience. This issue has also been humorously questioned and challenged by the celebrated American animator Chuck Jones's progressive and self-reflective work *Duck Amuck* (1953), in which Daffy Duck's actions, and thus the plot, are brutally interrupted and helplessly driven by the disruptively changing environments, including costumes, accessories, backgrounds, screen space, and even the frame! Although the work features a major American cartoon character, it is still an alternative piece in that genre.

Conversely, anime, the part of Japanese national cinema that has an increasingly international recognition and influence, exhibits more balance between character and space. Although cartoon characters and robots in anime such as Doraemon, Gundam, Astro Boy, and so on are definitely known to many people from the Asia Pacific, including North America, over a wide range of age groups, the unique settings and spaces depicted in anime also made an impression. For example, we could not possibly forget the imaginary floating "place" in *Laputa: Castle in the Sky* (1986), the bathhouse in *Spirited Away* (2001), the lively building in *Howl's Moving Castle* (2004), and others. In fact, many of Miyazaki Hayao's works have the plots closely tied with the locations. In *Spirited Away*, the protagonist Chihiro is trapped in the bathhouse and shuttled between different apartments. Each scene narrates some particular happenings in a particular place, which is then connected to the next through a bizarre corridor or eccentric path. The whole of Chihiro's journey is the plot, not unlike the storyline of a computer adventure game. The audience following Chihiro to travel the story world is like a particular player in the adventure game. Therefore, they remember the places no less than the characters and the events. In Miyazaki's work, the place usually has a role in the narrative as important as the character and the event. This location-based approach to narrative is more commonly employed in anime than in American mainstream animation. One might wonder why Western mainstream animated films are mostly character focused while anime can be more space oriented. I argue that the phenomenon is related to the more holistic Eastern visual culture. From the pictographs and ideographs in

Chinese characters and Japanese *kanji* to the multi-perspectival Chinese paintings, people of the East are accustomed to a more associative, analogical, and spatial perception; a more spatial way of thinking built upon everyday perceptual experience[1] is preferred to a linear and analytical one. To illustrate my point, I would introduce several cultural artifacts from different disciplines of the arts—namely, Japanese *haiku* poetry, Chinese handscroll painting, and some experimental animation films by Tezuka Osamu (1928–1989). These works exemplify the location-based narrative with both the comprehensive space design of the story world and the meticulous arrangement of the camera.

Japanese Poetry

The first cluster of cultural artifacts includes *haiku*, together with many of its cousins in Japanese poetry. The genre roughly emerged in the seventeenth century as a form of linked-verse poems, each of which was usually a long piece composed by a group of poets collaboratively. At the time of the celebrated poet Matsuo Basho (1644–1694), people tended to single out one verse and imposed vigorous rules on the form and content. The verses must follow a 5-7-5 phonetic pattern and the subject matter was restricted to nature, seasons, and human emotions. Later the themes covered a wider range and the art form remained popular in a more global context. Today the shortest form is called *haiku* and the linked form *renku*. Meanwhile, this peculiar literary art has received attention from the visual domain, because many pieces are praised for their fullness of metaphorical images that provoke a reader's emotions. For example, the following is one of Basho's masterpieces (Higginson, 1996: 51–53):

Rough sea
lying toward Sado Island
the River of Heaven

Literally, the verse describes an image: There is a rough sea between the author and Sado Island, just like the one between him and the Milky Way overhead. The cognitive linguist Hiraga Masako explicates the metaphor in the text and points out the analogy: The separation from someone on the island is compared to the distance between heaven and earth (Hiraga, 2005: 8–10). This analogical and spatial relation is parallel to the location-based narrative mentioned above. The places, here including the sea and the island, are used to symbolize the aspect of isolation, echoing Miyazaki's reliance on location in his films. Moreover, the poem is able to present a comparatively subtle camera movement from viewing the sea to looking up into the dark sky.

Renku, the linked-verse form of *haiku,* exhibits even more intriguingly the combination of camera movement and montage through its "link" and "shift," respectively. When composing a piece of *renku,* poets must preserve the linkage between successive verses by referring to certain common objects, environments, sounds, or even scents, in order to ensure a consistent mood. However, too many links might lead to regularity or repetition that poets definitely do not want. Therefore, they sometimes insert shifts, which can be reversals in themes, meanings, or emotions to complement consistency with variety. The art of *renku,* in short, is the balance of convergence and divergence, which can be illustrated by the following excerpt from a piece, again by Basho and his disciples (Higginson, 1996: 51–53):

Around the town
the smells of things . . .
summer moon
(link)
"It's hot, it's hot"—
the voices from gate to gate
(shift)
the second weeding
not yet done, and ears
out on the rice

The quoted verses start the piece with an elevated view of the town, followed by a camera track-down and pan movement to a succession of house gates in a neighborhood. The audience is able to "smell" and "hear" the hotness of the summer. Then, the camera lets the audience jump to a rice field. The audio track seems to transit from human voices to the sound of weeds waving in the field. The shift demonstrates a collision montage of the urban and the rural. A *renku* poem normally consists of thirty-six verses, and the whole piece can be perceived as a cinematic montage sequence, very much echoing Gilles Deleuze's "the movement-image." In his first volume of *Cinema,* Deleuze points out that natural human perception introduces "halts" or "fixed points" in everyday life (Deleuze, 1986: 22–23). We tend to "immobilize" the continuous flow of life, slowing down the intense "flux" of data, in order to think (Colebrook, 2002: 149). Hence, we see time as a connection of those fixed viewpoints within some ordered whole. That is why storyboards are used in narrative film production. He argues that the early cinema reached the movement-image, which frees our perception from fixed viewpoints by means of camera movement and montage. By the same token, the links and shifts in *renku* poetry enable an alternative to the conventional linear form of narrative.

However, the articulation of associated substances and subjects in *haiku* and *renku*, to some conservative narratologists, might not be legitimized as a form of narrative, because it apparently lacks explicit chronological and causal relationships. This view follows the conventional divide of poetry and narrative with which I contend that the two genres just belong to different parts of a continuum of narrative forms. The chronology and causality in a classical story are obviously manifested in a sequence of actions or events. In contrast, the two essential qualities of narrative exist subtly in a *renku* poem through the movement and juxtaposition of the point of view, like the motion camera and montage in the cinematic context. Sometimes, the viewpoint follows an action or event, while at other times it seems to move autonomously. In Basho's work mentioned above, the author's eyes move across the gates freely, and then jump to the field "because of" the sound of the weeds. In other words, the viewpoint is not only a passive observer, but also a protagonist, a character driving the viewer's journey. It conveys what the author saw and did; how he felt and thought, as articulated in the stanza. It immerses its reader (the viewer) in the author's story world, and even invites him to be a character. Hence, every reader experiences a story intended or imagined by the author.

Chinese Handscroll Painting

To further illustrate the entanglement of chronology and spatiality, let us turn to the second artifact: the Chinese handscroll painting. Chinese painting, especially landscape painting, is always said to have a convention of comprising multiple perspectives, as opposed to the linear perspective prevailing in Western art. The multiple vantage points, usually scattered over the canvas, form a constellation of attention points in which a viewer is free to navigate. A particular scan of the scattered attention points by the viewer constitutes a visual journey, like a *renku* poem, and the act also turns the work into a piece of time art. When the order of viewing is structured or arranged by the author, the painting becomes a work of sequential art, as in the case of handscroll painting. The handscroll, a distinguished format in Chinese painting, is an exceedingly long horizontal scroll. The long format not only allows the presentation of multiple points of attentions in a continuous space, but also specifies a particular order of reception from the right to the left. The most well known representative is the Sung Dynasty's *Along the River During the Qing-ming Festival*, the earliest version of which was drawn around the twelfth century, depicting various everyday lives in a city during that glorious period. The viewing experience of the painting parallels a walk-through of the suburban area, through the marketplace, to the main gate at the right end. In Japan, this distinctive type of painting is generally called *emakimono*, which literally means "picture-scroll." A widely mentioned example is a visual adaptation of the classic Japanese novel, *The Tale of Genji*. Japanese scholars regard the peculiar genre as "a form of painting where happenings and events are spoken through the act of illustrating" (Hu, 2010: 27). The animation theoretician Imamura Taihei sees it as an ancestor of manga and anime, and even draws a parallel to film, in that in order to lead the viewer's gaze the film camera moves while the emakimono artist simply changes his painting position (Hu, 2010: 29).

The art historian Wu Hung also compares the viewing of a handscroll to watching a movie, with "shifting moments and loci." He argues that not only does the viewer's gaze move, but the picture, too. The handscroll is literally a moving picture, and the process of viewing duplicates the process of painting (Wu, 1996: 59). I would add that the act of viewing actually simulates the act of panning the film camera. When not in use, a handscroll must be rolled up. On viewing, the beholder unrolls it, not to the end at once, but rather approximately an arm-length at a time. This length roughly defines the size of the viewing frame, which slides over the whole scroll, like the panning action in cel animation. Although the viewer is free to control the pace of the pan, the order of scenes revealed in front of the viewer is still prescribed by the painter. When this order is intended to align with the chronological order of the events depicted in the space, the viewer will experience a location-based narrative. A particular extraordinary work demonstrating this effect is Gu Hongzhong's *Night Entertainment of Han Xizai* created in the tenth century. The painting is a depiction, a narration, and a visual documentary of a notorious banquet held in the mansion of a governor named Han Xizai at that era. The pictorial narrative walks the viewer from a pipa-guitar performance at the dining room, through some small talk in a bedroom, to the eccentric behavior in the sitting room, concluded by the farewell at the entrance. In each of these locations, the host, guests, and female servants are recurrent. When the whole piece of the handscroll is unrolled, one can see that the painting is like storyboards of a moving camera sequence. The only intriguing difference is that the panel frames have already been dissolved from the scenes. Gu creatively utilized the screen panel, which is a traditional Chinese artifact used to divide space in a scene, to define the implicit viewing frame. The dissolution of the frame into the scene manifests the projection of the happenings from the temporal domain to the locations in the spatial domain, thus exemplifying the essence of spatial narrative.

Manga and Anime

The convolution between space and time through the manipulation of the panel has also been the focus of some progressive comic artists. The celebrated manga artist Tezuka Osamu, whose popular works include *Astro Boy*, produced many other experimental pieces that are very unconventional in both subject matter and representation. He never forgets the challenge to break the common practice of panel-based linear storytelling in comic strips. For example, in *Phoenix*, characters intermittently walk across the panels, or even literally "break" the "gutter" between. Adjacent panels might depict a continuous space, but each of them captures a different moment. As in Gu's masterpiece, some panels have the frame removed and the character becomes recurrent in the continuous picture space. All these atypical compositions attempt to tell events with the focus not only on action sequence but also on spatial relationship. The comic theorist Scott McCloud once conducted a formal analysis of Japanese manga, including Tezuka's *Phoenix*, as opposed to American comics. McCloud's result shows that the former statistically demonstrates a more balanced use of different transitions (which are comparable to montage in film), ranging from "action-to-action" to "aspect-to-aspect" (McCloud, 1994: 74–80). In other words, Japanese comic artists are used to "narrating" happenings from multiple points of view. One might attribute this practice to the spatial and nonlinear Eastern visual culture aforementioned, once again resonating with Deleuze's divergent perspective on cinematic perception.

This divergent and holistic perspective in Japanese manga was carried forward by Tezuka in his animated work, *Jumping* (1984). The award-winning work[2] employs a subjective and imaginative movement of the camera. With the cinematic drawing style and sound effects, the viewer is tricked into believing that the camera starts by following a bouncing basketball. The point-of-view (POV) shot then keeps jumping up and down through the whole film and leads the audience through a journey metaphorically encompassing convoluted human issues such as urbanization, erotica, ambition, war, death, and so on. Compared with the temporal visual journey documented in Gu's handscroll painting, the topical bouncing or "jumping" journey differs in that each bounce acts like a "jump" cut in film editing: a discontinuity in time and space, in contrast to the smooth camera pan in the former. In other words, the two artifacts represent the two fundamental manipulations of a camera for location-based narrative: movement and montage. Camera movement is analogous to character action. Montage can be compared to character sensation and cognition. As the animation scholar Paul Wells puts it, the "jump" in the Tezuka piece reflects the disruptive nature of human perception (Wells, 1998: 78). What the animation narrates is not a sequence of happenings, but rather a stream of consciousness presented as a metamorphosis of space, a peculiar hybrid of camera movement and cut distinguished in the art of animation. Nevertheless, no matter whether it is a series of events or happenings, or a static consciousness, space is still the key vehicle in this kind of narrative, and the camera/viewpoint is a character rather than an observer.

Conclusion

From *haiku*, the Gu handscroll painting, and Tezuka's work, I tracked down a subtle but fundamental difference in discourse in the East and that of the West. The comparatively holistic treatment of dichotomies of character and camera, action and space, happening and consciousness spans verbal, pictorial, and cinematic forms of creative works. This, in essence, is a trait that makes manga and anime so different from their Western counterparts.[3] In recent years, there has been a singular emphasis on character animation prevailing in many schools, especially those in Hong Kong, partly due to the recent worldwide popularity and commercial success of computer-generated imagery. When teaching animation from the East Asian perspective, this recent emphasis on character

1. A student's visual representation of the story about Icarus, a character in Greek mythology.

2. Another student's topographic representation of the fairy tale, *Three Little Pigs.*

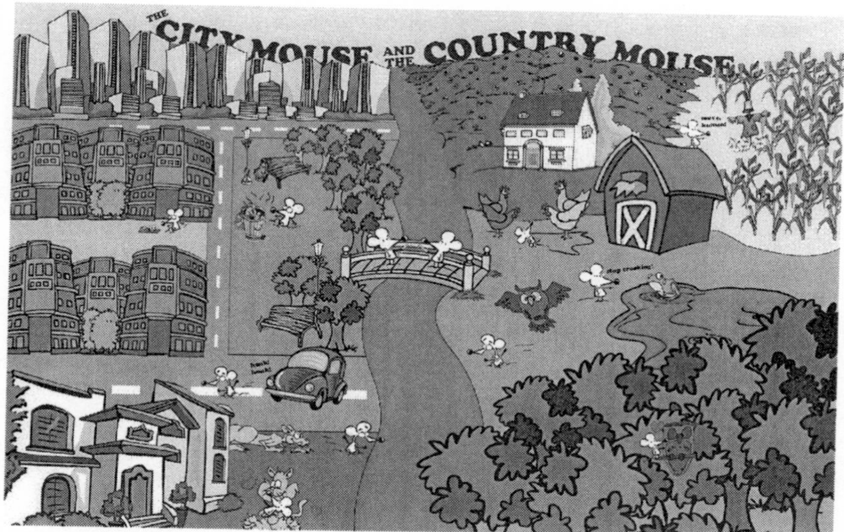

3. A topographic map showing and telling the story of the city mouse and the countryside mouse.

animation does not constitute a holistic meaning (or approach). I propose a complement, called "pan-imation," which turns more of our attention to space, camera, and consciousness. Through movement and montage, the camera is "animated" and acts as a character navigating in space, embodying a consciousness.

With this perspective, I have been designing animation courses focusing on camera and space. I once had a chance to teach a class of American students and guide them to appreciate spatial narrative with respect to the Eastern tradition. The outcome was encouraging.

One of the course projects is based on the pictorial narrative in the Gu painting and other intriguing comic works, like those by the French radical group Oubapo (Potential Workshop for Comic Strips). Students are assigned to tell a myth (based in their original culture) through a topographic map, with the sequence of events projected along the journey in space. The approach echoes the dissolution of frames by Gu and the breaking down of panels by Tezuka. To emphasize the nonlinearity of space, students are encouraged to explore additional narrative paths on the map and to contrive different versions of the myth. The output map works like a spatial storyboard of the possible outcomes in an interactive story world (see Figures 1–3). The learning experience is valuable for them to use on other projects like computer adventure games and interactive narratives.

Another project is about making animated *haiku*. The class is assigned a long *renku* poem. Each student is responsible for transforming one stanza into an animated movie, very much like the collaborative film project *Winter Days* (2003) initiated by the Japanese puppet master Kawamoto Kihachiro.[4] Students are directed to identify the objects, locations, happenings, time of day, and so on in the verses. They have to "picture" the moment, both imaginatively and literally, and describe emotions evoked by the images. The next and crucial stage is to instill the emotion in the camera. Students must animate the camera, using computer applications, to stage and enact the camera with other moving objects. For example, the camera might follow a flying bug and then change to focus on a house in the middle of its course. In short, the viewpoint should seem to have its own consciousness. Last, all student clips are put together in a montage forming a long linked animation in which the camera travels through a variety of spaces and times.

Through these exercises my students have become more aware of the interaction between the dichotomies: character and camera, action and space, happening and consciousness.[5]

Notes

1. About the experientialist perspective of human cognition, readers may refer to the works by George Lakoff, Mark Johnson, and others (Lakoff and Johnson, 1999).

2. The work won Tezuka the Grand Prize at the World Festival of Animated Films in Zagreb, Croatia, in 1984.

3. Here, I mean those Western animations and comics that are widely known to the general public and relatively well received.

4. Editors' note: See also in this collection Yokota's essay on Kawamoto's animation. Readers may also refer to Tze-yue G. Hu's paper, "Japanese Independent Animation: *Fuyu no hi* and Its Exclusivity," *International Journal of Comic Art* 7, no. 1 (2005): 389–403.

5. Editors' note: See the appendix section for the class assignment briefs provided by the author.

References

Arnheim, Rudolf. *Art and Visual Perception: A Psychology of the Creative Eye*. New, expanded and revised edition. Berkeley and Los Angeles: University of California Press, 1974.

Colebrook, Claire. *Understanding Deleuze* (Cultural Studies). Crows Nest, NSW: Allen & Unwin, 2002.

Deleuze, Gilles. *Cinema*. Minneapolis: University of Minnesota, 1986.

Eco, Umberto. *The Open Work*. Translated by Anna Cancogni. Cambridge, MA: Harvard University Press, 1989 (1962).

Higginson, William J. *The Haiku Seasons: Poetry of the Natural World*. 1st ed. Tokyo: Kodansha International, 1996.

Hiraga, Masako. *Metaphor and Iconicity: A Cognitive Approach to Analysing Texts*. Houndmills, Basingstoke, Hampshire; New York: Palgrave Macmillan, 2005.

Hu, Tze-yue G. *Frames of Anime: Culture and Image-Building*. Hong Kong: Hong Kong University Press, 2010.

Lakoff, George, and Mark Johnson. *Philosophy in the Flesh: The Embodied Mind and Its Challenge to Western Thought*. New York: Basic Books, 1999.

McCloud, Scott. *Understanding Comics*. 1st HarperPerennial ed. New York: HarperPerennial, 1994.

Wells, Paul. *Understanding Animation*. London: Routledge, 1998.

Wu, Hung. *The Double Screen: Medium and Representation in Chinese Painting*. London: Reaktion Books, 1996.

SECTION FOUR

Female Characters and Transnational Identities

Grotesque Cuteness of *Shōjo*

Representations of *Goth-Loli* in Japanese Contemporary TV *Anime*

—Akiko Sugawa-Shimada

Introduction

In this chapter I explore two interests: first, the way in which powerful *goth-loli shōjo* (gothic-Lolita girls) in Japanese *anime*[1] in the 2000s are represented to reconsider the changing "femininity" in the contexts of Japanese "postfeminism"; and second, the way in which powerfulness in girls is negotiated with child-like cuteness *kawaii* (one of the Japanese aesthetic values), suggesting a hybrid of masculinity and femininity. By analyzing representations of girl protagonists in the series of *Jigoku Shōjo* (Hell Girl) (2005–2008) and *Death Note* (2006–2007), I argue how these representations are linked to postfeminist *gender-free* (gender-equality) movements and the "*goth-loli* boom" in the 2000s youth culture.

Shōjo is one of the most complicated terms in Japanese pop culture. It not only conveys stereotypical images of female pureness, virginity, vulnerability, romanticism, and nostalgia, but it also represents female strength, decadence, and mysterious power, thereby producing a sense of the grotesque. According to *The Oxford English Dictionary*, grotesque means: "in a wider sense, of designs or forms: characterised by distortion or unnatural combinations; fantastically extravagant; bizarre, quaint" (874). *Shōjo* indeed has been represented with "unnatural combinations" in Japanese visual pop culture. In the above-mentioned anime programs, in particular, *shōjo* serves as a significant site through which positive and negative connotations about women are negotiated.

Shōjo in Japanese anime (which is often referred as *bishōjo* [pretty girl]) has been often characterized as girls with *kawaii* faces with large round eyes and hypersexualized bodies. *Bishōjo* in Japanese anime was negatively connoted in the discourses in the 1980s when *Loli-con*, the Japanese short form for the Lolita Complex,[2] began to be used to depict a pedophilic desire of *otaku* (male fans) toward two-dimensional, young, and cute female anime characters. It is not my intention, however, to discuss representations of *goth-loli shōjo* in the context of otaku culture. My focus is not on how otaku has consumed representations of *goth-loli shōjo* in anime, but on how representations of *goth-loli shōjo* in anime appeared concomitant with the trend of girl's popular fashion and on how they serve as sites in which Japanese postfeminist femininity are traced.

According to *The Oxford Advanced Learner's Dictionary*, femininity is defined as "the fact of being a woman; the qualities that are considered to be typical of women" (2000). In this chapter, however, I use femininity in a wider sense to mean the performances and constructed qualities and perception that are tightly associated with women. *Onna-rashisa* or *joseisei* (behavior, appearances, nature, diction, and elocution that are acknowledged as being feminine) is also included in this term.

Before discussing representations of *goth-loli shōjo* in anime, I will briefly explain Gothic and Lolita fashion in Japanese girl's culture as well as Japanese "postfeminism." "Lolita" fashion generally signifies a dress decorated with frills, a blouse, a headdress, and knee-high socks, which are based on Western aristocrat dresses in the Victorian era. The origin of this fashion first appeared in the 1970s. In the 1980s, Pink House[3] (the fashion label) produced dresses with frilled skirts and blouses with pink or white colors, which became familiar as Western romantic doll-like dresses. However, the term "Lolita fashion" to identify these kinds of girls' fashion was permeated in the next decade (Matsuura, 2007).

Derived from this Lolita fashion, *goth-loli* (a short form of gothic-Lolita) fashion means deftly symbolizes the binary features of *shōjo*[4]: *goth* denoting girls' occultist powerfulness and *loli* signifying girls' romantic cuteness are combined, being most visible in the form of girls in black leather jackets/black dresses with frilled knee-length skirts and bonnets. *Goth-loli* fashion was closely related to the costumes of X (present X Japan) and MALICE MIZER, male rock bands called the "visual type" bands. Japanese "visual type" bands were famous for their high appreciation of appearances: makeup, fashion, bodies, and hairstyles, which have been closely associated with femininity. Their female fans copied their fashion and makeup and went to their concerts (Koizumi, 2003).[5] Mana of MALICE MIZER, in particular, performed to be a long-haired girl in a black dress, a Western antique doll, a Western princess, or a prostitute, depending upon the concepts of their songs (Murota, 2003). The image of his gothic-romance fashion was called "elegant gothic Lolita" (Matsuura, 2007), which was later recognized as "*goth-loli* fashion." Thus, *goth-loli* fashion is symbolized by in-between or hybridity between masculinity and femininity. "Goth" (gothic) is often associated with darkness, decadence, death, and destruction. (Takahara, 2004; Maegawa, 2010). The Japanese *goth-loli* style entails two opposed images: being fearful and mysterious but cute and vulnerable. This fashion crystalizes performing child-like cute femininity and female peremptory policy conducted by girl agency. I will call it "grotesque cuteness."

In Japanese moving images, the grotesque cuteness (that is, being fearful but cute) is actually not a new trend, but it probably originated in 1960s TV anime programs for girls, whose heroines were Western-oriented witch girls, which will be discussed later. However, in recent Japanese pop-culture scenes, *goth-loli* girls serve as a site in which both female power and femininity (including visual feminine-ness and demure feminine behavior) are emphasized more strongly. They also serve to offer a positive image of femininity that challenges and simultaneously negotiates with a Japanese traditional female role model.

Here I should clarify Japanese "postfeminism." Takemura Kazuko (2003) suggests that the term *postfeminism* may be misinterpreted as "after" feminism (implying that feminism ended), or may allow antifeminists to eliminate feminism. However, by using this term instead of alternative terms of third-wave feminism, power relations exercised between women and men, the minority and the majority, and the public and the private can be observed (2003: 1–2). In order to understand this power relationship, I use postfeminism to signify movements and thoughts about gender in which powers are exercised after the late 1990s in Japan.

Japanese postfeminism is probably symbolized by the Basic Law for a Gender-Equal Society enforced in 2000. The Japanese government established the Gender Equality Bureau in the Cabinet Office, which has supported institutions, projects, and conferences organized by local communities in order to promote gender equality (Gender Equality Bureau, 2010). Ratios of public awareness about gender equality were reported as 63.4 percent in schools and educational institutions, 42 percent in the home, and 23.9 percent in the workplace (Cabinet Office, 2007). This partially resulted from renovated school "gender-free"(or gender-equal) education. The "gender-free" education has been exercised primarily through the innovation of curriculums and the change of conventions. Masculinity and femininity were partly nurtured through the curriculum of schools, especially through home economics, which used to exclude male students.[6] Home economics class, however, became compulsory for both boys and girls in public junior high and high schools in 1993 and 1994, respectively.[7]

Another noticeable "gender-free" educational movement was the introduction of a "mixed name list" (class roster), on which all the students' names are listed in Japanese alphabetical order. Japanese schools have traditionally used the class roster in co-ed classes, on which male names and female names were separately listed in alphabetical order, and the male names were located above the female ones.[8] In 1990, the feminist group "Committee for Actions" posited the gender-oriented listing style in schools as gender discrimination. They claimed that it hindered students from fostering a perception of gender equality in schools. Since 2000, the "mixed name list" has been introduced to all levels of schools.[9]

This gender-free education, however, has caused terrible backlash since 2000. Essentially, the term *gender free* was misinterpreted to be a negation of gender differences, allowing its opponents to claim that gender-free education would cause the downfall of masculinity and femininity and lead to societal instabilities (Ueno, 2006). In 2004, the Cabinet Office decided not to use the term gender-free because it was misleading. This policy further led to abstaining from the use of "gender free" in Tokyo as well as closing a public facility for women in Chiba (*Jendā furī fushiyō*, 2006). Therefore, while gender equality has improved in schools and workplaces, the backlash against the gender-free movements has caused a recurrence of conservative perspectives of gender roles, femininity and masculinity in the 2000s. Being both powerful and beautiful is one of the general attributes of Western postfeminist views. Japanese women, however, are still shackled by hegemonic femininity and gender roles, which enabled *goth-loli shōjo* to be represented as a powerful device to subvert hegemonic gender roles and to fulfill girls' desires to become *kawaii* (child-like cute) at the same time.

There are many representations of *goth-loli* girls in contemporary Japanese anime. In representations of *goth-loli* girls, images of death effectively highlight powerful femininity and ephemeral girlhood. In the next section I will explore the way in which *shōjo* is represented in Japanese girl culture to explain what sociocultural meanings have been produced through *shōjo*.

Representations of Shōjo in Japanese Girl Culture

What is a "girl"? In the physical human development, a girl is biologically a female in her prepuberty and adolescence, in between child and adult. However, as Catherine Driscoll (2002: 2) states, the definition of girlhood is always obscure (see also Shamoon, 2009: 132, and Shamoon, 2012: 2–3). The term *girl* is often translated into Japanese, *shōjo*, and occasionally, *onna-no-ko* (female child). The *onna-no-ko* primarily signifies preteen girls; however, it is sometimes used to address young women in relation to men as a verbal taunt or intimacy, since *ko* (child) implies immaturity and inferiority. The usage of *onna-no-ko* in the Japanese language differs from *shōjo* as well. Girls and young girls address themselves as an *onna-no-ko*, but almost never as a *shōjo*.[10] Thus, *shōjo* serves as an agent who is constructed and addressed by the third party (Yokokawa, 1991; Murase, 2000). In other words, *shōjo* has a function of an object, on which negative and positive images can be projected. Because of this attribute of the term, *shōjo* conveys more complicated connotations than the term girl of the English language does.

Japanese "*shōjo* culture" proliferating in the 1920s and 1930s signifies culture having "developed within the private world of girls' schools" (Shamoon, 2009: 133), which was established by segregating girls from the men-dominated society and enclosing them in a female homo-social world. Girls' magazines noticeably served to develop *shōjo* culture in two ways. They provided representations of Western culture by illustrations, novels, and articles. Girl readers created their original networks through exchanging their opinions on communication boards of the magazines and in fan conventions (Satō-Sakuma, 1996). Above all of the other Western countries, French culture was consistently introduced with positive connotations in magazines for girls in the 1920s. As a site where the early girl culture was embedded, girls' magazines in the 1910s, until the 1940s when other media took over, served to offer young women information on Western fashion, modern lifestyle, arts, and ideologies. The four major girls' magazines are *Shōjo no tomo* (*Friends of Girls*, 1908–1955), *Shōjo gaho* (*Girl's Picture Magazine*, 1912–1942), *Shōjo kurabu* (*Girl's Club*, 1923–1962) and *Reijokai* (*The World of Ladies*, 1922–1950).[11]

Reijokai, specifically targeting older-teen girls, featured a special column about France reported by Fukiya Kōji, the popular illustrator, who studied art during the art deco period in Paris in the 1920s (Yayoi Museum and Uchida, 2005: 7). Takabatake Kashou and Nakahara Jun'ichi played leading roles to provide alluring illustrations of girls, through which Western fashion was also introduced. An article with illustrated instructions of Nakahara, for instance, introduced ways of wearing Western clothes as ideal modern girls' fashion. Matsumoto Katsuji, one of the top illustrators and comic artists working for *Shōjo no tomo*, introduced a colorful Disney-type Western illustration style (Yayoi Museum and Uchida, 2006: 32). His motifs such as Western castles and landscapes in the sea and the sky in the exotic background decorated with fantastic images enchanted many girl readers in the 1930s (Endō, 2004: 53–54). Inagaki Kyōko (2007) suggests that girls' novels of Yoshiya Nobuko, the female novelist, which were published in magazines such as *Shōjo no tomo* and *Shōjo kurabu*, caused a surge of popularity among girls. The cover page of her novel, *Hana monogatari* (*Flower Story*, 1916), for instance, was filled with illustrations of art nouveau (69). Although girls' novels were underestimated due to their sentimentalism and romanticism, girl readers took pleasure in reading and appreciating the European illustrations inscribed in them (Inagaki, 2007: 76).

Images of West European culture positively connoted something fashionable, romantic, urban, modern, respectable, and sophisticated. Thus, images of Europe as Western modern culture were permeated throughout the country by visual media for girls, through which "fashion, hairstyle, bags and 'girls' language' were created and shared among girls" (Inagaki, 2007: 213; Kelsky, 2006). Mizutani Masaru published *How to Make Shōjo Poetry* in 1922, in which he notes on the specificity of girls' language in that "girls [had] unique life of mind. [. . .] In other words, girls [had] special sensitivity" (2009 [1922]: 14).

In the late 1920s and 1930s, young women called "modern girl" (or *moga*) were represented by Western clothes and short hair. The modern girl was "the result of a fascination with a fashionable new lifestyle triggered by World War I and the Great Earthquake [in 1923]" (Satō, 2003: 53). Associations between girls and Western representations served to symbolize social transformation at that time (Inagaki, 2007). The Western representations associated with girls were, however, faded out during wartime in the late 1930s and 1940s. In girls' magazines, for instance, illustrations of girls wearing fashionable Western clothes in their front pages were replaced by girls who served as a hard laborer or a fighter in monotonous costumes (Imada, 2007). The number of publications itself decreased due to the lack of paper. Western representations did not recur in girls' magazines and *manga* comics[12] until the postwar period.

To the extent that France had not directly given any traumatic experiences to Japan during the wartime unlike the United States, the UK, and Russia, the Japanese could accept West European culture without ruining their idealized images. Its geographic distance from Japan also helped the West European images to remain as fashionable and sophisticated. As a matter of fact, European imagery was often employed as settings in Japanese manga for girls since the 1950s and anime for girls since the 1960s.[13] As the Japanese economy grew rapidly in the 1960s, representations of the West (or of America) were associated with prosperity, superior status, and fashionableness, which Japanese girls emulated.

In 1963, *Shōjo Friend* and *Margaret*, weekly manga magazines for girls, were founded, which became sites in which young female artists published their manga works.[14] They were full of Western images; for the front pages of these magazines, foreign blonde girls were featured, and along with manga, "reports on journeys in Western countries and lifestyle of Western girls were overwhelmingly introduced" (Yonezawa, 2007 [1980]: 148). TV anime programs aimed at girls, such as *Mahōtsukai sarī* (Sally the Witch, 1966–1968), likewise introduced Western representations from 1966: witches, witchcraft, Western-style houses and lifestyle. *Majokko megu-chan* (Meg the Little Witch, 1974–1975), for instance, is set in an imaginary European city, and the hometown of the heroine of *Hananoko runrun* (*Lulu the Flower Angel*, 1979–1980) is located in southern France. *Candy Candy* (1976–1979) is set in America and Britain in the early twentieth century. Images of the thoroughbred, upright, fashionable, and lady-like are inscribed in narratives of printed and audiovisual works targeting girls.

Thus, elegance, purity, and vulnerability associated with the Western images are typically represented by *shōjo* in Japanese visual culture. This tendency is partly attributed to women's preference to Western fashion and lifestyle and to the fact that "the West" symbolizes the emancipation of women from the Japanese normative gender role. Western representations are also associated with supernatural power in *shōjo*. Although this association is not Japanese exclusive, Western-oriented witches and witchcraft, in particular, exemplify the frequent association between *shōjo* and supernatural power in Japanese popular culture. The next section explores how *shōjo* is associated with supernatural power by explicating the Japanese unique genre of "Magical Girl" (*mahō shōjo*) anime in order to connect it to *goth-loli shōjo* protagonists in anime in the 2000s. When "gothic" elements (fear, decadence, darkness, etc.) are added to Lolita girls (child-like cuteness), girls are represented as more powerful autonomous agents in *mahō shōjo* programs.

Western-Oriented Girls with Supernatural Power—Mahō Shōjo Anime (Magical Girl Animation Programs)

Western-oriented representations of mysterious and monstrous *goth-loli* girls in Japanese moving images may be first found in magical girl TV anime programs in 1966. *Mahō shōjo* anime (magical girl animation) is one of the unique subgenres of Japanese animated works targeting girl audiences. The protagonists are in most cases girls under twelve years old. Some are characterized as born witches (e.g., Meg of *Meg the Little Witch* [1974–75] and Lala-Belle of *Mahō shōjo raraberu* [*Lala-Belle the Magical Girl*, 1980–1981]) or witch princesses (e.g., Sally of *Sally the Witch* [1966–1968] and Chappi of *Mahōtsukai chappī* [*Chappy the Witch*, 1972]). Some are ordinary humans who happen to be granted magical powers as a reward of their good deeds (Akko of *Himitsu no akko-chan* [The Secrets of Akko-chan, 1969–1970] and Yū of *Mahō no tenshi kurīmī mami* [Magical Angel Creamy Mami, 1983–1984]).

Characteristics of witch protagonists of the Japanese *mahō shōjo* anime include nonreligious connotations in contrast to the Western ones. Witches in Western culture have two opposed conventional images. The first is portrayed as a Christian demonic, "old," and ugly female, who ruins good and innocent humans with her wicked magical strength. Especially during the Inquisition a number of women, who were mostly innocent, were falsely prosecuted for their witchcraft and ultimately killed by burning. Witches are stereotypically depicted as having a sharp nose and chin with a big mole and wearing a black pointed hat and a black cloak, which are exemplified by the Queen in Walt Disney's *Snow White and the Seven Dwarfs* (1937) and the Wicked Witch of the West in *The Wizard of Oz* (1939). The other way of portraying the witch is as an active, powerful, and fashionable "young" woman who rescues human beings by solving troubles with her magical powers, which are typified by the Good Witch of the North in *The Wizard of Oz*, the witch in *Cinderella* (1950), and the three fairies in *Sleeping Beauty* (1959), and young Caucasian witches with blonde and blue eyes in *Bewitched* (1964–1972) and *Sabrina, the Teenage Witch* (1996–2003).

In Japanese *mahō shōjo* anime, Western fashionableness and mysterious female power were positively adapted into the characterization of little witch heroines without Christian connotations. Female magical power is mysterious and fearful, but it does not remind Japanese viewers of negative Christian backgrounds. The magical power of girls in these works can symbolize female potential and mysterious strength. Powerful female leads were desired by girl audiences before the introduction of *mahō shōjo* anime. Lili, the female nurse robot, in *Reinbō sentai robin* (Rainbow Team Robin, 1966–1967), for instance, became popular among girl audiences due to her strength and fighting spirit ("*Joji ni ninki no 'onna robotto,'*" 1966).

Simultaneously, their magical power serves to highlight girls becoming fashionable. It is noted that young girls, rather than older teenagers or adult women, are used to project Japanese aesthetic values such as child-like cuteness and immatureness combined with mysterious fashionableness and monstrous strength, which are based on the Western representations of the witches. Representations of *goth-loli* girls also involve the combination of binary opposed images: powerfulness/strength and cuteness/fashionableness. In Japanese anime for girls, *shōjo* protagonists who are powerful and *kawaii* (child-like cute) have continued to attract girl audiences. These types of *shōjo* protagonists are also featured in anime for men. However, distinctive characteristics of *shōjo* in anime for men from those of anime for girls are that they are powerful, child-like cute, and often "hypersexualized," exemplified by fighting girls such as Honey in *Cutie Honey* (1973–1974), and most recently, Nanoha in *Magical Girl Lyrical Nanoha* (2007).[15] The emphasis on hypersexuality of *shōjo* protagonists are often criticized by feminist critics (Saitō, 1998; Murase, 2000). In anime for girl audiences, however, *shōjo* protagonists in general are not overly sexualized, and hence they are not portrayed as sexual objects. This speaks to the high popularity of powerful, cute, and desexualized *shōjo* protagonists in anime for girls among girl audiences.

Goth-loli girl protagonists indeed were not a central tendency in Japanese anime. However, the popularity of *goth-loli* girls among young women typifies girls' admiration for powerful, mysterious, but cute girls. Representations of *goth-loli* girls in contemporary Japanese TV anime serve as a site in which girls' desire for both power and cuteness in Japanese postfeminism can be traced. The next section will examine the way in which their representations of *goth-loli shōjo* configure an alternative female gender identity in relation to the Japanese postfeminist context and sociocultural meanings of female adolescence.

Lolita and/or Gothic Lolita as Performance in the Postfeminist Context

From the late 1980s to the late 1990s, Japan experienced drastic social and economic changes. The Showa era ended with the emperor's demise in 1989, enabling the Japanese to perceive the end of an old time and to anticipate an upcoming new era. Economic growth, or the economic bubble starting in the late 1980s, burst in the early 1990s, however, followed by a long recession. In 1990, Japan's birth rate dropped to 1.57, which was sensationally reported as "the 1.57 shock" in mass media. It was the lowest birth rate since 1947; however, the birth rate dropped further to 1.26 in 2005 (Cabinet Office Director-General for Policies on Cohesive Society, 2009). Women who had not experienced childbirth were often publicly blamed for the low birth rate.[16] In 1995, the Great Hanshin Earthquake and a terrorist attack by the cult group, Aum, in central Tokyo brought social anxiety and instability. Social pessimism caused by these incidents induced people's wish for a societal change. In these contexts, the term "gender" problems started to be alternatively used instead of "feminism" due to the gender-neutrality that the term "gender" connoted.[17] Gender-equality movements in the early 2000s familiarized the term *gender*, which had to do with men, women, and sexual minorities. While feminism was mistakenly regarded as a radical and hazardous ideology related merely to women, the gender problems contained issues of not only women but also men, sexuality, and masculinity and femininity (Ueno, 2006).

After the enforcement of the Equal Employment Opportunities Law in 1986, followed by amendments in 1997, 1999, and 2007, a notion of gender equality in the workplace, outwardly at least, has become established, although gender discriminations have not been eliminated completely. As mentioned above, in 2000, the Basic Law for a Gender-Equal Society was enforced; however, movements for gender equality resulted in a strong backlash.

In this postfeminist context, as briefly mentioned above, so-called visual-type rock bands in show business caused a surge in popularity among young women. Gender-blurring performances of X (X Japan) and MALICE MIZER served to question gender norms. Inoue Takako (2003) suggests that Japanese visual-type rock bands greatly influenced boys' culture in that teenage boys who are even uninterested in rock bands became so conscious about their appearances that they used cosmetics and paid much attention to fashion trend (35). In other words, cosmetics, makeup, and fashion that used to be closely associated with femininity are now also associated with men, which symbolized gender blurring. This enabled girls to be interested in visual-type rock bands. The most significant change in female fans, however, was that they wore *goth-loli* costumes when going to the concerts of their favorite bands. There were substantial numbers of female fans of rock bands already. However, it is noted that many girls showed a strong interest in visual-type rock bands that represented a hybrid of masculinity and femininity. In other words, normative masculinity represented by conventional rock bands no longer fascinated them.

In this sociocultural milieu, gothic Lolita fashion is highlighted in order to display girls' rejection to be controlled by normative femininity and simultaneously their desire for becoming *kawaii*. There are several types of Lolita fashions in Japan: gothic Lolita, sweet Lolita, punk Lolita, and so on. Especially, in the anime programs that have been selected for this paper in Japanese pop-cultural domain after 2004, elegant gothic Lolita serves as a site in which ambivalent configuration of female strength/powerfulness and cuteness/fashionableness (that is, "grotesque cuteness") are represented. A Japanese critic, Takahara Eiri (2007: 13) in *Gothic Spirit* suggests that "*Goth* is possibly carried out even if you are not gothic-Lolita, women in black, possessing dolls, getting into gothic rock music, or familiar with horror novels or movies." Takahara (2006: 9) also defines a "gothic spirit" as not only "expressions of death, the damaged body, [and] horror and decadence" but also "admiration for innocence" and "expressions of such admiration." One of the contemporary Japanese popular anime, the series of *Rozen Maiden* (2004–2006), portrays Lolita girls and a *goth-loli* girl.[18] In the story, seven female living dolls (Reiner Rubin [also known as Shinku], Jade Stern, Lapislazuli Stern, Mercury Lampe, etc.) made by a craftsman, Rozen, who are called "Father," are destined to fight with one another in a contest referred to as the Alice Game, in order to become a perfect and supreme girl called "Alice" for Rozen. They wear Lolita fashion with the exception of Mercury Lampe, who wears a *goth-loli* dress. Shinku's attire, in particular, is a Lolita-like scarlet Victorian dress with frills, a scarlet headdress, and a large green ribbon.

Dolls that speak and walk are often used to generate fear in many horror films.[19] Shinku could be an object of grotesqueness. On the one hand, her elegant fashion and manner mixed with grotesqueness serve to bring about a sense of the sublime, something highly virtuous and awesome. On the other hand, the dolls are destined to become perfect girls for their father, the male creator. The story ends up with the protagonist's withdrawal from the Alice Game. It suggests girls' struggles and negotiations under the control of male domination.

As another instance of *goth-loli* in anime, *Princess Princess* (2006) typically symbolizes gothic Lolita as performance.[20] In the storyline, three beautiful boys, Tōru, Mikoto, and Yūjiro, in a competitive boy's high school are forcefully designated by the students' authority to dress up as princesses to satisfy the fantasy of male students. They are often dressed to be Lolita or *goth-loli*-like girls for the students' requests. The other male students project their fantasized ideal girls on the three boys and enjoy unrealistic male princesses. Higuchi Hiroyuki (2007: 263), the Japanese art critic, argues that *Meido kafe* (Maid Café, or a café in which young waitresses attired in costumes of European elegant maids serve customers as their masters) typifies the way in which Japanese otaku culture consumes the icon of gothic-Lolita. Borrowing the situation set in British aristocracy in the Victorian Era, in the café, (male) customers take pleasure in fantasizing that the waitresses (maids) are in control of them through performing being their masters. Lolita girls are idealized and consumed as demure and submissive females. In a similar manner, representations of (*goth*)-*loli* boy princesses typically display that ideal girlhood is performatively constructed through Lolita or *goth-loli* as icons to the extent that male domination and control are inscribed in the figures.

Thus, on the one hand, (gothic) Lolita *shōjo* in these anime often represented a site through which idealized girls are constructed by male fantasy. On the other hand, despite these stereotypical representations, *goth-loli shōjo* also serve as a site in which girls' power/strength and cuteness/fashionableness are positively represented in order to avoid being controlled by male gaze. I focus on the latter case of representations of *goth-loli shōjo* because the positive representations of *goth-loli* serve to crystallize how *goth-loli shōjo* in anime represent that girls "choose" to have both strength and child-like cuteness rather than to be consumed as idealized sex objects. The element of "goth," in particular, entails horrific and monstrous power that threatens the idealized Lolita model. The next section will discuss how *goth-loli* girls are represented as positive power and "grotesque cuteness" in the series of *Hell Girl* and *Death Note* and how these representations differ from those in *Rozen Maiden* and *Princess Princess*.

The Series of *Hell Girl and Death Note*: Demonic Fairies and Performing Goth-Loli

In the series of *Hell Girl* (2005–2008) and *Death Note* (2006–2007), *goth-loli* girls as icons are performed by girl characters with honorable "gothic spirit."[21] Ai of *Hell Girl* and Misa of *Death Note* are depicted as grotesquely powerful but child-like cute girls with necromantic allusion (which will be discussed later). Performing *goth-loli* is symbolically associated with purification and death as Ai and Misa change their dresses before killing people. They are powerful enough to control death and terror, connoting their power to escape from traditional social norms concerning Japanese femininity.

The Series of *Hell Girl*: A Buddhism- and Shinto-Oriented Witch and Wa Goth-Loli

Hell Girl is a successful TV anime series due to its unique blend of Buddhism- and Shinto-oriented conventional horror motifs with cute and fashionable characterizations, and the mysteriously cute appearance of the protagonist, En'ma Ai (named after the Hell King in Buddhism, King En'ma), who is called "the hell girl."[22] In *Hell Girl*, is set in fifteenth-century Japan, Ai was offered as a sacrifice to the god of a small village, which at the time was a conventional rite of praying to the god to bring peace and harvest to the village. However, Ai secretly survived. Finding her alive, Ai's villagers buried her alive, along with her parents and therefore mercilessly killed them. After her death, Ai as a ghost sets fire to the whole village and kills all the villagers as an act of revenge. Because of her sin (karma), the King of Hell assigned her the duty of delivering humans to Hell for over four hundred years. In the twenty-first century where the main narrative takes place, Ai appears when someone accesses the Web site "Hell Correspondence" and hands the client a straw doll with a red string, which is a Japanese traditional doll for curses. If the client pulls the string, Ai sends the person whom the client wants to take revenge on to Hell even though the targeted person does not deserve this fate. However, a distinctive element of *Hell Girl* from the clichéd theme of punishment is that when you curse someone, "two holes are dug" (you will be also punished and sent to Hell after death).[23] This anime, thus, focuses on the darkness of human innate nature.

Ai represents female monstrous power to control people's death and terror. This power is profoundly contrasted with her child-like cute

1. Ai was crucified and made to wear a *goth-loli* dress.

appearance. She usually wears a sailor high-school uniform, which underlines innocent girlhood. The innocent girlhood is often represented through male sexual fantasy. Innocent, desexualized and passive girls as an idealized male sexual object have been repeatedly constructed and consumed, as typically seen in Japanese otaku culture. However, Ai shows a defiance of what male-dominant fantasy projects. For instance, in episode 20, a boy with supernatural power, Gil de Ronfer, challenges Ai in order to show his superiority to her. After torturing her, he puts a Lolita dress on her. Dressing a powerful girl in a Lolita costume and enjoying her as an object of the male desire metaphorically display male domination over females. However, unlike in the boy princesses in *Princess Princess*, Ai ignores his attempt and easily escapes from his imprisonment. Ai does not wish to be a desirable object to men and, is so unconcerned that she does not even struggle with this perception. This kind of transcendent attitude represents the strong will of girls to refuse to cater to the conventional male-led commodification of girls.

Fashioning *goth-loli* represents changing Ai's identity and her power. Ai conducts a traditional ritual of lustration, purifying her body in a river in front of her house surrounded by rhododendrons in the world for dead spirits and changing to her black *kimono* with a pattern of colorful flowers.[24] This is based on a Shinto ritual practice to purify pollution. This represents the changing process between the teenage girl's cuteness and the grotesquely strong girl's power. Ai, wearing the black *kimono* with

2. Ai in a black *kimono* with colorful flower designs.

colorful patterns of chrysanthemums, goes to the human world to send the target person to Hell. Lolita fashion combined with Japanese cultural factors such as a *kimono* is called *wa*-Lolita (Japanesque Lolita). In her attire, there are no frills and high socks that characterize *wa*-Lolita. However, her Japanesque gothic spirit well blended with Japanese Buddhist and Shinto's beliefs serve to signify the girl's self-assertion.

Death Note: A Goth-Loli Girl and Power, Terror, and Survival

Amane Misa of *Death Note* (2006–2007) is likewise performing *goth-loli*. She is characterized as an unintelligent and obedient girl to the male protagonist and her boyfriend, Yagami Raito (Light), in the first place. This typifies a Japanese traditional female role. However, like En'ma Ai, she plays an important role to portray girls' monstrous strength and child-like cuteness (grotesque cuteness), fleeing from the male gaze and even from the conventional dichotomous ideas of the good and the evil.

Light, who calls himself the new god, tries to create a utopia where no crimes and grief exist by using his Death Note, a notebook on which he writes the names of people he wants to kill and drives them into death. He, called "Kira" (killer) by his admirers, commits armchair murders of not only criminals but also those who are a hindrance to his plan. When he is unable to use his notebook, he orders Misa to use her Death Note and eliminate criminals and suspects. Like Ai, Misa changed her dress,

3. Misa in a *goth-loli* dress is wandering in a metropolitan city.

4. Misa in *goth-loli* dress stands on top of the building, viewing the city below.

dressing up as a *goth-loli* girl as if it is a ritual before killing. In a sequence of episode 25, Misa in a *goth-loli* dress is determined but emotionless, wandering around the town and singing a song with lyrics: "Be careful. God is watching you." Placing herself on the omnipotent position, she in the *goth-loli* dress refuses anybody to approach her in the city. This is symbolized by juxtaposing Misa in the *goth-loli* attire with her killing of suspects and criminals by writing their names on her Death Note at home. The sequence represents that Misa has a god-like power to control people's terror. This sequence is intentionally inserted as a side story of episode 25 prior to the sequence where the detective L, who has almost identified Light as a suspect, is killed. The *goth-loli* girl is positioned on the supreme/omnipotent level, viewing downward on human mortality.

In the final episode, in which Light is driven to his limit to reveal his true identity as Kira and is eventually killed, Misa again wears a *goth-loli* dress and stares at the beautiful sunset from the top of the building. Dying Light is juxtaposed with Misa attired in the *goth-loli* dress. This cross-cutting represents that Misa survives and is ultimately given a role of a storyteller to pass on the legend of Kira.[25] Although she has been manipulated by Light, she eventually escapes from his control, which is symbolized by her determined upright posture when Light dies. Thus, the *goth-loli* fashion serves as a defending device by which girls avoid being controlled by social norms in which males are dominant.

Furthermore, in episode 25 and the final episode, deaths of the two male leads are displayed: the death of L, supposedly representing the good and the death of Light supposedly representing the evil. In episode 25, L is killed (by Remu, another Death God, who was indirectly manipulated by Light). And in the final episode, the protagonist Light is also killed (by Ryuku, the Death God who has offered him a Death Note). When both symbol characters of the good and the evil are dying, Misa in a *goth-loli* attire is metaphorically positioned on the top of the building, viewing the metropolis stained red by sunset. Sunset, a conventional metaphor of the end of a day, also effectively signifies the end of the life of Kira and a start of her new life. She symbolically stands between the ends of the life of the binary opposition between good and evil. Therefore, she functions as a mediator who subverts our normative understanding of the dichotomy. The *goth-loli* girl, Misa, is positioned outside of the social norm in this narrative.

Conclusion

Since the late 1980s and the 1990s, *goth-loli shōjo* as a performance was profoundly popular as "visual type" male rock bands caused a new trend in Japanese music culture and influenced girls' fashion as well as gender images. In this postfeminist period, gender-blurring, which the visual type rock bands promoted, attracted young women who were unsatisfied with Japanese normative femininity. However, due to the aesthetic value of *kawaii* (child-like cuteness) in Japanese girls' culture, Japanese girls dare not to be "masculinized" in order to display powerfulness. While satisfying the desire for being child-like cute, *goth-loli* enables girls to perform to be powerful *and* child-like feminine at the same time, which suggests grotesque cuteness. In other words, *goth-loli* serves as a site in which masculinity and femininity are negotiated.

In Japanese contemporary anime, *goth-loli shōjo* are often used to display powerful but child-like cute femininity. Although they suggest an alternative powerful femininity, the living dolls in *Rozen Maiden* and the boy princesses in *Princess Princess* ultimately represent idealized femininity constructed by male sexual fantasy. Ai in the series of *Hell Girl* and Misa in *Death Note*, however, performatively construct themselves as being assertive, independent, and *kawaii* with gothic spirit.

It is often a case that representations of *shōjo* in anime are analyzed as sexual objects of male desire or consumed commodities. *Goth-loli shōjo* are indeed represented in such a clichéd way in anime in which *Rozen Maiden* and *Princess Princess* portrayed. However, Ai and Misa obviously control death (and birth), which emphasizes the terror and powerfulness of *goth-loli shōjo*. These representations serve to illustrate girls' empowerment when analyzed from a feminist perspective. Self-assertive *goth-loli shōjo* symbolizes the potential of a new perception of femininity in an emerging concept of gender equality in Japanese postfeminism. Girls' power and strength, their independence from patriarchal society, together with the ability to appear *kawaii* (child-like cuteness) are combined to offer a new gender identity. This change in power relation can provide a new perspective or alternative methodologies in teaching and researching animation; representations of powerful but cute *shōjo* should be argued by an interdisciplinary approach: through not only text analyses but also audience analyses, references to fashion, as well as fan culture of anime in relation to other fields of culture such as music, and so on.

On one hand, *goth-loli shōjo* represents the challenge toward Japanese normative femininity (being demure, obedient, and weak) in the postfeminist context. On the other hand, it serves as a site through which norms of femininity and masculinity are negotiated. One may argue that Japanese postfeminism still struggles with traditional gender images. However, the representations of *goth-loli shōjo* strategically function to avoid harsh criticisms of backlash toward "gender-free" (gender-equality) movements.

In the 2000s, *goth-loli shōjo* is one of the popular characters for "cosplayer" (people who are fond of "costume play" in which they copy their favorite characters of anime, manga, and video games or their favorite artists) all over the world. *EP3*, the Spanish newspaper for young readers,[26] for instance, reported that Spanish girls enjoyed performing *goth-loli* as imported fashion from Japan via anime and manga and localized it as their own culture (Ovelar, 2007: 20–21). They embraced *goth-loli* as a "foreign" exotic but European-oriented fashion. This "context-void" *goth-loli* has been consumed as one of the representation of Japanese girls. However, representations of *goth-loli* as a device have also conveyed Japanese aesthetic value of *kawaii* and powerful femininity to non-Japanese girls. This perhaps can posit another issue about *goth-loli*. Representations of *goth-loli* in anime in relation to postfeminism will offer us a site to crystallize the way in which Japanese *kawaii* and powerful femininity are negotiated with Western or other Asian hegemonic femininity in the postfeminist contexts.

Notes

This article is a modified version of the papers that were presented at the Asian Studies Conference in Japan in 2007 and the International Conference of European Association of Japanese Studies in 2008. I am grateful to the audience for their useful feedback and insightful suggestions.

1. Anime is used as the shortened form of the word animation in Japan. However, in the global context anime often signifies "Japanese-style" (two-dimensional) animated films and television programs.

2. The idea of the Lolita Complex stems from Vladimir Nabokov's novel, *Lolita* (1955). In 1969, the term *Lolita Complex* was first introduced to Japan with the translation of Russell Trainer's *The Lolita Complex* (New York: Citadel Press, 1966); Lolita Complex with the meaning of men's sexual desire for little girls was therefore permeated in Japanese society in the late 1960s and the early 1970s. "Lolita Boom" (a surge in popularity of seeing little girls as sexual objects) arrived in the late 1970s and the 1980s when many photo magazines dealing with girls called *loli-con* magazines, and porno magazines featuring girls' nudity were published (Takatsuki, 2009: 49–63). However, *Loli-con* (a shorten form of Lolita Complex) began to represent men's dangerous sexual desire for young girls when the serial murder case of little girls by the young (allegedly otaku) man terrified the public in 1989. The "Lolita Boom" ended in the late 1980s (Takatsuki, 2009: 65).

3. Pink House was founded by Kaneko Isao, the fashion designer, in 1973. The girls' fashion magazine, *Olive* (1982–), featured cute fashion for girls (who were called Olive

girls), which contributed to the building of the recognition of Pink House (Matsuura, 2007).

4. "So-called *goth-loli* consists of Gothic, Gothic and Lolita, and Lolita" (Maegawa, 2010: 91). I particularly argue the Gothic and Lolita type in this essay.

5. There is more tendency of *cos-play* ("costume play," copying attires and demeanors of musicians or anime and video game characters) of visual type bands for female fans than for male fans (Inoue, 2003b: 151). Male fans tended to organize their own bands in which they copied the music and performances of their favorite visual type bands (Koizumi, 2003).

6. In 1969, 79.5 percent of girls entered high schools; thus the ratio increased continuously.

7. In 1973, additional credits in home economics were required for female students in high schools, while the same number of credits was added to physical education for male students. In the curriculum of the lower grades of public elementary schools, the new course, Life Environment Studies, started in 1992 to replace sociology and science, with the goal that both boys and girls should learn general issues of life including aspects of the environment, communication, science, technology, and home economics. Concomitantly, home economics has been offered to the upper grades.

8. These issues were not overtly discussed until the late 1980s, although Japanese feminists such as Ichikawa Fusae posited them as gender inequality.

9. However, due to the backlash, it was reported that some public schools have abolished "the mixed name lists." See "*Jendā furī*," *kyoiku genba kara tettai* ["Gender-free" is to be withdrawn from education], *Sankei Newspaper*, August 13, 2004:1.

10. For instance, an English sentence, "I am a *girl*," should be translated into "*Watashi wa onna no ko desu*" in Japanese. Usually, no girls address themselves as "I am a *shōjo*." However, it is natural to express "She is a *shōjo*." Therefore, *shōjo* in Japanese usage is addressed by the third party.

11. *Shōjo gaho* was merged into *Shōjo no tomo* in 1942 (Yayoi Museum and Uchida, 2005: 6–7).

12. Manga is the name for Japanese graphic novels. Hereafter, manga is used to mean Japanese-style graphic novels. Girls' magazines that specialized in manga were published in the postwar period.

13. The renowned Japanese animation director Miyazaki Hayao often uses girl protagonists and European imagery in such films as *Lupin III: The Castle of Cagliostro* (1979), *Laputa: The Castle in the Sky* (1986), *Kiki's Delivery Service* (1989), and *Howl's Moving Castle* (2004).

14. Although monthly manga magazines for girls were also the locus of publication of their works, what distinguished them from weekly manga magazines was that target readers of the weekly magazines were older teen girls. Mizuno Hideko, Watanabe Masako, and Maki Miyako played the leads, introducing Western images and lifestyle (Yonezawa, 2007: 149–54; Shamoon, 2012: 96). Yonezawa suggests that the motives of the Western representations result from admiration for the West promoted by Western films such as *Roman Holiday* (1953) and *Sabrina* (1954) (2007: 148).

15. *Cutie Honey* is based on Nagai Gō's manga of the same title (1973–1974). It was adapted into animated short films (1974; 1997), Original Video Animations (OVAs) (1994–1995; 2004), a new TV series (1997–1998), and a live-action film (2004). *Magical Girl Lyrical Nanoha* is the spin-off from the R18 video games, the *Triangle Heart's* series (1998–2002). It was adapted into a film (2010) and three TV series (2004, 2005, and 2007).

16. Typified by the unreasonable remark of the then former prime minister, Mori Yoshirō, that "Women who do not give birth to children should not be supported by national pension when they are retired because they embrace freedom [without doing their duty of childbirth]" ("Aitsugu kanryo," 2003).

17. *Gendai Shisō* (*The Current Thoughts*), the well-known journal of Seidosha, featured "Gender Studies" in the January issue in 1999.

18. The TV anime series of *Rozen Maiden* is based on PEACH-PIT's manga of the same title (2002–2007). The first season of the anime version was substantially different from the original manga, regarding the characterization of heroines.

19. For instance, the series of feature films, *Child's Play* (1988, 1990, 1991, 1998, 2004 and 2010), typifies this fear. On the mysterious bodies of puppets, see Denison (2007).

20. *Princess Princess* is based on Tsuda Mikiyo's manga of the same title (2006–2007). It was adapted into a video game and a TV drama. In the anime version, there are new characters and episodes differing from the original manga.

21. *Hell Girl* was serialized in three seasons, originally created by Watanabe Hiroshi. It was adapted into manga, a TV drama, a video game, and a light novel (a popular novel that targets teen readers).

Death Note is based on Ohba Tsugumi's (story) and Obata Ken's (drawing) manga of the same title (2003–2006). In the anime version many different scenes and characterizations from those in the original manga were inserted. *Death Note* is adapted into two live-action films (2006) and a spin-off film (2008), video games (2007; 2008), and novels (2006; 2007).

22. The first season (2005) was aired from 1:55 to 2:25 a.m., recording a quite high viewing rate of 4.8 percent (Hiroichi, 2006). Target audiences were young adults. It is an unusually high rate in the midnight time slot, which was higher than expected (Hiroichi, 2006). It was also aired by another TV station and two other cable TVs in the evening slot. The second season was televised in the following year, gaining more popularity, which resulted in producing its sequel, the third season (2008).

23. This way of thinking is based on *Onmyōdo* (Japanese occultist esoteric officially introduced to the imperial court as part of the law system, *ritsuyō*, in the seventh century). *Onmyōji* (agents who conduct *Onmyōdo*) dealt with divination and magic.

24. In the Shinto practices, pollution (*kegare*) is purified by ritual ablutions (*misogi*). Buddhism also has the concept of pollution. For differences of *kegare* in Shinto and Buddhism, see Namihira (1974).

25. Misa's role as the storyteller is clearly depicted in the original manga, *Death Note*, on which the animation version is based. In the anime, however, the victory of the good represented by L is more emphasized by contrasting it with the death of the evil represented by Yagami Light.

26. *EP3* is a paper-based and online newspaper, which one of the major Spanish newspapers, *El Pais*, publishes for young readers. It specializes in entertainment and mode.

References

Cabinet Office, Government of Japan. "A Public Opinion on a Gender-Equal Society." August 2007. http://www8.cao.go.jp/survey/h19/h19-danjyo/2-1.html (Accessed on March 1, 2010).

———. "Seikatsu no teido" [The degree of life]. In *Kokumin seikatsu ni kansuru yoron chōsa* [*Public opinion polls about life*] (2009). http://www8.cao.go.jp/survey/h21/h21-life/images/z31.gif (Accessed on October 23, 2009).

Denison, Rayna. "The Muppet Show: Sex and Violence: Investigating the Complexity of the Television Body." *Intensities* 4 (2007): 1–17. http://intensities.org/Essays/Denison.pdf (Accessed on May 5, 2010).

Driscoll, Catherine. *Girls: Feminine Adolescence in Popular Culture and Cultural Theory*. New York: Columbia University Press, 2002.

Endō, Hiroko. *"Shōjo no tomo" to sono jidai: henshusha no yuuki Uchiyama Motoi* ["Girls' friends" and its time: Courage of the editor, Uchiyama Motoi]. Tokyo: Hon no izumi sha, 2004.

"Femininity." *The Oxford Advanced Learner's Dictionary*. 8th ed. London: Oxford University Press, 2010: 565.

Gender Equality Bureau, Cabinet Office. "Chihou tono renkei" [Cooperation with local communities]. *Gender Information Site* (2010). http://www.gender.go.jp/main_contents/category/chihou.html (Accessed on August 30, 2010).

"Grotesque." *The Oxford English Dictionary*. 2nd ed. Oxford: Clarendon Press, 1989: 873–74.

Higuchi, Hiroyuki. *Shiso no ketto—Gothic-Lolita no keifugaku* [The genealogy of Gothic-Lolita]. Kyoto: Tokyusha, 2007.

Hiroichi. "Samui fuyu wo sarani samukusuru!? Hora anime 'Jigoku shōjo' ni semaru" [It makes winter much colder?: The horror anime, *Hell Girl*]. An interview, *ITmedia+D Gamez*. Updated on February 13, 2006. http://gamez.itmedia.co.jp/games/articles/0602/13/news054.html (Accessed on August 25, 2010).

Imada, Erika. *Shōjo no shakaishi* [A social history of shōjo]. Tokyo: Keisō shobō, 2007.

Inagaki, Kyoko. *Jogakkou to jogakusei: kyōyō, tashinami, modan bunka* [Girls' schools and female students: Education, grace and modern culture]. Tokyo: Chūkō, 2007.

Inoue, Takako. "Bijuaru kei to jendā" [Visual type and gender]. In *Bijuaru kei no jidai: rokku, keshō, jendā* [The age of visual type: Rock, makeup, and gender], edited by Inoue Takako, 12–41. Tokyo: Seikyūsha, 2003a.

———. "Kakuchō sareta (otoko no bigaku)" [Expanded "Men's Aestheticism"]. In *Bijuaru kei no jidai: rokku, keshō, jendā* [The age of the visual Type: Rock, makeup, and gender], edited by Inoue Takako, 114–61. Tokyo: Seikyūsha, 2003b.

"Joji ni ninki no 'onna robotto'" [A popular "female robot" among girls]. *Asahi Newspaper*, June 14, 1966.

Kelsky, Karen. *Women on the Verge: Japanese Women, Western Dreams*. 3rd ed. Durham, NC: Duke University Press, 2006 (2001).

Koizumi, Kyoko. "Isei wo yosoou shōjo tachi: bijuaru rokku bando no kosupure fan" [Girls who perform to be opposite sex: Cos-play fans of the visual type rock bands]. In *Bijuaru kei no jidai: rokku, keshō, jendā* [The age of the visual type: Rock, makeup, and gender], edited by Inoue Takako, 207–45. Tokyo: Seikyūsha, 2003.

Maegawa, Masana. "Gosurori de iutokoro no 'seishinsei' ni tsuite—Henshin no hate ni arumono—" ["Spirituality" in the context of *goth-loli*: Beyond transformations]. *Annual Report of Girls Studies* 4 (2010): 90–103.

Matsuura, Momo. *Sekai to watashi to rorīta fashion* [The world, me and Lolita fashion]. Tokyo: Seikyūsha, 2007.

Mizutani, Masaru. *Shōjo shi no tsukurikata* [How to make shōjo poetry]. In Mizutani Maki's *Shōjo*. Tokyo: Yumani shobō, 2009 (1922): 5–173.

Murase, Hiromi. *Feminizumu sabukaruchā hihyō sengen* [A manifesto of feminist criticism on subculture]. Tokyo: Shunjū-sha, 2000.

Murota, Naoko. Shōjo tachi no ibasho sagashi [Girls' looking for a place to stay in]. In *Bijuaru kei no jidai: rokku, keshō, jendā* [The age of visual type: Rock, makeup, and gender], edited by Inoue Takako, 164–205. Tokyo: Seikyūsha, 2003.

Namihira, Emiko. *"Nihon no minkan shinko to sono koz"* [A study on the structure of Japanese folk belief]. *Minzokugaku kenkyu* [Japanese Journal of Ethnography] 38 (1974): 230–56.

Ovelar, María. "Flor en el Asfalto" [Flower in the asphalt]. *EP3*, September 14, 2007: 20–21.

Saitō, Minako. *Kō itten ron: Anime, tokusatsu, denki no hiroin zō* [The only girl in a group: Heroines of animations, "suits-mation" television programs and biographies]. Tokyo: Village Centre shuppankyoku, 1998.

Satō, Barbara. *The New Japanese Woman: Modernity, Media, and Women in Interwar Japan*. Durham, NC: Duke University Press, 2003.

Satō-Sakuma, Rika. "'Kiyoki shijō de gokousai o'—Meiji makki shōjo zasshi touko ran ni miru dokusha kyōdōtai no kenkyu" ["Relationships on the pure bulletin board: A study on the readership seen on the bulletin board of girls' magazines]. *Journal of Women's Studies* 4 (1996): 114–41.

Shamoon, Deborah. "Misora Hibari and the Girl Star in Postwar Japanese Cinema." *Signs: Journal of Women in Culture and Society* 35, no. 1 (2009): 131–55.

———. *Passionate Friendship: The Aesthetics of Girls' Culture in Japan*. Honolulu: University of Hawaii Press, 2012.

Shibusawa, Tatsuhiko. *Shōjo korekushon josetsu* [An introduction to the collection about girls]. Tokyo: Chūo Kōronsha, 1985 (1972).

Takahara, Eiri. *Gothic Heart*. Tokyo: Kodansha, 2004.

———. *Gothic Spirit*. Tokyo: Asahi Shimbunsha, 2007.

Takatsuki, Yasushi. *Rorikon: Nihon no shōjo shikōshatachi to sono sekai* [Loli-con: Japanese girls' lovers and their world]. Tokyo: Basilico, 2009.

Takemura, Kazuko. "Why Is 'Post' Feminism?" In *"Post"-Feminism*, edited by Takemura Kazuko, 1–4. Tokyo: Sakuhinsha, 2003.

Ueno, Chizuko. "Fuan na otokotachi no kimyō na rentai—jendā furī bassingu no haikei wo megutte" [Odd unifications among insecure men—about the background of gender-free backlash]. In *Bakkurasshu! naze jendā furī wa tatakareta noka?* [Backlash! Why was gender-free attacked?], edited by Sōfūsha, 378–439. Tokyo: Sōfūsha, 2006.

Yayoi Museum, and Uchida Shizue, eds. *Jogakusei techo: Taisho, showa, otome raifu* [Taisho, showa schoolgirl book]. Tokyo: Kawade shobō, 2005.

———. *Matsumoto Katsuji: showa no kawaii! wo tsukutta irasutorētā* [Matsumoto Katsuji: An illustrator who created kawaii in the showa era]. Tokyo: Kawadeshobōshinsha, 2006.

Yokokawa, Yumiko. *Shochō toiu kirifuda: "shōjo" ron hihyo jōsetsu* [Menarche as the last resort: An introduction to "shōjo" study]. Tokyo: JICC, 1991.

Yonezawa, Yoshihiro. *Sengo shōjo manga shi* [A history of postwar girls' manga comics]. Tokyo: Chikuma, 2007 (1980).

Animated Interracial Romantic Fantasies

Japanese Male and Non-Japanese Female Characters

—Joon Yang Kim

Introduction

There are some unusual, romantic couples featured as leading roles in the long history of Japanese animation. One side of the romantic binary relationship is a Japanese man, and the other a non-Japanese woman. The male character is definitely intended to have Japanese identity, marked by elements such as distinct black hair and a Japanese-style name, while his heterosexual partner is a Caucasian or non-Japanese Asian. Although the number of such a pattern of lovers, taken literally, might not be so large, the fact deserves to be brought to focus that they have made their appearance in these historically indicative as well as popular works: *Cyborg 009*, *Space Battleship Yamato*, and *The Super Dimension Fortress Macross*.

Japanese animation is often attributed to its a-nationality or nationless-ness (called as *mukokuseki* in Japanese).[1] For example, the presence of a multiracial cast including interracial lovers contributes to what the discourse is about. Conversely, it seems that the discourse has been so much abused as to regard Japanese animation as something apolitical and ahistorical. I wonder if it is a valid, acceptable concept with which to approach the subject. In the sense of mixing a variety of elements which (are supposed to) have a foreign origin, my question can be seen from what Karatani Kōjin points out about hybridity often referred to in Japanese culture. He suggests (2001: 143, 162) that one of the characteristics in Japanese culture would not be hybridity itself, but consist in the actual institution which reveals it in a visible way, in particular, of juxtaposing such scripts, *hiragana, katakana,* and Chinese characters in a phrase or a sentence, where the last two visualize the foreignness of a word and its notion, the first one set to be for traditional, pure Japanese, that is, *yamato* words. According to him (2001: 143, 164), such mode of writing institution, which has lasted about a thousand years along with Chinese characters, has had many effects on the structure of mind in the Japanese society, particularly, in the respect of externalizing and thereby excluding foreign things. Foreignness can be seen to be a matter of geopolitics and history in that it addresses the question on the one hand of the boundary of a community, and on the other of the origins. My suggestion here is that, likewise, the Japanese animation industry has developed and established its actual institution, which reveals foreignness in audiovisual ways like the naming of characters and the coloring and shaping strategy of their bodies.

It is not so surprising that the human figures with an externalized foreign identity in contrast with nationalized ones have not been dealt with in a more serious, intellectual way, particularly, in relation to the real world, since animation itself has long been thought of as being far from, furthermore, even as having nothing to do with, people's lived experience, as read between the lines in Paul Ward's essay ("Animated Interactions: Animation Aesthetics and the World of the 'Interactive' Documentary"). For the relationship of reality to animation, introducing a concept of "thickening," Ward (2006: 125–26) proposes an instructive idea that the real, the bodily presence of actual people, is never entirely absent or banished from animated representations, while attenuated in them.

Indeed, the Japanese animation industry did not only create non-Japanese female characters but also non-Japanese male characters. There are two ways in which I bring into focus the latter rather than the former, much inspired from Rey Chow's psychoanalytic, postcolonial investigations in her book *Writing Diaspora* (1993). First, their exotic, foreign identity is significant to my exploration as a device onto the surface of which a variety of political or historical fantasies are projected by male subjects and by spectators who are likely to identify themselves or empathize with them. Second, my attention is paid to the female and male characters who appeal a specific kind of emotional relationship between them to the spectators, not just to the former alone. In other words, the women are taken to be a mirror that reflects their heterosexual partners' subconscious, collective desires. This essay will explore what was and is dreamed of through hybrid romantic couples suggested in the three animated films each of which has kept its popularity for a long time with sequels in Japan.

Japan, Yamato, Okinawa, and Ezo

Before dealing with the animated texts, I hereby introduce something more about the significations of the words *Japanese* or *Japan.* Their usage, occupied by the perspective of the nation-state, would make the analysis regarded as too simple, reproducing the nation as the only mode of imagining a community. In fact, the Japanese society today has a variety of social, ethnic minorities within it: Okinawan, Ainu and Tohoku, and Korean-in-Japan usually called *zainichi.* However, the majority of Japanese people seem to have in common the national identity centered on Kyoto and/or Nara as the ancient cities of mainland Japan, and on Tokyo, once called Edo, as their extension. Their idea of identity is well represented by Yamato as another, old name of Japan, which has sometimes a more fundamental nationalist implication. Although by and large identifying themselves as Japanese, however, Okinawan people are inclined to separate themselves from the Yamato or mainland Japanese by calling themselves *uchinanchū,* and by calling them *yamatounchū* or *naichā.* Interestingly, *naichā,* the meaning of which is mainland people, is etymologically the same word as Korean people living under the Imperial Japanese government called Mainland Japanese people for a few decades in the first half of the twentieth century.

In spite of a common geographic condition with the northeastern province of the central island, *Honshu,* of mainland Japan, Tohoku people have a different view from those who have a Yamato-centric identity. A good example is *Aterui,* the 2002 animated feature about a hero and his people who resisted the invading Yamato government that scornfully called them *emishi* or *ezo* in the late eighth century; the two derogatory words imply foreign, primitive, and barbarian. The Yamato-centric perspective can be traced to Yanagida Kunio, the nineteenth-century ethnologist, who, according to Nishi Masahiko (2001: 127), regarded Tohoku people as foreign and uncivilized. In this sense, it is highly remarkable that, around the 1868 Meiji Restoration after more than a thousand year, Admiral Enomoto Takeaki established the Republic of Ezo in Hokkaido, only to cease to exist within a year; meanwhile, in the southwest, Okinawa had been the Ryukyu Kingdom reigned by the Shō Dynasty until 1879.

When its domestic signification and connotation are taken into consideration, the word *Japanese* (or *non-Japanese*), referred to in my essay, needs to be understood as a concept under Yamato-centric national ideology, the racist ideology of *tan'itsu minzoku* emphasizing a homogeneous nation in blood, which has marginalized, excluded, or subsumed minority groups by forcing them to erase their own identity. Although it today seems to some people that such ideology disappeared into history, it would be quite difficult to deny that it is still at work; for example, the national television network NHK still produces and broadcasts the historical fiction series under the title heading, *Taiga dorama*, which has taken Yamato-centric historical materials as its favorite subject.[2] The series was first aired in 1963. It serves as a form of ideological state apparatus, as suggested by Kang Sang-jung and Yoshimi Shun'ya (2001: 135). The ideological effect of the name *Yamato* also seems to remain somehow undiminished in private sectors; for example, like Yamato Un'yu, one of the biggest nationwide logistics service companies in Japan, which is delivering the name with parcels from door to door throughout the country.

Conventionally described as hybrid, yet modern Japan has not been so receptive to foreign East Asian cultures at least, whether they are inside or outside its boundary, as to Western cultures, differently from premodern Japan, which imported a lot from China, Korea, and other Asian neighbors. This sociopolitical landscape is likely to be invisible to the eyes that fail to imagine Japanese society as anything but *a* nation. Family names have been a site of such cultural politics for decades. Katō Norihiro (2001: 10–15) points out that Koreans-in-Japan have been induced to abandon their original family names, and to forge or adopt Yamato-styled ones by the authorities in the process of obtaining Japanese nationality; in fear of discrimination due to their own revealed Korean identity, a host of them have been compelled to use an alias that looks and sounds like a Yamato name.[3] As for Okinawa, there is a case in which native workers at nationwide call centers located on the province would be persuaded to do such naming by their managers for the reason that business talks might feel strange or uncomfortable for mainland Japanese customers at hearing their original family names, such as Kyān and Medoruma, which sound so different from mainland- or Yamato-styled ones. The name and naming in the Japanese society, which is made up of three factors—that is, character, pronunciation, and meaning—is likely to externalize the identity of someone who belongs to an ethnic minority in visual, acoustic, and semantic ways. This has also been used as a central, signifying strategy of cartoon characters in Japanese animation, which will be taken into account in the essay.[4]

A Japanese Hero Gazes at a French Swan on a Synthetic Lake

My first case of national-male and foreign-female lovers in Japanese animation is Shimamura Jō and Françoise in the animated feature *Cyborg 009*, produced by Toei Animation, and released in 1966. Shimamura alone, as the leading character with the code name 009 in the antiwar film, has Japanese identity among nine cyborg agents; the rest of them are Russian, American, French, German, Native American, Chinese, British, and African.[5] His family name is a usual mainland Japanese one, which would mean insular village. If it were Shimabukuro, he would be understood not as a Yamato mainlander but as an Okinawan; what would the Japanese audience's response to the hero's new naming be like?

He also has explicitly black hair, which can be said to be a color strategy of consolidating Japanese-ness—accurately Yamato—identifying with his family name. When it comes to the issue of identity related to his hair color, some people might like to argue that he is not purely Japanese, as he is set to be a child with brown hair, born of the interracial parents, in other texts under the same heading of *Cyborg 009*. Rather it is, however, necessary to note that the color of his hair is set to be black in the first feature of the series that Toei, the biggest major animation studio at that time, produced for children and their accompanying parents, as the studio's "B-class" project for the "domestic" market, not for an international distribution (Yamaguchi and Watanabe, 1977: 117–18). Pointing out that the Japanese people have tended to dislike to be Japanese since the modern Taisho period (1912–1925),[6] Oshii Mamoru states that there was a tendency of resisting against the black hair of the cyborg heroine Motoko in the production scene of his 1995 animated feature *Ghost in the Shell* (1996: 78–81). Given this cultural, aesthetic atmosphere of modern Japan, the color of Shimamura's hair in the 1966 film is black enough to imply that his identity is Japanese, even if not "purely" Japanese for some audience with a good, intertextual memory of his genealogy. Also, of interest is that his cyborg uniform is designed in the same colors, red and white, as the Japanese national flag Hinomaru.

For all his black hair and Yamato-styled family name, Shimamura does not look traditional, but modern and even Western, particularly in contrast to his Chinese cyborg colleague. Having the same black hair, this counter character has very tiny, dot-like eyes, distinct from those of his geographically closest neighbor, Shimamura. What is more interesting is that he is middle aged and secondary, while the Japanese cyborg is young and leading; they seem to embody Japan's view of China as old and as not hegemonic in East Asia since the late nineteenth century. Shimamura's given name Jō, sounding much like the Western name Joe, is another attribute of the national hero that represents modern Japan. The name looks and sounds modern, when written in *katakana* rather than in Chinese characters with the same Japanese pronunciation. The modern in Japan has been mostly understood as foreign, in particular, as Western in a geographic sense, and as Caucasian in a racial sense. The new foreignness excluded Chinese-ness, Korean-ness, and even Japanese-ness, as cited above from Oshii Mamoru, along with the de-Asianizing of Japan. It is not strange that today Japanese people have Western-sounding given names such as Ken, Naomi, and Erika.

The issue of modern Japan also calls attention to Shimamura Jō's career as a car racer in the beginning of the film. Speed and technology embodied by his professional activity can be said to have been a crucial factor for the national hero in postwar Japan that desired recovery from the Second World War, during which modernity was once denied in the postmodern discourse of *Kindai no chōkoku*, the "Overcoming of Modernity."[7] Given that Paul Virilio suggests that speed is a matter of power, and that accidents are the hidden face of technological progress, referring to the limit or excess of speed (1998: 107–8), his body, technologized through a cyborg operation after the accident in a car race, can be said to be a post-human embodiment of desire for more power.

A young blue-eyed female French cyborg, named Françoise, is exploited as an attribute of the national male subject dreaming of (re-)modernization of such kind. Except for her, the other eight cyborgs are or look male, whose age is various: baby, boy, youth, and middle aged. There is no other female member, either the same or different in age to her. Of the men, it is Shimamura alone who is allowed to have a romantic relationship with the one and only female member, who is, interestingly, depicted as a would-be ballet dancer from Versailles, as shown in her nostalgic vision of *Swan Lake*. Whether or not the production crew was conscious of modern European myths of automata, her national, professional, and corporeal settings evoke not so much the spellbound classical Princess Odette as the automaton Coppélia, who appears in the hermetic ballet of the same name, as a dancing mechanical version of Eve, invented and animated by and for the male gender.

Being of the same order of cyborg, she is not treated as equal to her male colleagues, while the Japanese cyborg Shimamura is in an exclusive position among the others. In comparison with theirs, her primary activity as a special agent is more passive than active and more mediate than immediate: to sense and report external physical changes with her bionic eyes and ears. But it is her secondary activity that makes clearer what she is: to care for a baby cyborg and the others as if she were a mother. She seems to be a docile, full-time housekeeping wife, or so-called *ryōsai kenbo* in Japanese. This word as a patriarchal discourse means a good wife and wise mother, who is said to have supported her male spouse as a corporate warrior, called *kigyō senshi,* in 1960s Japan. Is she French or Japanese? Why is it that she was set to be or look French, not Japanese in the film?

According to Rey Chow (1993: 40–41), there is a homoerotic link connecting "the third world" nationalist and "the first world" imperialist, which results in a perfect symmetry between their gazes that cross over the images of native women as silent objects, in the former's masculinist oedipal fantasy of envy and violence desiring for revenge to do to the enemy exactly what the enemy did to him, an envy of taking the same place as the latter. In *Cyborg 009*, the images of native women are replaced with that of an imperial woman. She enables Shimamura to take the place of a Western imperialist who is believed to be her legitimate heterosexual partner in a racial sense. This kind of role play realizes the national vision that Japan should and could be one member of Western powers, since it was set as semicivilized between the civilized West and the uncivilized East—somewhere between the first and the third world—by the early modern Japanese thinker Fukuzawa Yukichi (Komori, 2001: 16–19). Indeed, the quasi-imperial Japanese male cyborg Shimamura leads his colleagues, each of whom represents a specific race, nation, or ethnic group, with their unconditional consent. To put it conversely, there is a repressed political conflict. How could a subconscious fear about such reality be overcome? His answer would be the romantic relationship with the female cyborg from the West: love beyond reality. Shimamura Jō and Françoise is a synthetic, prosthetic dream of *yamato* and *yamato nadeshiko*[8] animated by postwar technologized Japan.

There Was No Geisha on the Two Islands for Which the Ship Left

The *Yamato* series, whose first theatrical production was successfully released in 1977, edited from the animation television series *Space Battleship Yamato* broadcast for the first time three years earlier, have been evaluated to have brought about the historic boom of animation in the 1970s Japan. As such, it seems highly significant that the series presents male protagonists with historically famous Japanese political heroes' family names such as Okita, Tokugawa, and Sanada, in a spectacle of collectivized black hair. For some audiences, it would not be a very new founding that the *Yamato* series do not look a-national, as a national characterization of them is too explicit to be unnoticed, even when there is no information given about the historical and ideological implication of Yamato, a constant element of the title.

The images of "the first world" women as romantic objects for Japanese male heroes are found in the series, too. In its 1977 first feature, Mori Yuki and Starsha and her younger sister Sarsha all have blonde hair, which makes a strong exotic, Western impression, surrounded by many male characters with black, sometimes brown-looking, hair.[9] However, their identity is a little more multiple than that of the French cyborg (only if putting aside cyborg discourses relating to the issue of identity). First, unlike what would be expected from her hair color, the family name Mori and the given name Yuki, given in Chinese characters on the screen, each of which means forest and snow in order, are quite common ones among mainland Japanese people; in addition, she has brown, not blue, eyes. A bit of scrutiny about who she would be, with the two clues combined, presents probable answers in two realistic ways; one is that she dyed her hair blonde, and the other that she is a child of interracial parents, called "half" (recently "double") in Japan. While a theory of hair dyeing might make the essay hilarious and deconstructive, it is a theory of genealogical background that is likely to be a better explanation for her hybrid setting in two respects. In an intratextual one, the film's happier-end edition, under the subheading "Starsha's Survival," suggests the interstellar, interracial marriage of an alien woman Starsha and a tellurian, Japanese man Kodai Mamoru; this implies that a child may be born of the interracial parents. In an intertextual one, a blond male soldier with the Yamato-styled, Japanese name Ijūin Shinobu, particularly, the family name of which seems to be much from the aristocracy, plays a leading role in *Haikara-san ga Tōru*, the animated television series broadcast in 1978, the year after the first theatrical release of the *Yamato* series. The hybrid hero is imagined as a child of interracial parents in the text where a modern, noble Japanese girl is supposed to marry him, set in the Taisho period.

According to Shimabuku Maria, romanticism for the "hybrid" or "half" characters in the middle of military conflicts is witnessed in the real world as well as in animated worlds. She points out that male-centric imperialist and nationalist gazes have increasingly expected children born of an American soldier father and a local mother in Okinawa to be an "attractive mediator" between two countries, in order to perpetuate the present military situation, effacing the fact that they have long condemned them as "filthy," on account of two factors; one is discomfort due to their body image *re*-presenting the colonialist rape, and the other is hatred due to a fear of national purity being damaged (2001: 159). Many children in a similar parental condition were to be seen in mainland Japan as well, much involved with the Japanese government's policy for official prostitution in excuse of protecting "good" women from foreign male soldiers in the aftermath of the Second World War (Yoshimi, 2007: 104–7).

Mori Yuki's attractive hybrid image is reinforced through the romantic, Western connotation of her Japanese name, as Mori (means Forest in English) is likely to be associated with *Sleeping Beauty* the Japanese title, *Nemureru "Mori" no bijo*, of which "in Forest" is added to, and Yuki (means Snow in English) with *Snow White* the Japanese title of which is *Shira "Yuki" hime*, though her name could also be from Japanese history like those of the other *Yamato* crewmembers. As with Shimamura in *Cyborg 009*, Kodai Susumu,[10] a Japanese male hero as elite officer in the film, can take the place of Western powers by virtue of a heterosexual relationship with the only female crewmember, in his gaze at "the first world" image she displays; like the French cyborg Françoise, she performs the role of a housekeeping wife as the leader of the living team, and that of a sensor as a radar operator in the battleship *Yamato*. Her being in the bridge of the ship can play a mediate role to attenuate some uneasy, political suspicion possibly caused by the resurrection of Imperial Japan's historical largest-scale warship of the same name, in the quasi-oedipal fantasy that Japan should be the representative force of the earth against alien enemies in the future. Then, what should be brought to focus is the Empire of Gamilas as the enemy of the battleship *Yamato* and Earth in the first of the series. The imperial leader's title is *Soto*, which is usually the Japanese word for the German *Führer* in the context of the Second World War. His name and those of his men, presented in *katakana* on the screen, are set to sound

German like Dessler, Schulz, Ganz, Kreuz, and Heidern. Implying that Gamilas could be Nazi Germany, these and other setting elements virtually take Japanese soldiers on the ship *Yamato*, along with Earth's Defence Fleet to which they belong, to the place of the United States in the military dynamic of world history. Yet, Earth, as an island of the universe, still seems to be more similar to Japan, which waited for the real battleship *Yamato*'s triumphal return from the final combat in Okinawa, while the island country was ruined by bombing from the sky, as with the planet under radioactive bombs in the film.

Starsha and Sarsha, among the-first-world-looking women in the animated world war, are presented as the royal sisters of a distant mysterious planet, called Iscandar, for which the battleship makes an adventurous voyage that promised to help the earth. Their names, looking and sounding Russian, much like Anastasia and Sasha in their Japanese *katakana* spelling and pronunciation, do not simply support their non-Japaneseness, but also intimate a romantic view of Russia, in the hierarchy of gender, formed through Imperial Japan's victory in the Russo- Japanese War (1904–1905), the victory of which it is said that the country defeated a Western power for the first time. At the same time, there is a question about whether their doomed planet kingdom is nothing but an imagined picture of Russia. Given that imagery is a complex of various, even contradictory, elements, a possible answer to the question is that the destination of the battleship *Yamato* in 1945 was the island Okinawa, the former kingdom Ryukyu, distant from mainland Japan, which was substituted by a fictional, celestial island far away from the empire of the earth in the film about thirty years later. Imperialism depicted colonies and colonized people as if they had been happy to make any sacrifice for colonizers, and so did Japanese-made animation in the Imperial period leading to the Second World War: *Kaikoku tarō shin nippon tō banzai* (Kaikoku Taro: Glory for the New Japanese Island [1938]); and *Momotarō umi no shinpei* (Momotaro, the Divine Soldier of the Sea [1945]). In the future imagined in the 1977 animated feature, Sarsha, princess of the planet kingdom in outer space, dies on the way to the earth in order to help it as shown in the beginning of the film; why should she die? Her elder sister Starsha, as queen of the kingdom, provides the earth with her resources for nothing. In the "Starsha's Survival" edition of the film, imperialist exploitative fantasy of the celestial colony is embellished with the romantic relationship, suggesting marriage between the alien queen who seems to be the only indigenous survivor and Kodai Mamoru, the Japanese soldier who, rescued by her, is eventually determined to stay with her forever, instead of going back to Earth with his younger brother Susumu, who is the ultimate hero of the story. Susumu says that they should be Adam and Eve of a new Iscandar: a fantasy of the *New World* as colony. Is this a postcolonial Japanese sci-fi version of *Pocahontas*, or an inflected inversion of *Madame Butterfly*? Indeed, two more "butterflies" are found in two works that follow: they are Chinese.

Does He Remember the Chinese Girl?

My third case is the 1984 animated feature *The Super Dimension Fortress Macross: Do You Remember Love?*, the first feature of the *Macross* series, released a few years later after the first television series was broadcast in the middle of the boom of animation since *Space Battleship Yamato*. A triangular love affair in the film is depicted among three characters in a multinational manner. They are a Chinese female pop singer Ling Mingmei, a Japanese male soldier Ichijō Hikaru, and a Japanese female officer Hayase Misa. Here, too, their names present their own national identity. Of them, the first two have in common black, sometimes near to dark blue, hair, while the last has explicitly brown hair, which, together with her fashionable given name Misa, makes her seem to be less traditional and more liberal. Not being as much introduced as in its preceding television series, their biographic information in the feature suffices to understand and discuss the relationship between them.

In the spectacular beginning of the film, the playful pilot Ichijō Hikaru argues with his senior Hayase Misa for his unruly behavior in a battle against enemies. Being angry with her, seized by a prejudice that women should be obedient and sexy, the hero suddenly falls in love with a popular singer, Ling Mingmei, whose life he saved from giant aliens' indiscriminate attack. His male colleagues, who share his sexist view in common, incite him to have an affair with her, arguing that a sexual experience with a woman should be the evidence of what it is to be a man. In their mischievous dialogues, which are likely to have much to do with the early 1980s discourse, on men's sexuality, of *Yarahata*[11] (Shibuya, 2003: 161–81) that men have to discard their chastity before the age of twenty, my primary concern is the Japanese military boy's romantic, even pornographic, gaze upon the Chinese girl who is forged as a feeble, docile, emotional, and bashful character. The early scenes of the film have her full nude in a shower exposed to his gaze, and his hesitant seduction of her to a motel on their first date.

Such characters and scenes are found in the 1941 animated short *Mābō no tairiku senbutai* [Mābō's Continental Propaganda Brigade], too, directed by Chiba Yōji.[12] In the short, a Chinese girl is abducted by a group of mounted bandits who plundered her hometown, possibly in Manchuria, and later rescued by a Japanese boy hero named Mābō, defeating the enemies, who, as an acrobat, came to the continent for propaganda activities of the Imperial Japanese army during the Second World War, as given in the title. It is not clear whether he is a military spy in disguise, or a naive artist exploited by the army. In the triumphant end, he offers his hand to her in a naive manner suggesting that their handshake should someday result in a romantic relationship. At that time, Manchuria and other Chinese regions were invaded and colonized as a "new frontier" by Imperial Japan, where some of mounted bandits actually attacked the army and settlers from the overseas empire, though they are only depicted to harass local people in the film. Forty-three years later, the insular, flying fortress in the first feature of the *Macross* series holds an urban space whose population is multinational and multiracial, and aims at immigration from Earth to other planets in the war with aliens. However, the film does not show the fortress finding and conquering a "New World" in outer space, but it features the return to Earth; no colony seems to exist there in the 1984 animated version of the imagined geography or celestial map.

The fortress city named Macross is like the space battleship *Yamato*, and at the same time, different from it, seemingly in a more cosmopolitan than national atmosphere. The crew as well as the inhabitants speak various languages, as heard clearly from the bridge of the urban battleship in the introducing scenes, which is similar to the scenes of the postmodern city L.A. in the 1982 film *Blade Runner*. The fictional organization of the U.N. Spacy, to which Macross belongs, seems to be a military succession, in a sci-fi sense, of the United Nations. Symbolically, the captain's name is Global.

Despite a good relationship with his new Chinese girlfriend, however, the hero Ichijō Hikaru paves a nationalist way to which his predecessor Mābō missed a chance to lead after a *happy* end of the 1941 short. While lost on the ruined earth with his arguing senior officer Hayase Misa alone in the middle of the story, he has an affair with her. He disliked her initially for being self-disciplined, unemotional, disobedient, and rational, and now he suddenly thinks of her as if he has found his true love in her, consequently to leave his exotic girlfriend. Moreover, the progressive, subjective female officer, who seems to portray a face of the contemporary Japanese urban woman, in a degree, from a male-centric perspective, comes to be obedient to, and supportive of him in the next morning after their affair, as if she were a docile housekeeper. Her new boyfriend is no longer ruthless or playful, but gets serious, literally heroic. Persuaded by her ex-boyfriend, the young Chinese diva Ling Mingmei, who cannot soon discard her attachment to him even after the one-sided breakup—he also seems to have a clandestine affection for her—sings a legendary song found by him, in order to disarm the alien enemies. The title of the song is "Do You Remember Love?" which in effect asks simultaneously for love in the enemies and in the Japanese hero who dumped her. Here, the Chinese girl serves as a propagandist subject for the military action of a futuristic version of Mābō, not being an object that should be liberated by the Japanese boy.

The two women, who differ in national identity, personality, and job but who have Asian identity in common, are successfully subsumed under his oedipal strategy of achieving what it is to be a man, by means of the myth of romance; this can be seen as a project of restoring masculinity, which is attempted in the course of the degradation of nationalist discourse, as Kim Soyoung (2001: 30–31) points out in her discussion about Chinese or North Korean women who began to appear, replacing South Korean counterparts in the 1990s live-action films in South Korea. In the nationalist discourse, much backed up by the traditional Confucian patriarchy of the East Asian region, men have regarded themselves as active, national subjects and women as their passive supporters rather than as their equal colleagues, and tend to feel their masculinity as such damaged and to find new others in sex/gender, as the female supporters get more and more modernized, Westernized, urbanized, and self-determining and subjective for themselves, ceasing to be obedient any longer to the male subjects of the same national community (imagined), in spite of hatred and blame from them. In the 1984 film *The Super Dimension Fortress Macross: Do You Remember Love?* a nationalist project of that kind also dreams that a contemporary liberal female subject who has the same national identity with a male subject retrogresses to the traditional other who assists him at home. A paternal model for the black-haired Japanese hero with Yamato-style name is his phallocentric senior pilot Roy Focker, who is a blond-haired Caucasian man in love with an African female officer, Claudia LaSalle, displaying his kissing her as a masculine sign, whether she agrees or not, in the presence of his men. Roy is killed in a battle in the middle of the film, and Ichijō Hikaru takes his place as a male subject as well as a soldier. Who did the boy love, the girls or the pseudo-father?

Conclusion

In this essay, I explored some types of romantic relationships suggested between Japanese men and non-Japanese women, intending to make clear their historical, political, and ideological meanings and implications. It is said in the Japanese animation industry that their characterizations and visual features are just superficial signifiers, that it is neither significant nor essential whether the color of their hair is blonde or green (Kim, 2006: 85–86). I do not believe that a person's identity can be separated so simply from her/his physical conditions, in order to externalize and exclude them; however, they might look hybrid or strange in the real world. Keeping in mind Paul Ward's realist view, animated characters can be said to be an extension of real people, which raises a question: who were or are they?

In the sense, what is interesting is that the 1977 film *Space Battleship Yamato* treats three exotic, foreign women as if they were triplets, particularly when a *Yamato* crewmember says that on seeing the alien queen Starsha, she resembles Mori Yuki, and when she takes Yuki for her twin-like sister Sarsha in her "Survival" edition. Her "Death" edition of the same film shows Yuki alone shed tears on seeing the queen's electronic apparition as if she had any memory of her, or understood a meaning of her death, beyond such indescribable distance of light years from the earth to the *unchartered* land. Riddles of three similar women, Mori Yuki's tears were part of what led me to write the essay about them.

I expect that my essay should raise questions in the following three directions. First, there is a question possibly directed to non-Japanese, non-Yamato, particularly Caucasian-looking, male leading characters that have Japanese-looking girlfriends, as with *Haikara-san Ga Tōru*, the television series referred to in short above. Second, questions addressed in the essay can shift from non-Japanese to Asian girls; for example, Lalah Sune with a bindi on the forehead and brown-colored skin, and Fa Yuiry and Chan Agi, who have Chinese-sounding names and dark blue, looking much near black, hair in the *Mobile Suit Gundam* series that have so far been produced since 1979. The third direction will put into question a multinational, multiracial secret service team, as seen in *Cyborg*

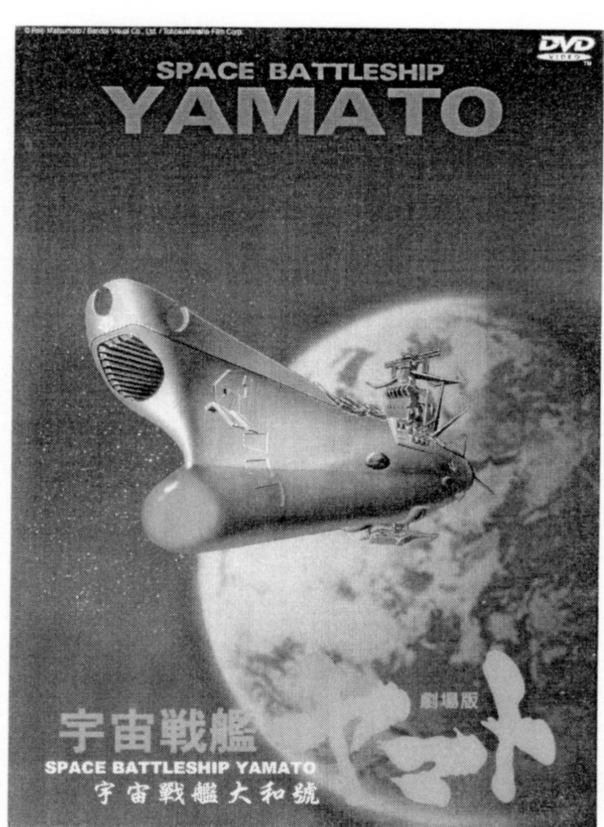

1. Editors' note: DVD covers of the *Space Battleship Yamato* (1977) in Taiwan. The film is also known as *Space Cruiser Yamato* in English.

2. Editors' note: DVD covers of the *Space Battleship Yamato The Final Battle* (1983) in Taiwan. The film is also known as *Final Yamato* in English.

009. Remarkable is the fact that the 2001 film *Sakura Wars: The Movie*, directed by Hongō Mitsuru, presents secret agent girls of the Imperial Japanese government, who are respectively from China, Okinawa, Russia, France, and Spain, along with two leading agents from mainland Japan. I hope that my introductory exploration acts as motivation for these kinds of questions to take a steady step with an iconographic and iconological study of characters portrayed in the field of animation, of which Japanese animation is regarded as an important part.

Notes

1. Editors' note: The term *mukokuseki* is also covered in Yamanashi's article in this collection while Hu's book *Frames of Anime: Culture and Image-Building* (2010: 4), discusses the term *kokusaika* ("internationalism") used in describing Japanese animation.

2. Note that *Ryukyu no kaze* (1993), one of the series, took up a history with Okinawa as a dynasty from the late sixteenth to early seventeenth century. Its English title is known as *Dragon Spirit*.

3. Recently, some Koreans-in-Japan, among whom well-known entertainers are included, started to reveal in public their Korean identity and family names, which had been concealed. This recognition of Korean identity in Japan seems to have been to a degree encouraged by the South Korean wave, called *Hallyu*, with the television drama series *Winter Sonata* (2002), which has obtained a great popularity in Japan since 2003.

4. Animated characters' original names are transliterated into the Roman alphabet in the essay. The spelling has a possibility of being in a degree different from that in other literary texts. The name order follows their original condition in the films.

5. In the film, the national identities of the cyborgs that are Native American, Chinese, and African are visualized in a physical manner, and that of the French cyborg and the British one is suggested in a verbal way. The others' national identities are given in external texts or materials. Detailed information about them is found in the film's official Web site (http://www.009ing.com/about/004/).

6. Editors' note: Here, Kim is referring to the continual modernization process of Japanese life where the learning and adoption of Western civilization lifestyles, values, and so forth are viewed highly. The modern identity of the Japanese is a complex one partly due to the establishment of a new form of government since the Meiji period (1868–1912) that follows the Western style of constitutional democracy. The Taisho period is considered as a historical period in Japanese modern history where the influence of Western culture was at its highest in the fields of art, philosophy, technology, and the like.

7. This postmodern discourse proposed officially in Imperial Japan in 1942 was at that time imagined as a resistance against and a cure for the so-called morbid,

pathological situation of Japan that had been "contaminated" by the Western/modern culture since the late nineteenth century (Kang, 1997: 178).

8. The traditional Japanese word refers to women who were evaluated from male-centric, feudal perspectives in mainland Japan, as well as to the flower of native dianthus in Japan.

9. There being a degree of variation in hair colors, this essay gives priority to those articulated and signified specifically in the film.

10. Kodai, his family name, means ancient times, and Susumu, his given name, progress. As for his elder brother Kodai Mamoru referred to later, Mamoru means conserve. Susumu and Mamoru are usual given names for men in Japan, while the family name Kodai, which is not so easy to imagine a Japanese person with, is suggestive of what the two male soldier characters have in common, historically and genealogically. The combination of the family name with each of the given names makes a synthetic implication about the personality of each of the brothers. Like his younger brother, Mamoru has a romantic relationship with a "first world" lady.

11. The Japanese word *yarahata* is an abbreviation of the phrase *yarazuni hatachi*. The former means no experience of a sexual intercourse, and the latter means the age of twenty.

12. This short is one of the animated series of Mābō that lasted from 1936 to 1955. Satō Kinjirō, the producer of the short, also directed some other shorts in the series.

References

Amino, Yoshihiko. *Nihon shakai no rekishi* [History of Japanese society]. Tokyo: Iwanami Shoten, 2004.

Chow, Rey. *Writing Diaspora*. Bloomington: Indiana University Press, 1993.

Hardt, Michael, and Negri, Antonio. *Jeguk* [Empire], translated by Yun Soo-Jong. Seoul: Ehak, 2001.

Hashiya, Hiroshi. *Teikoku nihon to shokuminchi toshi* [Imperial Japan and colonial cities]. Tokyo: Yoshikawa Kōbunkan, 2004.

Kang, Sang-jung. *Orientalism Ul Neomeoseo* [Overcoming orientalism]. Seoul: Isan, 1997.

Kang, Sang-jung, and Yoshimi Shun'ya. *Grōbaru-ka no enkinhō* [Perspective of globalization]. Tokyo: Iwanami Shoten, 2001.

Karatani, Kōjin. *"Senzen" no shikō* [Ideas of the "pre-war"]. Tokyo: Kōdansha, 2001.

Katō, Norihiro. *"Tennō hōgyo" no zuzōgaku* [Iconography of "tennō's demise"]. Tokyo: Heibonsha, 2001.

Kim, Joon Yang. *Imiji ui jeguk: Ilbon yeoldo wi ui animation* [Empire of images: Animation on Japanese islands]. Seoul: Hannarae, 2006.

Kim, Soyoung. "Sarajinun namhan yeoseongdul" [South Korean Women Disappear]. In *Hanguk-hyung Blockbuster: Atlantis Hogun America* [Korean Blockbusters: Atlantis or America], edited by Kim Soyoung, 17–39. Seoul: Hyunshil Munhwa Yeongu, 2001.

Komori, Yōichi. *Posutokoroniaru* [Postcolonial]. Tokyo: Iwanami Shoten, 2001.

Monma, Takashi. *ōbei eiga ni miru nippon* [Japan found in Euro-American cinema]. Tokyo: Shakai Hyōronsha, 1995.

Nishi, Masahiko. "Atokusare no tochi toshite" [As a Land with troubles unsolved]. In *Posutokoroniarizumu* [Postcolonialism], edited by Kang Sang-jung, 127–29. Tokyo: Sakuhinsha, 2001.

Oshii, Mamoru, et al. "Eiga towa jitsu wa anime-shon datta" [In fact, cinema has been animation]. In *Eureka rinji zōkan japanimeishon!* [Eureka Extra Edition: Japanimation!], 50–81. Tokyo: Seidosha, 1996.

Shibuya, Tomomi. *Nihon no dōtei* [Male chastity in Japan]. Tokyo: Bungeishunjū, 2003.

Shimabuku, Maria. "Konketsuji wo miryokukasuru otokotachi no kyōbō" [Men's conspiracy that makes hybrid children attractive]. In *Posutokoniarizumu* [Postcolonialism], edited by Kang Sang-jung, 159–61. Tokyo: Sakuhinsha, 2001.

Virilio, Paul. *Dennō sekai, saiaku no sinario heno taiō* [Cybermonde, la politique du pire][Cyberworld, the policy of worst], translated by Honma Kunio. Tokyo: Sangyō Tosho, 1998.

Ward, Paul. "Animated Interactions: Animation Aesthetics and the World of the 'Interactive' Documentary." In *Animated "Worlds,"* edited by Suzanne Buchan, 113–29. Eastleigh: John Libbey Publishing, 2006.

Yamaguchi, Katsunori, and Watanabe Yasushi. *Nihon anime-shon eigashi* [The history of Japanese animation]. Osaka: Yūbunsha, 1977.

Yoshimi, Shun'ya. *Shinbei to hanbei* [Pro-America and anti-America]. Tokyo: Iwanami Shoten, 2007.

SECTION FIVE

Artistic Animation and Expression in Japan

3-D Computer Graphics

Creating and Teaching Professional Animated Techniques in *Innocence* and *Doraemon*

—IKIF (Tokumitsu Kifune + Sonoko Ishida)

Translated by Joon Yang Kim

Introduction

The digitalization of animation methodology has created advanced techniques of animation production. Basically, as for animated features, depending on budgets, schedules, and production crew, their methodology of production often takes on a variety, which seems to be much more widened by digitalization. Furthermore, it is now possible for people of little experience to be involved with some work in the production scenes of animated films for theatrical release, which were once open only to animators who are long trained and sufficiently skillful. Working at the production scenes of commercial animations, IKIF (comprising animators Ishida Sonoko and Kifune Tokumitsu) is involved with animation education at Tokyo Zokei University and Tokyo Polytechnic University. Many teachers, as well as us, of the two schools are working as artists or creators in practical scenes. For art universities, this is the case found not just in the field of animation but also in many others. However, it is clear that digitalization has increased opportunities to allow students to participate in the scenes of animation production.

We want to unveil a face of such diversification and the way it was made best use of in education by elucidating the situations of our production work in *Ghost in the Shell 2: Innocence* (2004) and *Doraemon* (2004), the animated films in which we, IKIF/IKIF+ (IKIF is the name of the unit that

consists of Kifune Tokumitsu and Ishida Sonoko. IKIF+ is the name of the company that IKIF established in 1997).

Innocence was a big project, which an unusual huge budget was invested in Japanese animation to date. In a sense, the director of the film, Oshii Mamoru, controlled all the works efficiently, although at times, he appeared to direct inefficiently in order to achieve the highest effect by adapting to the work condition and circumstance. The chapter partly discusses the creative processes of the Chinese festival parade's scenes and those of the inside of the factory ship, both of which IKIF+ took charge of for the film, *Innocence*.

Adapted from a popular manga of the same title, the *Doraemon* animated series has been in production since the 1980s. Part of this chapter will also discuss the *Doraemon* features that IKIF/IKIF+ took part in around the period in 2004 called "Renewal," when the voice actors of its television were changed, and when a *Doraemon* feature was produced by a new crew in 2006 after introducing its new production system. As animated features, the series was somehow in good condition, yet being of an average scale, and attempting different things, little by little. Another goal of ours is to focus on the animated opening title sequences, too, which enabled artists to challenge visual experiments. Such contractual work also gave opportunities to students to participate in making the animation.

3-D Computer Graphics in the *Ghost in the Shell 2: Innocence*

In making *Innocence*, I, Kifune, think that the aim of creating refined images in a short period of time led to setting more than one deadline by dividing the production schedule into three stages and more than one production scene where a number of personal computers are operated, and then to seek a congruous style by raising an expressive degree of each scene, each shot, and each picture, at the same time deliberately turning aside consistency in the directing of animation, production design, the supervising of animation, 3-D computer graphics, and others.

To achieve the aim, the film involved two animation directors, Nishikubo Toshihiko and Kusumi Naoko; two production designers, Hirata Shuichi and Taneda Yōhei—yet Ogura Hiromasa, the production designer of *Ghost in the Shell* (1995), took part in one scene of this sequel; and three supervising animators, Kise Kazuchika, Nishio Tetsuya, and Okiura

Hiroyuki. Also, the effects work of determining the final visual condition of the picture was done by Ezura Hisashi's team, with After Effects, who belongs to Production I.G, and by Omnibus Japan with Domino, and some of the work was done by the production designer Hirata Shuichi.

We were involved with and were assigned to the 3-D CG work, and we made it in more than one studio without interfering with one another: the opening title sequence by Polygon Pictures; the old streets of the slum district, the convenience store, and Kim's mansion by the 3-D CG team of Production I.G; the skies over the streets and Iturup, and the middle of the sea by Motor/lieZ; and the allies and festival of Iturup, and the inside of the factory ship by IKIF+. It seems that the director Oshii Mamoru anticipated that a stylistic inconsistency in the 3-D CG images rendered with respective different aesthetic senses should nonetheless give birth to visual diversity and eventually lead to the fertility of the film.

I will give a bit of close explanation about the scenes which I was involved with.

The scene of the streets/festival of Iturup was created as a loose scene in the middle of the film. Such a scene that only shows landscapes with few words is almost always inserted around the middle of Oshii's films; for example, *Patlabor: The Movie* (1989), *Patlabor: The Movie 2* (1993), and *Ghost in the Shell*. Its function is supposed as a time for reflecting on the meanings of the scenes spectators have seen.

In *Innocence*, too, the scene was created for the same effect, of which Kusumi took charge in the directing of animation. Since they had worked together as a team for *Metropolis* (2001), she and the production designer Hirata started to undertake it with the method of completing a scene by digitizing and pasting hand-drawn artistic materials—although there was an instance of drawing on a computer display in Photoshop—onto the 3-D CG plane, while bringing various elements from 3-D computer graphics, and then by compositing them in After Effects, as an extension of the method used in their preceding co-work: there was even an instance in which they stacked more than one hundred layered materials.

Furthermore, the director intended to express noisy urbanity in the scene. The plan was to present a city full of noises, by means, not of adding noises to hackneyed imagery of such kind, but of creating details through 3-D computer graphics and the artwork of Hirata's team, based on the layouts with high-density detail designed by Takeuchi Atsushi; and to create an image of purgatory and a magical sense in scale, with giant structures making a parade in the city, flowers drifting incessantly, and human beings so treated as to look faint by means of slow motion in which their movements look overlapped.

The featured 3-D CG imagery of the drifting flowers needed to be modified and animated shot by shot as it was not created automatically by computer software programs. Basic works for each shot were, therefore, done by several students interested in 3-D computer graphics. There are also some shots in which final movements were created by the students who supposedly had a high aptitude and could comparatively afford to take the time to animate them.

As for characters closed in on by the supervising animator Kise, who took charge of the scene, in order to make their impressions clearer, only a monk and a main character were so planned as to show their own skin, while each of the others put on a mask.

At the beginning, the movement of the background was supposed to be rendered with the method of the closely overlapped multilayers, which is traditional in Japanese animation, but was increasingly done with that of the camera mapping of 3-D computer graphics as long as it conformed to the 3-D CG shots that were being finished.

In the early stage of production, Oshii said that the scene would be the most loved one especially with the foreign viewers. It seems that his prediction proved true insofar as the scene of Iturup streets/festival alone was selected among some others as 3-D CG images of *Innocence* submitted to the Electronic Theatre of SIGGRAPH in Los Angeles on August 8–12, 2004.

I would like to give a further explanation in detail about remarkable shots in the scene.

Scene 36, Shot 01

Floats, *dashi*, in the festival parade were created as 3-D CG models because they were to appear more than one time not only in this shot but also in others. 3-D CG artists created rough models in order to look into an overall balance of the rough designs drawn by Takeuchi, and continued to give them much elaboration, based on additional details that Takeuchi put onto the line drawings of the printed models. Once the models were in a degree established, Hirata's team drew texture maps with the original printed images; dozens of maps were drawn.

Once the maps were applied to the models, a change was made in the setting of 3-D computer graphics for the material of each part of the floats.

For a difference in reflection of light on glass, wood, and metal, a close adjustment is made for both the modeling and textures. The plan was to make 3-D CG data perfect to the last detail by exchanging them many times among the workplaces of layout, 3-D computer graphics, and art. It took about a year to complete the 3-D CG data.

The background work was carried out at the same time as the others. The rough layouts and the rough models of the floats were put onto the 3-D CG space, and then the camerawork and the lighting were decided after their simulation. The test for the drifting flowers was repeatedly performed; the flowers in the back were given their movements through physical calculation, while the large petals in the front were animated through hand drawing.

This was followed by checking the range of framing, with the camera moved on a rough layout, which led to the drawing of an original background picture that has to be available. All of them were composited in 3-D computer graphics; rendered separately for various elements such as shade, shadows, colors, and reflection; and organized as an After Effects project by 3-D CG artists, followed by Hirata's effect work: finally, a shot was finished.

Scene 36, Shot 03

The elephant that appears in some shots went through the same rendering process with the floats. Yet, unlike the floats, the elephant has moving parts. Moreover, in the shot that has camerawork, it took some time to fix the movement of its nose. The moving speed of the nose felt different, whether its movement was finished in rough modeling, or given to the final model with much information full of details. This caused the position of the nose to change, requiring a close adjustment, when another change was given to the camerawork. The lighting and the drifting flowers, added to the shot, brought about a repetitive adjusting process.

The elephant standing on a boat was set to move along a large canal. The layouts drawn by Takeuchi for the camera maps of the background were entirely dark, filled up with a number of lines because there were intrigue-constructions drawn in them. More than one month was invested in drawing them. It took more than one month, even for a crewmember in Hirata's team, called "speedstar" for drawing quickly the background pictures. To recompose them in 3-D computer graphics cost the same time and carried the same laborious work. In expressing the surface of the water, such elements as reflection and transparency were separated and then composited in a painterly manner. The images of the displays at the bridges, for which experts were hired, were rendered in 2-D computer graphics and then put in the 3-D CG space.

Scene 36, Shot 08

All in this shot with a number of moving objects as well as camerawork were created in 3-D computer graphics, while 3-D CG modeling only for one single shot is not a usual case because it is hard work. It took about a year for the modeling process, which was carried out by just one 3-D CG artist.

Scene 36, Shot 12

In this shot, which has a camera movement of 130 degrees around a signal, more than one camera was used in order to process the background by means of camera mapping. When the drifting flowers from one and the same direction were shot by the 130-degree camerawork, their motion came to seemingly flow in a reverse direction on the screen. Despite a 3-D computer graphics presentation, it did not look good as the flowers were set to flow from the left upper side of the screen, no matter how many degrees the camera moves round by.

Scene 36, Shot 14

By means of camera mapping, perspective in change was made according to camerawork. In this shot, the hand protruding in the front of the divine statue was drawn by the art crew. The drifting flowers tuned to the camera moving back, was set to always flow from the left upper side of the screen with a trick.

Scene 36, Shot 17

The background and the treasure ship in this shot were created by means of camera mapping, and the foreground by means of 3-D CG modeling borrowed from part of the materials of the floats in shot 1. The modeling of the foreground was done no less closely than that of the floats, only to be made invisible, shaded by an adjustment of lighting in the final picture.

The director's judgment was that it is impossible to know what to abandon if all are not created; and the approach taken was to treat even points whose resultant qualitative improvement may be seen almost invisible in comparison with efforts made for them entirely contrary to the usual approach made in the scenes of animation production, that which ignores works whose effect is not conspicuous in spite of efforts, with emphasis placed on cost performance.

Scene 36, Shot 19/21/22

There being live-action footage of a Taiwanese festival as reference for this shot, it was successful in creating more refined 3-D CG images by elaborating it. For the Generals of Thousand Mile Sight and the Chinese-styled Robotans, there is an aspect that took much time for presenting in 3-D computer graphics the characteristic dynamics of Japanese animation such as an exaggerated motion for their gigantic sense and the motion of their seeming to close in on the camera, as well as for modeling of them.

The 3-D computer graphics of the inside of the factory ship was rendered when the production of the film reached its last third period. Nishikubo directed this animation part, while Okiura, the supervising animator of this scene, created all the layouts in 3-D CG applications along with 3-D CG artists. As the production actually faced its final moment with no more room in the schedule, it was impossible to invest more time in the festival scene. The backgrounds of all the shots in this scene including those without camerawork were created in 3-D computer graphics. However, only a minimum number of textures and image boards for each section were finished as the background art unit could only afford to draw that amount given the time limit. It seems that the best animators in Japan worked together to draw this scene as the drawing crew of the other scenes took part later in helping out after finishing their own work. There were nonetheless sections in which the shape of characters was much changed by each artist in charge of them, but a high quality of hand-drawn animation made such change not so serious. Although the 3-D CG work here was done in a shorter period than the other scenes in *Innocence*, while it was given a sufficient time in comparison with other usual films, this scene was enough for a climax without looking poor as it was covered by a high quality of animation. Oshii said that there was no problem; in the editing, he would cut shots with conflicting, low expressive levels if they had resulted from the limit of time. In the end, he did not cut any shot in this scene.

For human characters in the defensive wall supposed to be drawn in a usual way in the stage of storyboard, there was the change of creating them, too, in 3-D computer graphics, in order to lessen the burden of drawing as they were set to be completely surrounded by the wall. And while Matsumoto Kaoru created indicators or displays for a specialist crewmember of Production I.G to follow through the drawing process, IKIF+ took charge of those that appeared to overlap with a structure so as to lessen the overall load of work. This is how each crewmember made changes in her/his own role, adapting to circumstances in order to be on time to the end.

Scene 54, the aisle in the ship

This scene was set by Watabe Takashi. There were data rendered with his original 3-D CG application, not drawn on a usual paper. Based on them, 3-D CG artists set up a rough scene and then after putting details onto its printout, Watabe determined the final design of the scene. He created layouts in cooperation with Okiura putting the temporary models of characters in a 3-D CG space at the same time with ordering the required minimum number of textures. Additionally, given the line of sight and grids so that perspective might be understood in either a horizontal or vertical way, the determined layout was developed to a line drawing, which was taken as an original layout drawing. As they appeared to be merely 3-D CG images, despite the rendering after mapping them to the textures sent from the art unit, the models were made to approximate to the background art by adding light for a colored reflection or an improbable shade, in order to make them congruous with their hand-drawn backgrounds.

Scene 55, the security flat

As for the setting of the flat, Takeuchi alone was aware how it would move so he drew some of the storyboard images. For the indicators created by Matsumoto in this scene where there are cylindrical surfaces in the center, a trick was to make use of 3-D computer graphics so that they might fall beautifully on the bodies of operators. They were so set as to look better on a screen, with their position and size changed for each shot.

Scene 56, the inside of the gallery

The setting and final shape of the empty center were much changed in accordance with the camerawork of each shot. Some floors were omitted for a sense of speed, and the bottom of the factory ship was made open, or the empty center taller, for a more powerful impression in a shot from the top. This section was finished much approximate to hand-drawn backgrounds, although it is originally of 3-D CG imagery; since it was completed in an early stage, enough time was available for working on it through trial and error. However, most of the 3-D CG backgrounds were made invisible via the overlapping presence of figures of indicators that were hand-drawn in two-dimensional cel animation describing the building destruction scene.

Scene 58, the assembly line of the gynoid

Hard work was required in this scene to create a presentation of water. As 3-D computer graphics alone makes it different, distant from hand-drawn characters, the work of compositing was done in a close adjustment of reflection and shade, transparent-looking things, and others, after separating them from each other. The gynoid-manufacturing pots' coming up and that of their hatches' opening were animated with movements whose speed is controlled faster or slower, given extreme acceleration and deceleration like *tsume* (squeezing) and *tame* (charging) specific to animation.

Scene 58b, the gun room

This is a scene in which the hand-drawn security guards pick out guns and arm themselves with them one after another. Here two-dimensional images and three-dimensional ones are intricately mixed with each other; the guards and the guns are of two dimensions, and the place from which the guns are picked are of three dimensions.

Scene 59b, the gallery

This scene was created in the last stage of all the production. As the art unit had no more time to draw images for it, consequently, the preceding and following scenes were used as a guide without reference images. Despite a prior discussion on lighting (its direction) with the director of animation Nishikubo, shadows in the finished animation were depicted in the opposite direction. As the background was created in 3-D computer graphics, it was possible to adjust its lighting in the reverse direction to that of the animation. This animated procedure might have come near being a crucial failure if it had been hand-drawn.

Scene 59a, the top of the catwalk

Utsunomiya Satoru, an experienced animator, took charge of key animation of this scene and he was interested in 3-D computer graphics at that time so he performed the animation based on a printout of the data of gynoids that were used for a reference. In other words, he imparted movement to them in 3-D computer graphics CG software. While supported by the IKIF+ crew as he was not accustomed to the computer software, Utsunomiya attempted to create movements acceptable to himself, controlling all the instant poses of characters by way of inserting a key frame every two frames with his saying that he did not trust computer interpolation, unlike 3-D CG artists who try to control movement with the required minimum number of key frames. They were much surprised at his methodological difference.

Scene 62, various places in the ship

The motion of the doors that close one after another was at first set to a slow speed, in consideration of their size and weight. However, Oshii in his final check directed his crew to increase the speed more than three times, placing emphasis on the flow of the shots in this scene. An objection was made by Okiura, who took charge of key animation, and also Nishikubo, the director of animation, but this scene when shown on the screen was successful in the quick motion of the doors creating suspense, somehow by virtue of a sound effect. Ultimately, priority was given to the effect on screen—that is, with no complete devotion to reality, although such elements as lighting and the size of characters were intended to be manipulated as little as possible, taking into account even the position of camera and the caliber of lens, which are likely to be done in 3-D computer graphics.

Scene 64, the development lab in the ship

In order to make clear the setting of a place with little noise, a change of lighting was made from the preceding sections and the flickering gauges were almost eliminated. Girls' faces were required to show a subtle, continuous change in perspective resulting from slow camerawork. The faces on the front of every pot, in each of which a girl is locked, were depicted in 3-D computer graphics. Such a change was to be closer than the pencil

1. Editors' note: Publicity print image of *Ghost in the Shell 2: Innocence* (2004) on a cinema book cover on sale when the film was first screened in Japan.

2. DVD cover image of *Ghost in the Shell 2: Innocence* in Taiwan.

3. A poster-advertisement of *Ghost in the Shell 2: Innocence* in Japan.

4. Editors' note: A publicity print image of the characters found in the popular manga, *Doraemon*.

line of hand-drawn animation. First, the hand-drawn girl characters were placed onto 3-D computer graphics. Later, this work led to 3-D CG modeling, to which lines drawn on cels were applied onto the faces modeled in 3-D computer graphics, by means of camera mapping in order to make the technically different elements congruous with each other.

A First Conclusion

It seems that the arts in Japan are likely to turn to a craft, to be obsessed with details, to put too much importance on subtle distinctions, to lead to such work as washing every single grain of rice. The work of *Innocence* was performed in such a direction. However, it might have been a right methodology for creating digital images that would last ten years at least,

5. Editors' note: A postal stamp image of *Doraemon*.

through a long series of manual, analog labor, among many others that are likely to be out of date with the increasing version number of 3-D CG software programs. Computer graphics was made use of as if it were a brush in painting: the setting of lighting and surface was closely adjusted; some pictures were rendered with Photoshop; and images were modified with After Effects[1]—as if a picture had been painted. In the method of making a final picture, the film was exactly opposite to Otomo Katushiro's *Steamboy* (2004), in which IKIF+ were involved at the same time with it; among them were crewmembers who joined in the former after finishing their work in the latter. In *Innocence*, the effect unit added much change to the images rendered by the 3-D CG unit—their picture making presupposed some change possible, while in *Steamboy*, most of the images made by a unit of the same kind led to the completion of final pictures with little change as there was an aspect in which 3-D CG artists took an additional charge of effect work. Despite such a difference, in both films it seems to have been possible to show the characteristic of IKIF+ in the sense of 3-D computer graphics as painting a picture, bearing in mind the unity of style in using it surrounded by 2-D animation.

3-D Computer Graphics in the Main Body of the Feature Film Series *Doraemon*

Compared to others, about one and a half times more in budget and production time has been invested to the feature theatrical film series of *Doraemon,* mainly for families with preschool children or elementary students than to general animated features.

In this second part of the chapter, we will discuss 3-D CG presentation in theatrical animated features, different from that which is magnificent, visually elaborated, with investment of time and a large budget, as in *Ghost in the Shell 2.* IKIF+ became involved with the 3-D computer graphics in the main body of the feature film series *Doraemon* after *Nobita's Dinosaur 2006* (2006). At that time, the animated feature series made a full change of the production crew and the voice artists of the *Doraemon* television series. The beginning was followed by *Nobita's New Great Adventure into the Underworld: The Seven Magic Users* (2007), *Nobita and the Green Giant Legend* (2008), and *The New Record of Nobita: Starblazer,* the fourth work of the feature film series released in spring 2009.

A common theme among the four *Doraemon* films in the 3-D CG production of their main bodies is to make 3-D computer graphics not look incongruous with two-dimensional, hand-drawn animation in the commercial animated work aimed at children in whom the worldview of the *Doraemon* series is established. Keeping his characters and worldview, the animated comics by the creators Fujiko Fujio F show main characters' adventure with a story and a setting, both of which can be expanded from a television series to film. Required to make powerful visuals that deserve to be seen in a cinema equipped with a big screen and sound facilities, 3-D computer graphics can make the visuals look isolated, failing to aim at the consistency of the series' worldview, if it has a live-action look. 3-D computer graphics in the films aimed at an expression that has regard for congruity with the hand-drawn, two-dimensional 2-D animation character drawing and it depends on the world of art in animation.

Furthermore, there was a difference in the theme of 3-D CG expression, according to the narrative of and the director's needs of each film. Making a positive introduction of 3-D computer graphics, the first post-Renewal film, *Nobita's Dinosaur 2006*, employed a 3-D CG presentation of the time tunnel, differing a bit from that of the television series, and comparatively a lot of background animation was included.

In the second post-*Renewal* film, *Nobita's New Great Adventure into the Underworld,* 3-D computer graphics was not supposed to be so much used in the beginning, except for the required minimum quantity of background animation and the inner space of Doraemon's four-dimensional pocket, but plenty of 3-D CG background art was created in the presentations of the cosmic space, the planet, and the moon, in order to cover the section of background art, particularly due to a delay in production.

In the third post-*Renewal* film, *Nobita and the Green Giant Legend* (2008), an attempt was made to sway trees, which had not been possible to put into motion until then, in the background with 3-D computer graphics. There was an attempt at a 3-D CG presentation of characters as well as 3-D CG background art in the mob scene of botanic people in a meeting venue.

In the fourth post-*Renewal* film, *The New Record of Nobita: Starblazer,* an attempt for vehicles, devices, and others was made at outlines with stress and looseness in hand-drawn style, not simply relying on Cel Shader and Cel Edge2 (software programs).[2] 3-D computer graphics was rendered to look so congruously as directly touched in the cel animation of the analogical age, in a close adjustment of stains and the color of shade, instead of painting separate colors. 3-D CG background art was created in hand-drawn style, by not relying on texture mapping, but by controlling reflection and reflected images, as with the inside of the cockpit of the spaceship that the main characters get on.

The method of work changed with this flexibility, adjusted to the director and the situation of production, and any of the four films could be successful in using 3-D computer graphics in creating the worldview of Doraemon.

The Opening Title Sequences of the *Doraemon* Films Animated by 3-D Computer Graphics

In the four job assignments that were given, IKIF and IKIF+ took charge of creating the opening title sequences in the *Doraemon* film series.

The title sequences of the film series have taken a form of an original animation status by which each *Doraemon* film presents the main production crew in a series of superimposed text along with the same theme song with the television series, linking the introduction to its actual beginning.

Unlike the main body of the film with respect to 3-D computer graphics, the sequence allows artistic play and experimentation, which seems to result somehow from seeking an effective method available in a short period of time as its framework of production. IKIF and IKIF+ were involved in the following films making the title sequences:

Doraemon: Nobita in the Wan-Nyan Spacetime Odyssey (2004)
Doraemon: Nobita's New Great Adventure into the Underworld—The Seven Magic Users (2007)
Doraemon: Nobita and the Green Giant Legend (2008)
Doraemon: The New Record of Nobita: Starblazer (2009)

Title Sequence of *Doraemon*: Nobita in the Wan-Nyan Spacetime Odyssey

In 2003, we took the first charge of creating the opening title sequence of a *Doraemon* film (I, Ishida Sonoko, was the animation director of the contracted *Doraemon* filmwork), whose release was scheduled in the March of the next year, at the same time with that of Oshii Mamoru's *Ghost in the Shell 2: Innocence*, in which 3-D computer graphics were rendered by Tokumitsu Kifune and IKIF+.

We proposed that paper puppets act in a theatrical space, as in *Mini-Pat* released in 2002, making our presentation for it clearer by showing the previous work as an example of 3-D CG expression radiating warmth for the child audience. Taking children's play and dream as a theme, the plan was that the characters themselves make their own dream a performance looking like the puppet play of *Peipu Satō*.[3] Figures such as dogs, cats, and spaceships, appearing in the main body of the film, were introduced in the developmental course of linking hand drawings and the play of children's (character's) own making in their dream.

In a technological aspect, an attempt was made to reconstruct the analogical techniques of expression in a digital way. The stage for the puppet play was set to include the optical toy of zoetrope with moving images and the cine-calligraphy of scratching film in both of which IKIF had formed their own works until then. As for the cine-calligraphy, 35mm black film was scratched horizontally and then scanned as a material for compositing.

Motives of the optical toy, the paper puppets with the feeling of crayon, and mobiles were merged in a digital system giving a presentation of three-dimensionality, light and shadow, and bubbles specific to 3-D CG computer graphics expression. Further attention was paid to presenting the materiality of paper and handwriting, and the warmth of hand-made objects, instead of the feeling of hardness in CG images.

Made of real paper, the puppets were shot in being moved to songs and a storyboard. The footages edited as animatics were referred to in creating 3-D CG shots. It took three months to finish the title sequence.

Title Sequence of *Doraemon: Nobita's New Great Adventure into the Underworld*

At the time when an innovation of the television series took place (use of wonderful animation tools and change of the background animation process, etc.), following the *Renewal* period where a full change of voice artists was enacted in the *Doraemon* television series, IKIF+ came to be involved in 3-D CG production for the main body of the film *Doraemon: Nobita's Dinosaur 2006* released in March 2006, a year later after a post-*Renewal* series had made its first appearance on television.

We did not take charge of the opening title sequence in this first post-*Renewal Doraemon* feature. However, in the autumn when its 3-D CG work was in progress, we were asked to plan and create the title sequence of the second post-*Renewal* film, *Doraemon: Nobita's New Great Adventure into the Underworld,* released in March 2007.

We chose the expression of the silhouette animation of cutout paper by means of 3-D computer graphics as a method of presenting images of the underworld and the cosmic space setting a different feeling from the film's main body. Impossible to invest a time in modeling, owing to a short period of production, we took the workflow of compositing movements with 2-D objects. For the same reason, a development was taken into consideration for reusing as silhouette materials the wonderful tools designed for the television series, and for reusing the moon, and the objects and scenes of the space of Doraemon's pocket for the main body of the film. An attempt was made at the beauty of a real silhouette image, or of a transmitted light as in stained glass. Attention was paid to representing the optical diffusion, haze, and blur, as in a silhouette against a light background.

Title Sequence of *Doraemon: Nobita and the Green Giant Legend*

The expression of clay animation developed by means of 3-D computer graphics was adopted in order to avoid repeating the techniques of expression used thus far, albeit as short a period of production as before.

Clay work was put into action (which IKIF played a central part) by directing five to six students, as part-time crewmembers, recruited from Tokyo Zokei University and Tokyo Polytechnic University. They were directed to make clay puppets with the parts of an element supposed to be composited with 3-D computer graphics, in accordance to the design plan, and then to composite the animated footages of the parts (carried out by IKIF) onto pictures close to their final condition. They could carry out the work in ways similar to the two-dimensional animation that they learned, through digitalizing the parts even if they were made of clay. It was possible to let the students learn the methods of three-dimensional (not CG) animation and relief animation, different from two-dimensional animation, as various examples of an application of digital animation.

Nobita and main characters and materials for artwork were created in clay relief, or in a three-dimensional way, and the parts—faces, bodies, arms, and hands—of each of them by means of a sequential or individual photography for CG data. A reuse of 3-D CG objects for the main body of the film brought many of the 3-D CG characters of botanical people from their original place to the title sequence, which were rendered to look like clay puppets by mapping the texture of clay to their surface in order to get rid of incongruity when composited with the clay elements, and which were again composited with the other clay elements and those of animation in 3-D CG software programs or After Effects. The animated words of the title song obtained a good response.

Title Sequence of *Doraemon: The New Record of Nobita: Starblazer*

Unlike hand-drawn cel animation, cutout animation was made with original pictures drawn in water-soluble crayons. Deforming characters drawn with a few lines in crayons, an attempt was made to present a lovely, pictorial world with the feeling of hand drawing as shown in picture books. A picture with a deep and warm sense was possible to construct, with additions of lighting, sparkling effects, and a sense of depth, by using 3-D computer graphics in imparting and compositing movements.

A choice of presenting such cutout animation can be said to have been made to minimize the working time of the 3-D CG crew. It was required to make the title sequence in 3-D computer graphics based on the storyboard by the director of animation, Kaneko Shizue, with an early plan of making it in traditional, two-dimensional cel animation. In addition, the production period of the title sequence was shorter than any of the previous ones. Moreover, 3-D CG work for the main body of the film was in progress under a very tight production schedule. The two people of IKIF began to draw original pictures in water-soluble crayons that were scanned for rendering 3-D CG objects. Rendering 3-D CG scenes, animating, and compositing were done intensively when the shots of the main body reached their finish. The IKIF+ crew's technological accumulation and its achievement in skill contributed to the high efficiency and acceleration of work.

A Second Conclusion

Besides *Ghost in the Shell 2* and the *Doraemon* film series, each film has its own production, schedule, and narrative, which makes it different what it is required to, and possible to, present with 3-D computer graphics. However, we have paid attention to creating a picture congruous with the worldview and pictorial world of a film in response to the director's needs under various conditions, and to imparting a movement proper to the art of animation, that it will not look mechanical with 3-D computer graphics created in the middle of the traditional, hand-drawn two-dimensional animation. And we will keep creating 3-D computer graphics for animated works, aiming at as large an effect and result as possible with high efficiency in a working process. Moreover, our hope is to seek and realize the new, interesting expression of 3-D CG animation.

Notes

1. Adobe After Effects is a standard editing software of moving images used in the production scenes of Japanese animation.

2. These are methods of depicting images using 3-D CG softwares. Cel Shader expresses shadows by way of color coding, not gradation, and Cel Edge expresses outlines in such a way that they are seen in hand-drawn animation.

3. The play is performed by manipulating puppets, each of which is made of a figure drawn on a small paperboard set onto a rod. A human or animal figure is usually drawn on the paperboard.

Animation and Psychology

The Midlife Crisis of Kawamoto Kihachiro

—Masao Yokota

Introduction: Animation and Clinical Psychology

A midlife crisis is a well-known psychological event in the human life cycle. Japan's renowned master puppet animation director, the late Kawamoto Kihachiro (1925–2010), changed his career in midlife: He quit his job as a successful animator at Shiba Productions where he worked with his senior colleague, Iizawa Tadasu, and went to Czechoslovakia to study puppet animation with the great Jiri Trnka, thereafter becoming an independent director. After coming back to Japan, he directed *Breaking of Branches Is Forbidden*, which is based on Mibu Noh-farce. He changed his career from an animator to an independent animation director. This career change indicates his midlife crisis, and making independent animation was the solution to it. Kawamoto's latest animation is *The Book of the Dead* (2005). In this animation, the heroine, Iratsume, who keeps copying sutra (a Buddhist teaching), sees the image of a nobleman that appears among the peaks of two mountains nearby. She wants to weave the yarn into a cloth because the nobleman is naked. It seems that Kawamoto's creative process is reflected in Iratsume's behavior. There are many unfinished animation plans among the *Breaking of Branches is Forbidden* and *The Book of the Dead* projects. These unfinished plans indicated that Kawamoto had developed his lifestyle of Zen.

Animation is deeply related to psychology. For example, movement in animation is explained by perception in psychology. There are so many fields in psychology. All of them may be differently related to animation. This article focuses on clinical psychology. In clinical psychology, a client

Table 1. Kawamoto's Works and Related Events

Year	Age	Event
1925		Born in Tokyo
1963	38 years old	came to Czechoslovakia to see Trnka and prepared for *Breaking of Branches is Forbidden* based on the Mibu-farce
1964	39 years old	finished a continuity with pictures of *People Who Saw a Dragon* based on a story of Iizawa Tadasu at the age of 17
1966	41 years old	*Breaking of Branches is Forbidden* was finished in the third-floor study of Iizawa's house
1973	48 years old	*Travel* that reflected Kawamoto's experiences in Czechoslovakia was released
Unknown	unknown	*A Dream of a Butterfly* was prepared for animation but unfinished
1991	66 years old	"The Dragon" based on Iizawa's story was prepared for animation but unfinished
2005	80 years old	*The Book of the Dead*

with psychological trouble may be assessed by a clinical psychologist using psychological tests, observation methods, interviews, materials, and so on. Usually, the clinical psychologist assesses personality traits and an intelligent level of the client. However, this chapter tries to understand the creativity of an animator by assessing his animations and materials that he prepared for creating those animations. This method is a clinical psychological one. I conducted several interviews with an animator and was able to refer to his materials permitted by him. He is the late Kawamoto Kihachiro.

The Late Master Puppet Animator: Kawamoto Kihachiro and His Animation Films

Before beginning to describe Kawamoto, I shall explain a basic frame of reference that I use in clinical psychology studies. It is the human life cycle. The human being usually changes his or her life structure periodically (Levinson, 1980). One of the structural changes that appears in one's midlife is known as a midlife crisis. When the human being enters into his or her midlife, he or she is expected to look back over the past, sometimes realizing that certain past desires were not attained. And then he may change his career to another. The career change may be a result of a solution to his midlife crisis. Or, sometimes the sudden change of life direction may appear during a midlife crisis.

Kawamoto is arguably the most famous artistic animation director in Japan (Yokota, 2003; 2006a; 2006b). Born in Tokyo in 1925, he made puppets since his childhood. When he was in his twenties, Kawamoto was struck by Jiri Trnka's poetic puppet animation, and he believed that he, too, could compose poetry with puppet animation if given the opportunity. At that time, however, he was too busy making commercial films. He wanted to take some time to study Trnka's work carefully. Finally he wrote to Trnka, and Trnka replied, encouraging Kawamoto to come to Czechoslovakia. At thirty-eight years of age, Kawamoto had already established a fine career, but he quit his job at Shiba Productions making commercial films, left Japan, and went to Czechoslovakia to work with Jiri Trnka. This is certainly a midlife crisis (Yokota, 2006a).

After getting a reply from Trnka, Kawamoto did not hesitate to go to Czechoslovakia to learn what he could about puppet animation. When he returned to Japan, he became an independent director of puppet animation films. This was the wish he had had in his youth; this was the consequent result of his midlife crisis.

Kawamoto's first project after arriving in Czechoslovakia was based on an old traditional Japanese play. Kawamoto had a friend in Japan, Iizawa Tadasu (his former boss at Shiba), who had once taken him to see a Mibu-farce, *Breaking of Branches is Forbidden*,[1] and Kawamoto wanted to make a poetic puppet animation film of this story. Kawamoto wrote a letter from Czechoslovakia to Japan asking Iizawa about theatrical costumes of a Noh-farce (Kawamoto, 2002), and his friend sent back detailed information (figs. 1 and 2). Kawamoto planned to shoot the film while in Eastern Europe, but his wish was not realized.

In 1966, after returning to Japan, the film was completed in the third-floor study of Iizawa's house. Kawamoto's design for the camera setting still remains, as well as the original patterns for the puppet costumes he made and dyed (Kawamoto, 2009; fig. 3). Kawamoto studied the Noh-farce and carefully applied it to his animation as much as possible.

In *Breaking of Branches is Forbidden*, four characters appear: an old monk (fig. 4), a young monk (fig. 5), a samurai (fig. 6), and his servant (fig. 7). The setting is a walled garden centered by a large old cherry tree in full blossom. The old monk orders the young monk to chant a sutra, warning him not to break any branches off the cherry tree. The old monk puts a sign on one of the lower branches: "BREAKING OF BRANCHES IS

FORBIDDEN," then goes out. The young monk chants the sutra, but soon begins to grow drowsy and doze. The samurai and his servant come to see the cherry blossoms. They knock at the gate, waking the young monk, but he refuses them entry. The samurai and his servant begin to drink sake outside the gate. The sweet odor of the sake is irresistible to the young monk, and he reaches for the sake cup. The samurai grabs the monk's arm, terrifying and threatening him, and forces him to unlock the gate (fig. 8). Once inside the garden, the samurai orders his servant to make the young monk drunk, and the monk cannot resist the sake. When the young monk is drunk and unconscious, they dress him in female clothing and tip a straw hat over his face. Despite the warning sign, the samurai breaks a branch of blossoms from the old tree, and they go out. The old monk returns, mistakes the young monk for a girl, and imagines that she is smiling coyly under the brim of her hat (fig. 9). The young monk awakens to a difficult situation. The old monk soon realizes it is the young monk and flies into a rage.

Kawamoto wrote many letters from Czechoslovakia to Iizawa in Japan, saying he wanted to make puppet animation with symbolic stories. Trnka had inspired him to think that a puppet could play a typical person in a historical setting and have a more poetic effect than a real actor. The puppet could have a symbolic meaning of a nation. Thus, the puppet was ideal for the old stories that indicated typicality across the nation.

Breaking of Branches is Forbidden can have a symbolic meaning. The Mibu-farce is a funny story that shows a type of master-pupil relationship: The old and the young monks have a master and pupil relationship. Kawamoto was planning his version before Trnka suggested to him that he should consider using Japanese culture in puppet animation. When Kawamoto left Japan, he also left Iizawa Tadasu, whom he held in high esteem. Iizawa had had the same dream at one time, to make puppet animation. Iizawa had founded Shiba Productions with Kawamoto and they had a master-pupil relationship at Shiba for many years. Then Kawamoto left Shiba and left Japan. He was eager to see Trnka, cut his relationship with Shiba, but later shot his animation in Iizawa's private home when he returned from Czechoslovakia. This is similar to the young monk who likes sake, got drunk, unwillingly assumed a disguise, and was then scolded by the old monk.

Another project in 1964, *People Who Saw a Dragon* is a story that Iizawa Tadasu wrote at the age of seventeen, and Kawamoto wanted to adapt it into a puppet animation film. He asked Trnka to read it, and Trnka advised Kawamoto that a small number of puppets would be suitable for its animation, but in the end many puppets were necessary for the film.

The story is as follows: An emperor rules ancient China. The people live in safety and there are no criminals. A delegation arrives from Africa to pay tribute to the emperor, and presents him with a gift of a lion (fig. 10). The emperor appoints a young man to take care of it. The young man goes to the delegation, and they tell him that the lion eats the human body of a criminal every day. The young man has a problem because there are no criminals in his country. He tries to give the lion many other foods, but the lion will not eat them and grows weaker day by day. At last, the young man gives the lion his own arms (fig. 11), legs, and torso. The lion grows stronger. The young man has only his head remaining. At the moment he is giving his head to the lion (fig. 12), the emperor comes in and watches as the lion changes into a dragon (fig. 13). The young man has sacrificed himself for the lion, and the self-sacrifice transformed the lion into a dragon.

The young man is another one of Kawamoto's self-images. From youth, Kawamoto wanted to devote his life to puppet animation, just as the young man sacrificed himself for the lion. The dragon that the lion became symbolizes the poetic animation that Kawamoto wanted to produce. The young man is an idealized personality for Kawamoto. Thus, Kawamoto described two self-images while he was in Czechoslovakia: One is the young monk who has a weakness for sake, and the other is a young man who sacrifices his body.

By showing the puppet performing almost in a trance, Kawamoto believed that the puppet is eminently suitable for showing a person who sets his heart on something. From the beginning, Kawamoto seemed to know what the puppet could do. The puppet is a medium that helps people see the truth through the image that the puppet reflects.

Another story, *The Dragon*, was listed as a project that Kawamoto planned to create in 1991. The project was introduced on a pamphlet of *Briar-Rose, or Sleeping Beauty* that was released in a theater.[2] The story seems to be similar to the original one written by Iizawa, *People Who Saw a Dragon*. But according to Kawamoto, the last scene is slightly different. In 1991, Kawamoto was sixty-six years old, and he described the emperor as a poet. The emperor's desire is to compose a poem of the highest sentiment, but he has not been able to do so. In the last scene, the emperor sees the transformed dragon in the sky (fig. 14), and learns that the young caretaker has given up his body on the rainbow (fig. 15). When he sees all this, the emperor is inspired to write his poem.

Over the years, Kawamoto's personal point of view shifted from the devotion of the self-sacrificing young man in *People Who Saw a Dragon* to the inspiration of the emperor-poet in *The Dragon* or from the young man to the old man. Now, in his senescence, he was more interested in the creative process similar to how the emperor obtains his poem. Unfortunately, the project of *The Dragon* has yet to be completed as an animation film.

The Book of the Dead is Kawamoto's latest animation film that has been analyzed in detail elsewhere in the literature (Yokota, 2006b), so my comments on it will be brief.

The heroine Iratsume makes handwritten copies of a sutra. The poet Ohtomo-no-Yakamochi is her admirer; he is devoted to her but does not meet her. Like the emperor in *The Dragon*, Yakamochi watches from a distance. Iratsume keeps copying out the sutra and occasionally sees the image of a nobleman that appears between the peaks of two mountains nearby (fig. 16). After seeing his image several times, she decides she wants to make a cloth for him; she has noticed he is naked. She spins thread from lotus stalks and weaves it on her loom (figs. 17, 18), but she is not satisfied with the cloth. She draws an image of the nobleman on the cloth. We witness the creative process of art—from spinning thread, to weaving cloth, to drawing the image—and the creative process symbolizes Kawamoto's own life. Kawamoto reviewed his artistic and creative life as an animation director (Yokota, 2008). Iratsume is brought toward spiritual enlightenment by devoting herself to creating the cloth for the nobleman.

There is another unfinished project, *A Dream of a Butterfly*, that is based on the Noh-drama *Kantan* and also a Daoist philosophical writing by Zhuangzi. The little story goes like this:

A monkey-show man comes to a tea store in his travels, located at the highest point on a mountain road. He asks the host for a cup of rice gruel, and notices a small butterfly hovering around him. With his monkey nearby, he lies down to rest on a bench (fig. 19). Some people march by in a procession. The monkey-show man is awakened and beckoned to a palanquin. The people march on in procession. The monkey-show man becomes an emperor, the wealthiest in the land, and he notices a small butterfly hovering around him. He transforms his own body into that of the butterfly. It flutters around, and then stops. At the same time, the tea shop host appears (fig. 20), carrying the cup of rice gruel, in front of the tea shop. The monkey-show man notices that the prosperity was in a dream.

The Japanese like this drama story. Within a few moments a person sees his whole life and reviews it clearly, to see that life is something transient and empty. Kawamoto kept creating puppet animation films in which not only the heroines but also the heroes devoted their entire lives to doing something, and at last the great truth about life dawned upon them. However, the monkey-show man dreams his whole life and understands his life to be transient and empty. He does not devote himself to creating anything. This story shows that all achievements in life are like dreams. The aging Kawamoto is suggesting that his artistic life was as transient as the dream of the monkey-show man. Kawamoto feels that his life of creating animation, as transient as a dream, is the same way a typical Japanese person feels about his own life.

Kawamoto was interested in Zen Buddhism. During his stay in Czechoslovakia, he cited a poem (*shige*) in his diary about Su Shi (also known as Su Dongpo: 1037–1101), who was a famous Chinese poet (Kawamoto, 2002).[3] In Japanese Zen Buddhism, the *shige* is usually composed by a spiritually awakened Zen priest. The *shige* that Kawamoto cited is as follows:

> Misty rain on Mount Lu,
> And waves surging in Che Kiang;
> When you have not yet been there,
> Many a regret you have;
> But once there and homeward you went,
> How matter-of-fact things look!
> Misty rain on Mount Lu,
> And waves surging in Che Kiang. (Suzuki, 2001)

Suzuki (2001: 15) explained this *shige*,

> The misty rain on Mount Lu and the surging waves of the Che Kiang remain the same whether or not you have Zen; as the poet sings, "there is nothing special" before and after your arrival there. The same old world with Zen or without Zen, yet there must be something new in your consciousness, for otherwise you cannot say, "It is all the same."

Kawamoto cited the *shige* in his animated film, *Travel*, made in 1973. In *Travel*, a young woman suddenly wants to travel abroad when she sees a poster of a travel in a train. The *shige* that suggests the mind of the young woman appears. An airplane flies. She arrives at a foreign country and is guided by a blind man. He takes her to the top of a building and later she comes down from the top of the building. She is shocked to see that surrounding architecture is completely broken. She is perplexed, wandering from place to place, and experiences extraordinary events. She sees a boy who eats babies, a tank and servicepersons with a rifle, a man who is burning himself to death, and monks who travel. She transforms herself into a statute in despair. Audiences hear a sutra reciting. The young woman sits in Zen meditation in the center of a mandala. This means that she is spiritually awakened. An airplane flies. She comes back to Tokyo. The *shige* appears again. It indicates that the young woman has experienced a sense of spiritual awakening during her travels abroad. This *shige* recurs again in the unfinished film project *A Dream of a Butterfly*; it ultimately portrays a state of being spiritually awakened as Kawamoto had expressed in *Travel*.

Conclusion

Here, I have discussed Kawamoto's first and last puppet animation films as well as Kawamoto's unpublished and unfinished projects.[4] As he aged, Kawamoto's films reflected more and more specifically on the theme of the human life cycle. The earlier films show how people experience an individualistic obsessive desire to get something, while the later projects depict people with an open-minded wish to take care of others. Even later, Kawamoto's films made during his old age tend to give a summary that a human life is like an empty dream and it is influenced by Zen Buddhism, which Japanese audiences recognize.

I want to also mention that there is a group of animation directors in Japan whose animated works are reflective of their age advancement. This group consists of famous animation directors like Takahata Isao, Miyazaki Hayao, and Oshii Mamoru. When Takahata was sixty-three years old, he directed *My Neighbors the Yamadas* (1999). In *My Neighbors the Yamadas*, Takahata Isao describes how members of a family depend on one another. When Miyazaki Hayao was sixty-three years old, he directed *Howl's Moving Castle* (2004). In this animation, Miyazaki describes how a heroine integrates several isolated people into one family. Miyazaki sent the message that the broken family system should be "fixed" in *Howl's Moving Castle*. Both directors had described a hero and heroine in past animated works before, but their ages have advanced, and they both have changed their themes from the individual to the family (Yokota, 2010). In another significant example, *Innocence* is a story of a hero who forms a deep friendship with a dog after the loss of an intimate relationship with a heroine. This loss experience symbolizes the death of a loved one, or it may mean that director Oshii was sub- or un-consciously thinking about his own mortality as he made the film. Contemplating mortality is a psychological theme common in middle age, an integral subplot of the midlife crisis. Oshii was fifty-three years old when he directed the animation *Innocence* in 2004.

These Japanese animation directors have changed their themes in accordance with the progress of the human life cycle (Yokota, 2006a), shifting from the focus on the "self" to the focus on "others."

I lecture about psychology and animation at both the psychology and the cinema departments in Nihon University. In my courses, I mention not only Kawamoto but also Takahata Isao, Miyazaki Hayao, and Oshii Mamoru. The other animation directors whom I introduce in my lectures are the late Kon Satoshi (1963–2010), Mori Yasuji (1925–1992), and Jiri Trnka (1912–1969). All of them change their themes in animation according to their life cycle.

Lastly, I want to mention a ceremony held on November 20 in 2010 in memory of Kawamoto, who passed away on August 23, 2010. Five hundred people came together. The chairperson of the ceremony, the animation director Mori Masaaki, announced to guests that the ceremony should be presented pleasantly as Kawamoto would usually want to entertain visitors sincerely. The warmhearted ceremony indicated that Kawamoto's life was in full bloom like the cherry blossom depicted in the film project, *Breaking of Branches is Forbidden*. Even if Kawamoto summed up the human life as an empty dream in his later animated works, his artistic contributions to Japanese animation and world puppet animation are permanent.

Notes

1. The Mibu-farce is a pantomime played annually at the Mibu temple in Kyoto for ten days beginning April 21. There are thirty Mibu-farce stories. It is said that the Buddhist monk Saint Enkaku (1223–1311) began the Mibu-farce to help people more easily understand the teachings of Buddha some seven hundred years ago.

2. *A Dragon* is an unfinished project that was introduced on the pamphlet. The pamphlet was published in 1991.

3. Su Dongpo is also known for his travel literature writings where they often contain narratives of his philosophical and moral insights.

4. My analyses of Kawamoto's other animation works are published in Japanese (see Yokota 2006a; 2006b; 2008).

References

Kawamoto, Kihachiro. Interview with the author at his studio in Tokyo on March 23, 2009.

Kawamoto, Kihachiro. *Czechoslovakia Letters & Memories* (2002, in Japanese). In author's office in Tokyo.

Levinson, Daniel J. *Jinsei no siki: Chunen wo ikani ikiruka* [The Seasons of a Man's Life], translated by Minami Hiroshi. Tokyo: Kōdansha, 1980.

Suzuki, Daisetz T. *Living by Zen*. New Delhi: Munshiram Manoharlal Publishers Pte. Ltd., 2001.

Yokota, Masao. "The Japanese Puppet Animation Master Kihachiro Kawamoto." *Asian Cinema* 14, no. 1 (2003): 28–44.

———. *Animation no rinnsho-sinnrigaku* [Clinical Psychology of Animation]. Kyoto: Seishin Shobo, 2006a.

———. "Kawamoto Kihachiro no ninngyo-animation *shisha-no-sho*" [Kawamoto Kihachiro's puppet animation *The Book of the Dead*]. In *Studies in Humanities and Social Sciences, The Institute of Humanities and Social Sciences, Nihon University* 71 (2006b): 59–68.

———. *Animation to raihu-saikuru no sinnrigaku* [Animation and Psychology of Life-cycle]. Kyoto: Rinsen-Shoten, 2008.

———. "Sutajio-Gyibuli no animation no rinnsho-sinnrigaku: Miyazaki Hayao and Takahata Isao" [Clinical Psychology of Studio Ghibli's Animation: Miyazaki Hayao and Takahata Isao]. In *Nihon daigaku bunnrigakubu sinnri rinnsho senta kiyou* [Studies in Humanities and Social Sciences] 7, no. 1 (2010): 5–15.

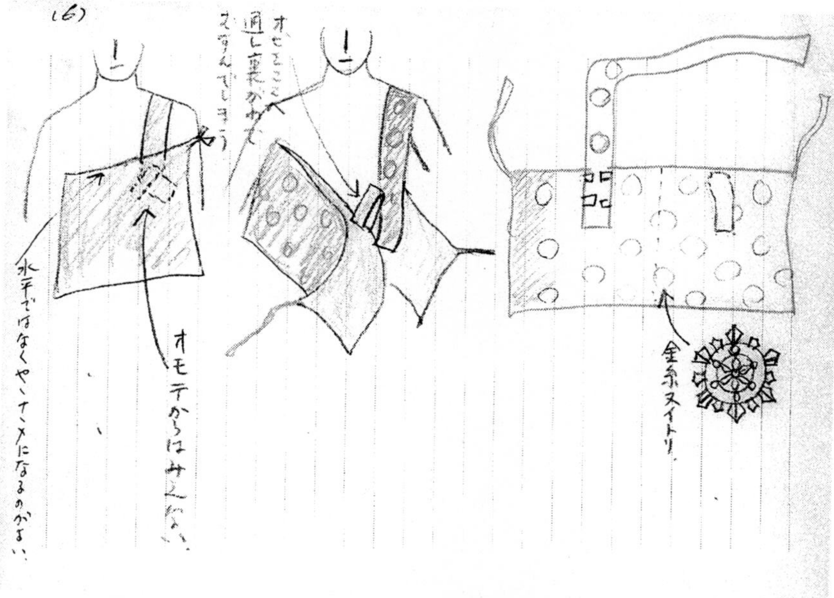

1. Kawamoto received sketches of clothes in the letter from Japan. Figures 1–20 are reprinted by permission from the late Kawamoto Kihachiro.

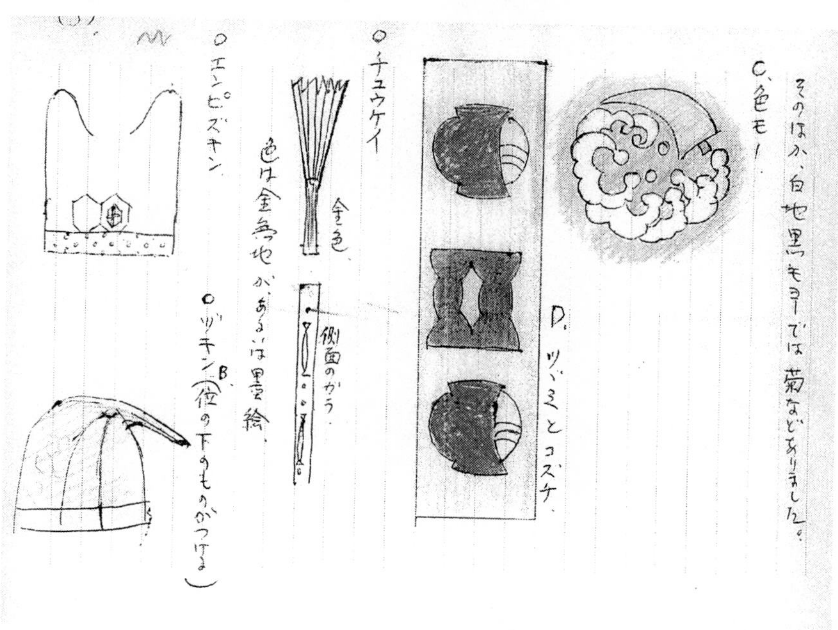

2. Kawamoto received other sketches in the letter from Japan.

3. Design patterns used in *Breaking of Branches is Forbidden*.

4. Kawamoto's sketch of the old monk.

5. Kawamoto's sketch of the young monk.

6. Kawamoto's sketch of the samurai.

7. Kawamoto's sketch of the servant.

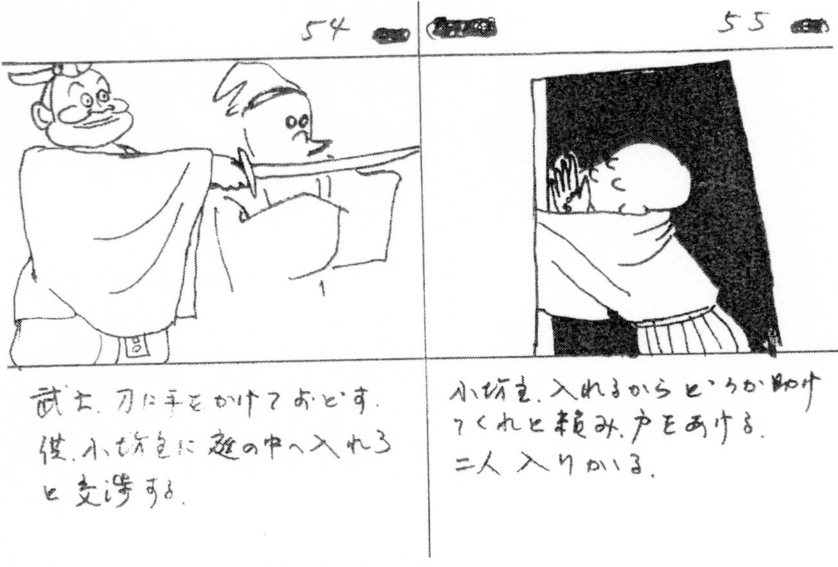

8. The samurai terrifies the young monk into allowing him to enter.

9. The old monk mistakes the young monk for a girl.

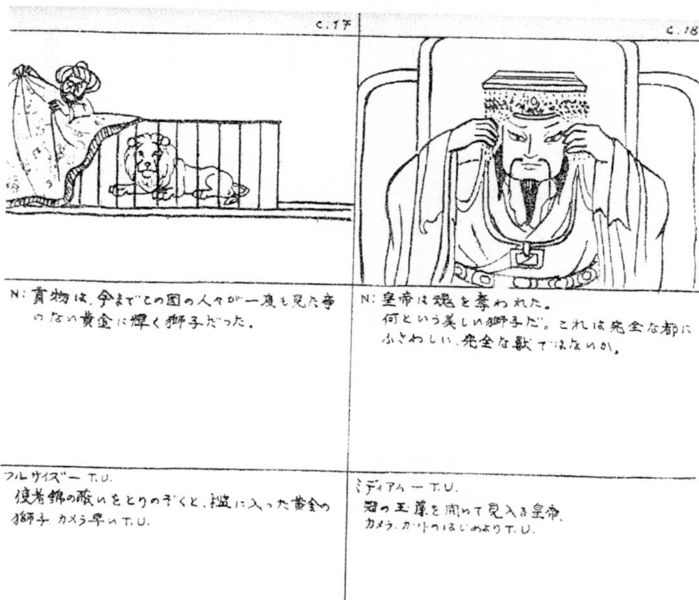

10. The emperor receives a lion as tribute.

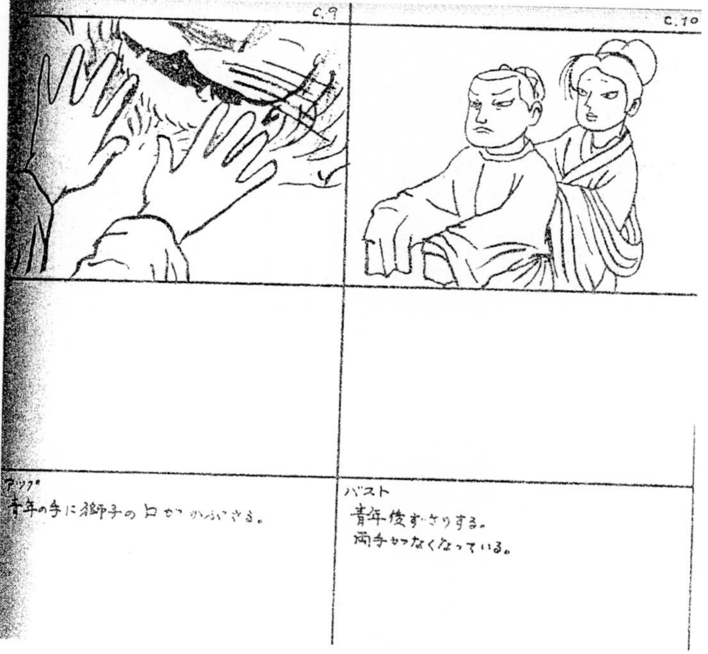

11. The young man makes the lion eat his arms.

12. The young man gives his head to the lion as the emperor watches.

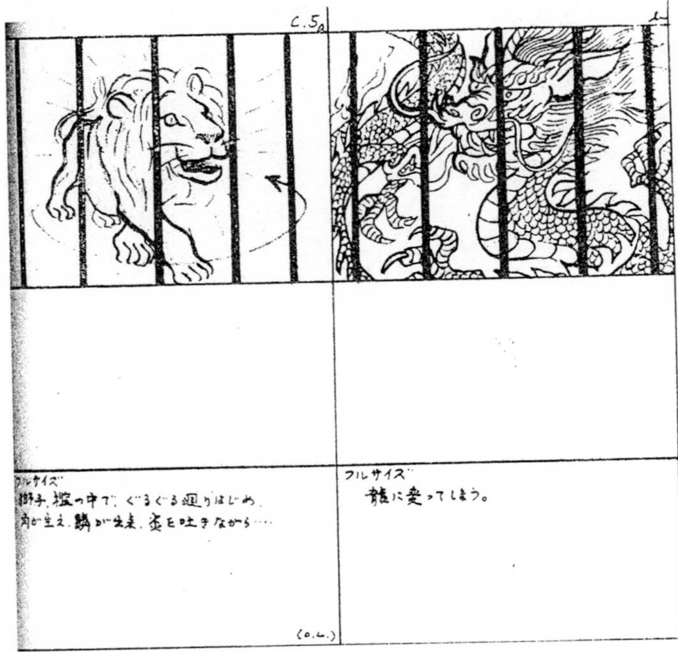

13. The lion changes its figure into a dragon.

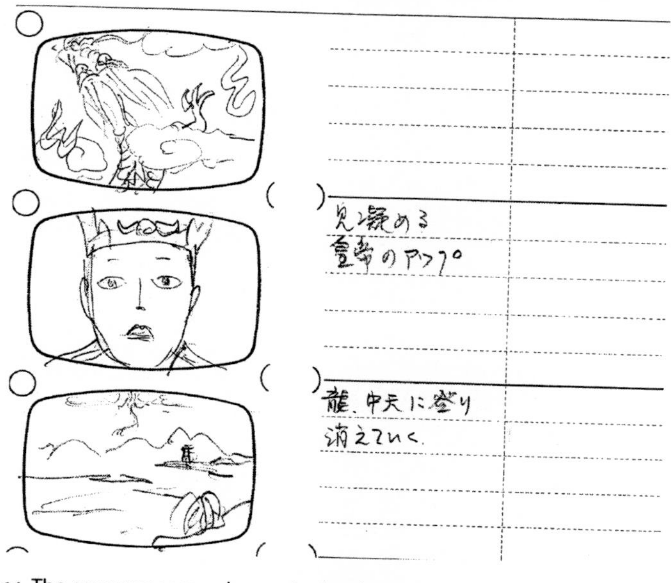

14. The emperor sees a dragon in the sky.

15. The emperor sees a young man on the rainbow.

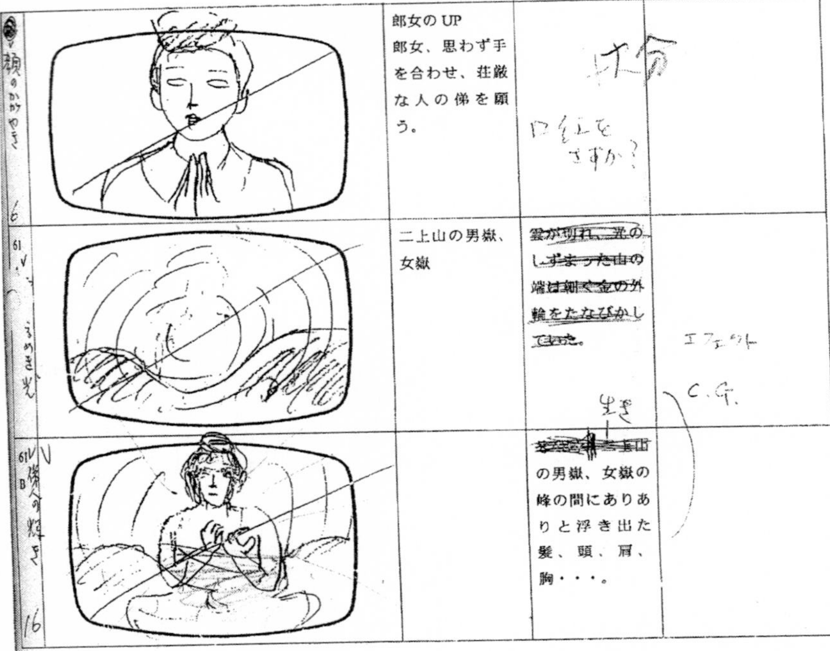

16. Iratsume sees an image of a nobleman between two mountaintops.

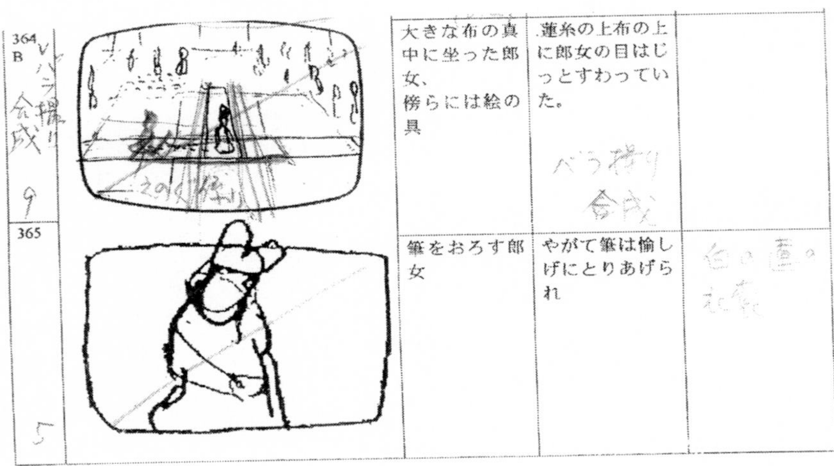

17. Iratsume tries to draw in *The Book of the Dead*.

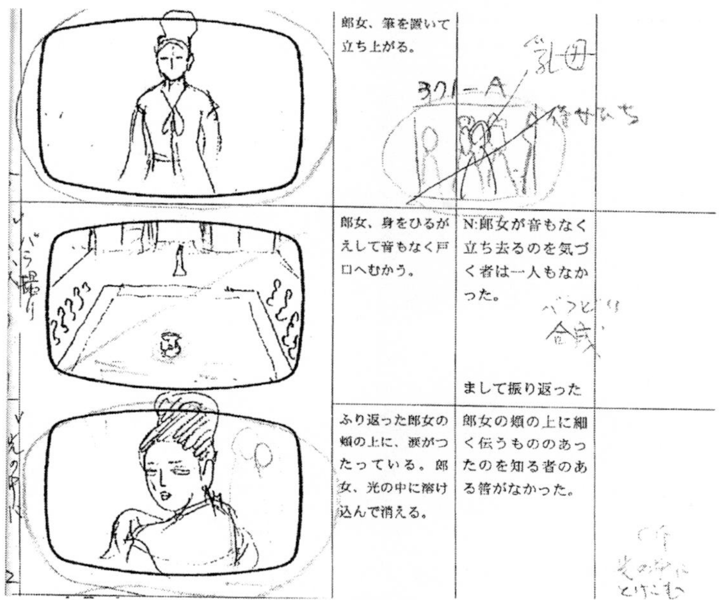

18. Iratsume completes the image of the nobleman.

19. A monkey-show man lies down and a butterfly flies around him.

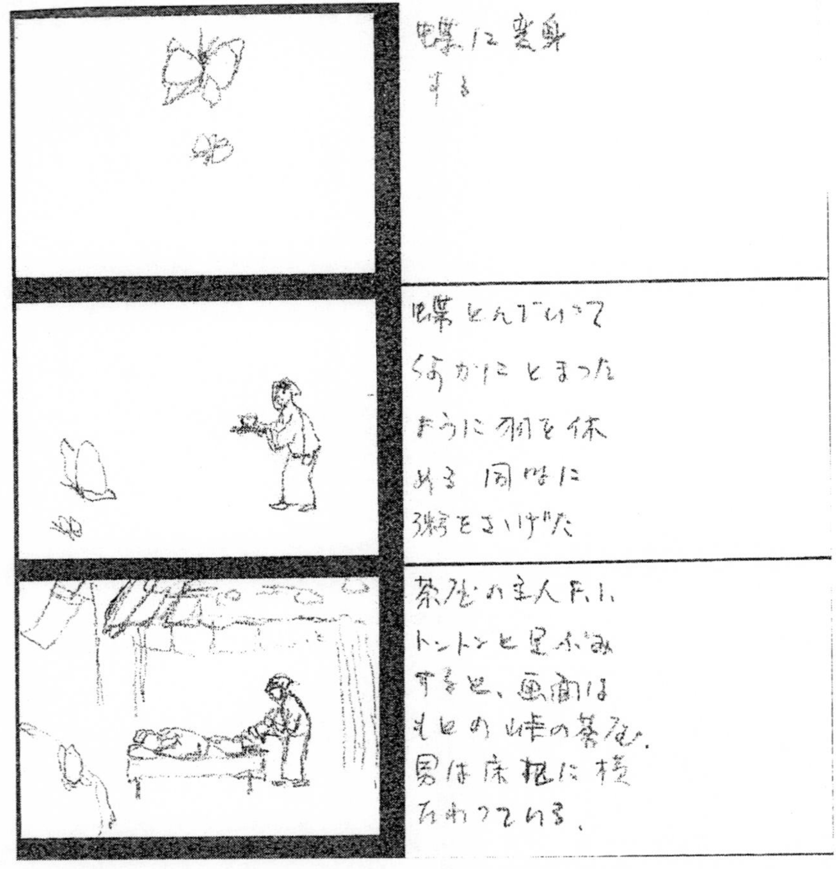

蝶に変身
する
蝶とんでいって
何かにとまった
ように羽を休
める 同時に
粥をさゝげた
茶屋の主人が、
トントンと足ぶみ
すると、画面は
もとの峠の茶屋。
男は床几に横
たわっている。

20. A butterfly flies in the sky and the monkey-show man reappears.

Section Six

Japan's First Commercial Animation Studio after the Second World War: Toei

The Background of the Making of *Flying Phantom Ship*

—Hiroshi Ikeda

Translated by Masao Yokota and Tze-yue G. Hu

From the editors:

This chapter is adapted from the presentation script and notes given by Hiroshi Ikeda in a lecture meeting at Tokyo Zokei University on May 2, 2008. The editors express their sincere appreciation to Masayo Bowles and Akiko Sugawa-Shimada for their initial assistance and translation of certain parts of the article.

Readers should refer to Appendix 3 for explanatory notes of local terms and historical events mentioned in the article.

Introduction

Flying Phantom Ship was released by Toei Film Company (Toei Co. Ltd.) in 1969, which differentiated its storyline from that of the comic book of the same name by Ishimori Shoutarou (later renamed Ishinomori Shoutarou, 1938–1998) upon which the film was based. Although till today, Toei has produced animated films aimed at a child audience since its first feature film, the *White Snake Tale* (1958), the *Flying Phantom Ship* as well as *Prince of the Sun: The Great Adventures of Hols* (1968) contain diverse messages targeted at not only children but also young adults. It was made in a period in Toei Animation Studio[1] where young animation directors and animators like Takahata Isao, Miyazaki Hayao, and Ikeda Hiroshi were given tasks to work on their animation film projects that included greater responsibilities.

I will examine the background and motivations for producing the *Flying Phantom Ship* in two sections.

Section One: The Production Environment of *Flying Phantom Ship*

The Toei Film Company was established in 1951, and it was the latest of the major film enterprises to be founded in Japan after the Second World War. The animated film, *Flying Phantom Ship*, was produced in 1969 by Toei. During the period after the war, in order to survive in the competitive movie business, the company had to find directors (working in the live-action dimension and others) who had their own original style and talent.

Let me just highlight several live-action directors who made a strong impact socially through their works:

Table 1. Directors and Film Titles

Name of Director (live-action film)	Film Title(s)
Sekigawa Hideo (1908–1977)	*Listen to the Roar of the Ocean* (1950), *Overcome the War Flames* (1950), *Dawn, Fifteenth of August* (1952), *The Great Journey* (1960), *Great Dash* (1960)
Kamei Fumio (1908–1997)	*Being a Mother Being a Woman* (1952)
Tadashi Imai (1912–1991)	*The Tower of the Lilies* (1953), *Rice* (1957), *A Story of Pure Love* (1957), *That Harbor Lights* (1961), *Bushido* ["Cruel Story" (1963)], *A Story of Echigo* (1964)
Yamamoto Satsuo (1910–1984)	*Avalanche* (1956), *Japan Thief Story* (1964)
Ieki Miyoji (1911–1976)	*The Naked Sun* (1958)
Uchida Tomu (1898–1970)	*Chikamatsu's Love in Osaka* (1959)
Tasaka Tomotaka (1902–1974)	*Run Geta Run* (1961), *A Carpenter and Children* (1962), *A House of Shame* (1963)

The above directors were interested in social events and issues that included not only antiwar sentiments but also themes such as injustice, poverty, prostitution, and immorality and their works carried a strong social message. Young directors, like Takahata Isao and Ikeda Hiroshi, who worked in Toei Animation Studio, situated adjacent to the parent movie studio of Toei Co. Ltd., had the opportunity to watch the above-mentioned experienced directors directing their live-action films through a window of the building of the animation studio. As a result, they were strongly influenced by the directing style of the directors as well as their interest in social issues.

In addition to the influence of the directors, it is also important to underline the impact of the social context of the film(s) they were producing. See the following table, which shows the series of political and international events that occurred from 1949 to 1968:

Table 2. Political and International Happenings

Year	Events and Developments
1949	Democracy Liberal Party landslide victory / Japanese National Railway large personnel redundancy / Yamashita Case / Mitaka Case / Matsukawa Case
1950	Red Purge / The establishment of a police reserve force
1951	Regulations on the ethics of filmmaking / Intensification of Korean War
1952	Peace Treaty / U.S.-Japan Security Treaty / Subversive Activities Prevention Law / May Day of the Blood
1953	Stalin's death / Fool (*bakayarou*) dissolution / The summit of Mount Everest is reached for the first time
1954	Daigo Fukuryu Maru (Lucky Dragon 5) / Japan Congress against A- and H-Bombs World Meeting / Tōya Maru accident / Shipbuilding scandal / Professional wrestler Rikidouzan
1955	Jinmu economy / Publication of the *Season of the Sun* novel
1956	*The Suez Crisis*
1957	100 million total idiocy (mental illness) / Three kinds of sacred weapons / Disturbance in Suez / Atomic fire of Tokai village / Sputnik launch
1958	Prostitution Prohibition Law / NASA established / Kano River typhoon
1959	Marriage of crown prince / Iwato economy / Isewan typhoon / Cuban Revolution / Minamata Disease
1960	Anpo Treaty protests / Personal income redoubling / Asanuma assassination
1961	*Ue wo muite arukou* ("Walk Upwards," Sukiyaki song by Sakamoto Kyū) released / Project Apollo
1962	Cuban Missile Crisis / Japanese Horie Pacific Crossing / Vietnam War
1963	Japan-U.S. TV satellite broadcasting / Kennedy assassination / Nuclear-Test Ban Treaty
1964	Tokyo Olympics / Niigata earthquake
1965	Bombing of North Vietnam becoming more serious
1966	Protests against building Narita Airport / Nuclear submarine arrival in Port Yokosuka / Black Mist scandal / Beatles coming to Japan
1967	Protest sit—in front of the American Department of Defense in Washington, D.C. / Anti–Vietnam War Movement
1968	University campus dispute especially in Tokyo / Civil resistance against the occupation in Czechoslovakia / Nuclear submarine arrival in port Sasebo / Martin Luther King Jr. assassination / Screening of *Prince of the Sun: The Great Adventures of Hols*

The string of the above such mentioned incidents, events, and developments influenced the film directors' filmmaking as they were no longer able to remain indifferent to the social situations and circumstances of that time.

During that period, the Toei Film Company built a permanent open-air film studio for live-action filming at Tokyo and also, next to the live-action studio, a three-story animation studio was constructed. As mentioned before, from the windows of the animation studio's third floor, one was able to see the photographic design sets made by the well-known live-action directors for their ongoing film projects.

It was stimulating and challenging for the young directors of the animation studio to see the production process of the experienced film directors. Their impressive works and their looming presence generated a dynamic environmental difference that influenced the animation directors' creative spirit and output. This created and resulted in a vital difference as compared to other animation directors working in other parts of Japan.

In 1968, the animated feature film *Prince of the Sun: The Great Adventures of Hols* was screened in public. The film was promoted as a feature film for children as it had been an industry practice in regard to the medium of animation but the film failed to attract its target audience. In contrast, in 1958, Toei's first color animated feature film, *White Snake Tale*, successfully attracted children audiences around the age of six. The *Hols* film actually attracted a number of sixteen-year-old high-school student-spectators, as did the previously screened *White Snake Tale*, where the audience also included eleven to twelve-year-old school students and twenty-year-old adults. However, the marketing and promotion department staff had overlooked the diversity of age groups that had actually attended the screening of the 1958 animation film. Even later on, the release of the animated film *Space Battleship Yamato* in 1977 clearly demonstrated the changing demographic of animation cinema spectatorship. (*Editors' Note*: Refer to Kim's article in this collection for analysis of the film.)

Section Two: The Film Direction of *Flying Phantom Ship*

In 1955, director Ikeda started to work on his graduation thesis focusing on the theme of "neorealism" under the supervision of the late film director Ushihara Kiyohiko (1897–1985).[2] The theme of neorealism essentially focused on the social problems of the day. Western European film directors like Roberto Rossellini (1906–1977) and Vittorio De Sica (1901–1974) and their works are representative of that film movement. For example, *Rome, Open City* (1945), *Paisà* (1946), *Shoeshine* (1946), and *The Bicycle Thief* (1948) reflected this documentary method of filmmaking.

During that period, director Ushihara had recognized the similar filmmaking direction of East European filmmakers, including products such as Czech and Polish animation films, where works displayed strong neorealist elements featuring the fundamental contradictions in real life. When Toei Animation Studio posted its first recruitment notice of assistant directors in 1959, graduating student Ikeda applied and was successfully offered a position with the recommendation of his teacher-director Ushihara. Ikeda aspired to produce animation influenced by the documentary method of filmmaking and its ideology.

As noted before, in 1968 the completed animated feature film *Prince of the Sun: The Great Adventures of Hols* was screened to the public, creating a big shock to the animation industry. Especially within Toei, among the other criticisms from the industry, the film was considered difficult to understand and the audience was astonished at the film's contents.[3] In the years following the release of Toei's *White Snake Tale* in 1958, the animation audience in Japan had become increasingly diverse and had broadened from a primarily children audience to a young adult audience and beyond. This demographic change in the audience became an arresting point within the animation filmmaking community. The commonplace wisdom of thinking of animation as a children's genre had to change. The animated film *Prince of the Sun: The Great Adventures of Hols*, like the subsequent animated film *Flying Phantom Ship*, was "lost" due to the failure of industry leaders to appreciate the change in audience behavior. The former became the lowest income-earning film in Toei Animation Studio's history and was only screened for ten days at cinema theaters. *Prince of the Sun: The Great Adventure of Hols* had a strong sociopolitical message. The next animation film, *Flying Phantom Ship*, also continued in this vein.

The Embedded Messages and Expressions of *Flying Phantom Ship*

In an abstract sense, the film *Flying Phantom Ship* looks into the origins of evil in relation to the subject of science and humankind. The animated characters symbolized the darkness of that era where national political and financial powers were misused regardless of existing social and public demands. Boa is an evil entity corporation that does not directly control human society but the Boa juice, which it manufactures itself, is a mega hit item that symbolically reflects its secret growing power. The film shows that the existence of such heinous juice needs to be brought to the general public's notice and be exposed by such individual heroes as represented by Hayato.

The film strongly reflected the social conditions of the period. The Boa juice can be understood as alluding to the food and drink safety issue as raised by the Minamata Disease incident in 1959. Director Ikeda was fearful of the residents' health due to the food they consumed that was contaminated by the industrial waste produced by the incident. The animated film indirectly pursued the Minamata Disease incident and the food problems caused by irresponsible industrial activities. Within the film, the hero, Hayato, fought against drinking the Boa juice. If he were to become addicted to Boa juice, he would be poisoned and subsequently, his body would change into liquid.

The film also uses the military as a symbol of power and authority through its appearance in tense situations as an "enforcer" of social order. In *Flying Phantom Ship*, there were film segments portraying the active presence of military vehicles in the midst of busy city streets of people and other kinds of public transport. Through this, the film also reflects on the attack of Czechoslovakia; that is, the armed intervention by the Warsaw Treaty forces. In 1968, Communist Allied forces and tanks invaded Prague. It might be believed that the main aim of the army is to protect people from invaders. However, the tanks shown in *Flying Phantom Ship* trample down cars in the streets similarly to what was done in Prague.

The use of the ghost ship motif and its violent capabilities also indirectly reflect the scenario of the Manchurian Incident in 1931. The Manchurian Incident happened in accordance with the hidden intentions of the Japanese army. In the animated film, the robot Golem first appeared as a combat robot against Kuroshio's group (a kind of an enforcement organization that actually served the Boa juice corporation, its name means the "Dark Force Group"). However, in reality it was Kuroshio's group that controlled Golem. In a way, Golem is reflective of the Japanese army during the imperialistic era of Japanese history.[4] Through this, *Flying Phantom Ship* reflects the idea and the act of a "self-made and self-performed" event. As can be seen, all in all the film is an amalgamation of images and historic reflections influenced by the theme of neorealism.

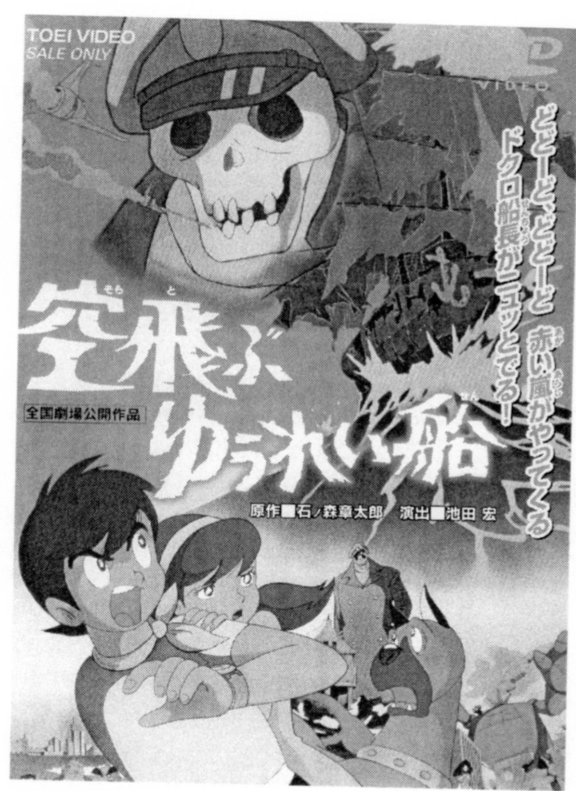

1. Editors' note: DVD covers of *Flying Phantom Ship*.

Conclusion

The animated work of *Flying Phantom Ship* differed from the original story, and film reviewers criticized the film. The original story describes the personal revenge of a captain of the phantom ship. In contrast, the story of the animation film features the fight for social justice of a young boy. Later, Ikeda's subsequent work at Toei, the animated feature film *Animal Treasure Island* (1971), did not reflect international issues as planned (for example, big powerful nations versus the pirates at seas as a proxy for highlighting interreligious and interethnic group conflicts and the support of big powerful nations and their relationships and connections). A senior animator, Mori Yasuji, did not agree with Ikeda's original planning. Though Mori did not express his reasons, it was thought that he opposed the social messages embedded within and just wanted to describe a funny story.

At Toei Animation Studio, during the late 1960s and the early 1970s, two important animated works were produced in the form of *Prince of the Sun: The Great Adventures of Hols* and the *Flying Phantom Ship*. Later, Takahata Isao and Miyazaki Hayao, who were the key production members of the 1968 film, would subsequently leave the studio and carry on to make animated works with social messages and aspirations, this time bringing critical value to the medium of animation in Japan and worldwide.

Notes

1. Toei Film Company is the parent company of Toei Animation Studio.

2. Editors' note: Ushihara Kiyohiko was a famous silent film director in Japan. It is widely known in the Japanese film industry that he studied Hollywood filmmaking in the United States in the mid-1920s and he also studied the production of the film, *The Circus* (1928), which starred the world-famous film artist Charlie Chaplin (1889–1977).

3. Editors' note: The film carries anti–Vietnam War sentiments and other social messages, readers may refer to Hu's *Frames of Anime: Culture and Image-Building* (2010): 109–10 for further details of the *Hols* film.

4. Editors' note: See, for example, http://www.archives.gov/iwg/japanese-war-crimes/introductory-essays.pdf (accessed on January 25, 2012), for accounts of Japanese atrocities committed during the Second World War and book publication, *The Nanjing Massacre: A Japanese Journalist Confronts Japan's National Shame*, by Honda Katsuichi, translated by Karen Sandness, and edited by Frank Gibney (Armonk, NY: M. E. Sharpe, 1999).

References

Gojū nenshi jikkōiinkai [Fifty years implementation editorial committee]. *Toei anime-shon gojūnenshi* [Toei animation fifty years]. Tokyo: Toei Animation Studio, 2006.

Ishimori, Shōtarō. *Flying Phantom Ship*. Tokyo: Kodamapuresu, 1966.

Souristu yonjū shūnen kinen jigyō iinkai hen [Forty years of enterprise founding editorial committee]. *Toei Dōga yonjûnen no ayumi* [Toei animation forty-year steps]. Tokyo: Toei Animation Studio, 1997.

Toei Co. Ltd. *Daiichikai manga eiga seisaku kenkyu iinkai shiryō* [First manga film production research member group materials]. Tokyo: Toei Co. Ltd., 1956.

Toei Co. Ltd., ed. *Toei Eiga sanjūnen* [Toei film thirty years]. Tokyo: Toei Co. Ltd., 1981.

Tsuji, Masaki, and Ikeda Hiroshi. *Flying Phantom Ship*. Tokyo: Asahi Sonorama, 1982.

Toei jūnenshi [Toei ten years history by "Toei Editorial Committee"]. Tokyo: Toei Co. Ltd., 1962.

Yamaguchi, Katsunori, and Watanabe Yasushi. *Nihon anime-shon eiga shi* [The History of Japanese Animation]. Osaka: Yubunsha, 1977.

Appendix 1

First sample of Kenny N. Chow's class assignment for his students

LCC2720 Principles of Visual Design
Spring 2008

Project Two (Due March 11)

Myths are traditional stories concerning usually histories, conventions, or rituals of certain groups of people. Meanwhile, the term can also be used to mean a widely held but false belief or idea, which can be promising topics subject to our appropriation and reiteration.

Dissolving Frames: Projecting "time" onto "space"

In this project, you look for a myth with a simple storyline that can be fitted into four or five sequential frames. The myth, similar to other stories, is happening in certain places or locations. With reference to the topographic narratives and Anders Nilsen's comics shown in the class, you dissolve the frames and stitch the panels to form a "temporal map" or "spatial itinerary" that tells the myth.

Multiple Retelling Myth

Then, you explore the space on your "map" and investigate the possibilities of retelling the myth visually in multiple directions that demonstrate your imaginations. It can be:

- A branching from a critical moment in the plot;
- Another parallel universe intersecting the original plot on a particular moment;
- A circular narrative loops the end back to the beginning.

You are encouraged to use "found" images as long as you make acknowledgment of them. The materials are manipulated and combined with the techniques of digital compositing.

Please keep in mind what you have learned about visual communication because the assessment is still based on your choice of representational styles, the demonstration of compositional awareness, the novelty of storytelling, and the finishing of the final output.

The image resolution of the final output should not be less than 1200 by 1200. Submit the **JPEG** file to T-square before noon of the due date.

Present your work during the class; make your arguments explicitly with respect to the contrived story, narrative techniques, and representational styles (max. 3 mins.).

Appendix 2

Second sample of Kenny N. Chow's class assignment for his students

LCC2720 Principles of Visual Design
Spring 2008

Project Three (Due Apr. 22)
In this assignment, you have to produce a montage (both spatial and temporal) sequence based on a piece of haiku.

Time Frames: Motion Haiku
Haiku is one of the most significant kinds of Japanese poetry. Haiku poems are mostly about nature and seasons. The traditional form is made of verse with a strong sense in visuals, sounds, and emotions.

Each of you is given a particular haiku poem. Read, interpret, and imagine. Pay attention to the objects, environments, sounds, and emotions. Then associate imagery and graphics to represent your mental image of the literary work.

All visual elements, including colors, textures, graphics, and photographic images should be under your considerations. You should also think about the camera movement. The length of your work should not be shorter than 10 seconds.

The audio track is required to enhance the rhythm and emotion.

Technical specification of the deliverable:

File name: proj3_*yourlastname*.mov
File type: QuickTime movie
Compressor: MPEG4
Frame aspect ratio: 4:3
Resolution: 320 h 240 v
Pixel aspect ratio: 1.0
Frame rate: 30

Please submit your movie file to T-Square before noon of due date.

Appendix 3

The following selected explanatory notes are provided by the editors and Ikeda Hiroshi.

1954

Shipbuilding Scandal

It revealed widespread corruption among politicians and bureaucrats who engaged the shipbuilding companies to pay bribes for the benefits of the ship-transportation industries.

Daigo Fukuryu Maru ("Lucky Dragon 5")

Daigo Fukuryu Maru is the name of a Japanese pelagic tuna fishing boat that was exposed to plenty of nuclear fallout from an American nuclear test. All the crewmembers of Daigo Fukuryu Maru became victims of radiation sickness caused by the nuclear fallout.

1955

Jinmu Economy

Under the leadership of the Liberal Democratic Party, the economy expanded dramatically in the period 1955–58 with heavy industrial spending, dynamic growth of the manufacturing sectors, and the strong appreciation of the yen currency.

1956

Suez Crisis

It was a war in which Britain, France, and Israel fought against Egypt, which had decided earlier to nationalize the Suez Canal.

1959

Iwato Economy

Another phase of economic boom in Japan from 1959 to 1961 with an average growth rate of over 12 percent, exports of electric products escalated; e.g., sale of Sony's transistor radio.

Minamata Disease

This poisoning caused by organic mercury effused from chemical plants in prefectures like Kumamoto and Niigata led to rising citizens' and residents' movements around Japan.

1960

Anpo Treaty Protests

In English, it is known as the Treaty of Mutual Cooperation and Security between the United States and Japan (1960). It strengthened Japan's security-military ties with the USA during the Cold War era. The protests were against such arrangements and the Japanese government's support of American interests in the region.

Asanuma Assassination

Asanuma Inejiro (1898–1960) was the head of the Japanese Socialist Party and a popular politician known for his socialist ideals. In 1960, he was assassinated in broad daylight on television by an extreme rightist during an election rally.

1962

Cuban Missile Crisis

The Cuban Missile Crisis was a confrontation between the Soviet Union, Cuba, and the United States in which the Cold War might have turned into a nuclear war.

Vietnam War

The Vietnam War followed after the First Indochina War, and the aim was to reunify North and South Vietnam under a communist government.

1963

John F. Kennedy Assassination

John F. Kennedy, the President of the United States, was assassinated in Dallas, Texas.

1966

Struggle against Building Narita Airport

It refers to local farmers protests against the development of an international airport in their farmlands.

Black Mist Scandal

It refers to a corruption scandal among Liberal Democratic Party politicians in regard to sale of public land in downtown Tokyo. The string of connections was darkly complex and thus the "Black Mist" description.

1967

Protest Sit—in front of the American Department of Defense in Washington, D.C.

Several American demonstrations and protests were held in front of the Pentagon in 1967 calling for the end of the Vietnam War.

1968

University Campus Dispute, especially in Tokyo

University students protested against elements of authoritarianism and bureaucracy in Japanese society, also a continuation of the antiwar movement that had begun in the early 1960s.

Civil Resistance against the Occupation in Czechoslovakia

In response to a brief period of liberalization known as the Prague Spring, members of the Warsaw Pact invaded Czechoslovakia. After invasion, a spontaneous campaign of civil resistance against the occupation occurred.

Martin Luther King Jr. Assassination

A leader of modern American liberalism, Martin Luther King Jr. was assassinated in Memphis, Tennessee.

Contributors

Kenny K. N. Chow is currently a lecturer in the School of Design at the Hong Kong Polytechnic University. He obtained a Ph.D. in Digital Media at the Georgia Institute of Technology in 2010, an M.F.A. degree from the City University of Hong Kong in 2007, and a M.Sc. degree from the University of Hong Kong in 2002. His research interests include digital visual culture, generative art, interactive narrative, film, and animation. He has extensive practical experience in motion graphic design, animation, and film production over ten years. He is also an independent filmmaker. His latest works include "Sword, Pigeon, and Bicycle," which was selected as the Opening Guest Film at the Osaka Asian Film Festival 2006 and included in the Hong Kong Panorama Section of the thirty-first Hong Kong International Film Festival. Another work "Play Again," as a part of the collaborative film *The Moon*, was selected in the sixth Hong Kong Asian Film Festival 2009.

Hiroshi Ikeda is a former Toei Animation Studio director. Besides directing the animated feature films, *The Flying Phantom Ship* (1969) and *Animal Treasure Island* (1971), he also directed over fifty animated works at Toei. He has been an active animation lecturer in several universities and currently still teaches on a part-time basis at Nihon University, Graduate School.

Sonoko Ishida and **Tokumitsu Kifune** began to create experimental animations in 8mm and 16mm film after the formation of IKIF in 1979. They have worked on experiments of animation with a variety of materials and techniques and on installations of the moving image. They started IKIF+ as a company in 1997, as their work has gotten more and more involved with animation production as a business, participating in the production scenes of PC-based animations for children, CG title sequences, and commercial animations (original video animations, opening title sequence animations for computer games, animated features) in the late 1980s. Now teaching at Tokyo Zokei University and Tokyo Polytechnic University, they are members of the Japan Society for Animation Studies and of the Japan Animation Association (of which Kifune is a board member).

Joon Yang Kim is a Seoul-based critic and scholar of animation. He is the author of *Animation, Alchemy of Images* (2001), and *Empire of Images: Animation on Japanese Islands* (2006). The latter was awarded the Poranabi Prize by the Japan Foundation in 2008. He is an associate editor of *Animation: An Interdisciplinary Journal* (Sage Publications) and a visiting researcher of the Institute for Japanese Studies, Seoul National University, while being involved with Cinema Digital Seoul Film Festival and other related events. He also teaches at the Korean National University of Arts and the Korean Academy of Film Arts.

Dong-Yeon Koh is currently a lecturer at Korea National University of Arts in Seoul. For her Ph.D. in art history at the City University of New York, Graduate Center, she specialized in the study about male sexualities within the New York avant-garde during the 1950s. Her work on art history and Asian Studies now focuses on issues of nationalism, popular culture, and the development of contemporary arts in Asia and also subjects on the recurring themes and artistic methods related to nostalgia in East Asian pop art.

Masashi Koide is a professor at the Tokyo Zokei University, Faculty of Art and Design, Department of Design. He is a key founding and management member of the Japan Society for Animation Studies. His research interests include animation theory and animation education.

Nobuyuki Tsugata is an associate professor at Kyoto Seika University, Department of Animation. He teaches animation history and is the author of several books on subjects related to the history of Japanese animation. He is a board member of the Japan Society for Animation Studies.

Akiko Sano is a lecturer at the Department of International Liberal Studies in St. Andrew University in Osaka (Momoyama Gakuin University). She has a Ph.D. degree in language and culture from Osaka University. She is currently researching the history of Japanese animation.

Akiko Sugawa-Shimada is an assistant professor at Kansai Gaidai University, Department of Foreign Languages. She completed her Ph.D. work at the University of Warwick, Department of Film and TV Studies, in January 2012 and her thesis topic covered the subjects of Japanese *magical girl anime* and female audiences. She is the author of a number of articles on anime and cultural studies, including "Double-Imaging of Girls: Hayao Miyazaki's *Kiki's Delivery Service*" in *Cinema and Literature* (2010), "Rebel with Causes and Laughter for Relief: 'Essay Manga' of Tenten Hosokawa and Rieko Saibara, and Japanese Female Readership" in the *Journal of Graphic Novels and Comics* (2011), and "Animation and Culture" in the *Encyclopedia of Animation* (forthcoming).

Yasushi Watanabe is an animation historian and independent scholar. He is the coauthor of *Nihon anime-shon eiga shi* (The history of Japanese animation, 1977) published by Yubunsha in Osaka. He has been a part-time lecturer at Otemae University since 2005, teaching an introductory course on animation, and a selection committee member of the Mainichi Eiga competition for animation for twenty years. Currently, he is researching the history of released feature animation in Japan after World War II.

Makiko Yamanashi is an independent scholar and has taught at universities in Denmark, Britain, and Japan, and given both public and academic seminars on Takarazuka. She now lectures at Waseda University, and is also in charge of the Japanese Popular Culture course for overseas students at Tokiwa University. Currently, she is a visiting academic researcher at Hosei University, Research Centre for International Japanese Studies. She has published a monograph entitled *A History of Takarazuka Since 1914: Modernity, Girls' Culture, Japan Pop* (2012).

Editors

Masao Yokota is a professor of psychology at the Department of Psychology, Human Sciences and Humanities, Nihon University. He lectures on animation and psychology at the departments of psychology and cinema in Nihon University. He is also the former chair of the Japan Society for Animation Studies and author of several book publications and a number of research papers on the subject of animation, and some of the latter have been translated into Korean, French and English.

Tze-yue G. Hu is an independent scholar and author of *Frames of Anime: Culture and Image-Building* published by the Hong Kong University Press in 2010. She is a member of the editorial board of *Animation: An Interdisciplinary Journal* and the Society for Animation Studies Grants Committee. Some of her essays on East Asian animation have been translated into Chinese, French, and Japanese. Her current research covers the spiritual aspects of Chinese water-and-ink animation made in the second half of the twentieth century as well as the theme of peace in animation. She also volunteers her time as an educational coordinator for the Japan-America Society of Oklahoma and is the project director of Japan in a Suitcase, an educational project sponsored by the Japan Foundation, Center for Global Partnership, promoting Japanese studies subjects to underserved communities in Oklahoma City.

Index